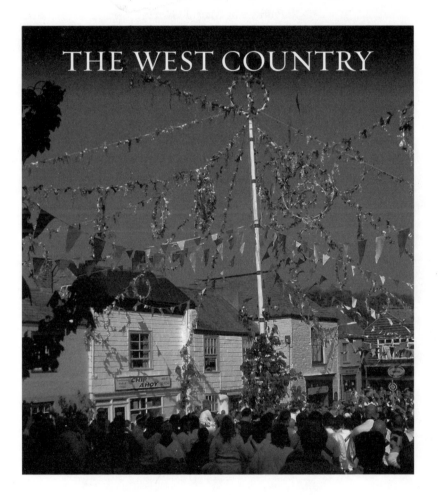

THE WEST COUNTRY

Landscapes of the Imagination

Landscapes

THE WEST COUNTRY

A *Cultural History*

JOHN PAYNE

Signal Books
Oxford

First published in 2009 by
Signal Books Limited
36 Minster Road
Oxford OX4 1LY
www.signalbooks.co.uk

A catalogue record for this book is available from the British Library

ISBN 978-1-904955-61-0 Paper

Cover Design: Devdan Sen
Production: Devdan Sen
Cover Images: fotoVoyager.com/istockphoto.com; John Payne
Illustrations: John Payne i, 16, 38, 60, 68, 55, 98, 147, 155, 171, 207, 230; dreamstime.com xiii, xx, 1, 11, 21, 41, 49, 61, 88, 101, 125, 132, 139, 144, 160, 191, 198, 213, 224, 234; istockphoto.com xiv, 81, 115, 169, 187, 233
Printed in India

Contents

Preface and Acknowledgements

This book is about the five south-western counties of England. From east to west they are Wiltshire, Dorset, Somerset, Devon and Cornwall. There is perhaps something arbitrary in the choice of these five counties. Others might prefer to include sea-going, cricket-loving Hampshire and the lovely city of Winchester, ancient capital of the kingdom of Wessex. Still others will be shocked to find Gloucestershire excluded, and this perhaps requires rather more comment. Most of Gloucestershire is Cotswold country, where everything seems determined by the underlying limestone beds. The villages lurk among the rolling hills, like a chameleon fading into the grey stillness of a winter afternoon or the golden brightness of a summer morning. Much of the history of the English Arts-and-Crafts movement, a subject dear to my heart, intertwines with the history of Cotswold England, one of the few places where vernacular architecture is still the chosen style for most new house building. Yet the Cotswolds do not respect boundaries: they intrude into Warwickshire and the English Midlands, into Oxfordshire and the headwaters of the Thames and into Oxford itself. It seemed wise to devote a whole volume in the Landscapes of the Imagination series to the very complicated English phenomenon of the Cotswolds.

Bath, of course, which was a Roman city and then a Cotswold city long before it was a Georgian city, has always been in the historical county of Somerset, and the bishop from his cathedral and palace in little Wells still retains the title of Bishop of Bath and Wells. Besides, the author was born, brought up and educated in Bath, and the Queen of the West remains a personal starting-point for these explorations. Bristol is unique in having had county status since the Middle Ages, yet its importance to the economic and cultural history of the West Country demanded its inclusion. The West Country is not just villages and market towns, but also cities such as Bath and Bristol, Exeter and Plymouth, Poole and Penzance.

So what then do these five counties chosen here to represent the English West Country have in common? Well, they are distant. Distant that is from London and the ways and thoughts of the metropolis. Yet they have been linked from earliest times to the rest of England by trackways, and later by turnpikes, canals and railways. This tension between belonging and not belonging, between local distinctiveness and participation in a wider world is of the essence of the West Country. Even before the Romans, Cornwall was trading tin with Mediterranean Europe. During the Roman period a settled Roman way-of-life grew up here, with important cities at Exeter and Bath, copper and tin mines in Cornwall and Devon, and lead and gold in the Somerset Mendip Hills. Later, North Devon kept Catholic, Mediterranean Europe supplied with salted fish for Friday observance.

The "British" people, driven west by post-Roman invasions of Anglo-Saxon tribes, have given the West Country a stronger Celtic patina than any other part of England. Cornwall retained its own Celtic language until the dawn of the Railway Age and widespread schooling in English. In recent years the language has been revived, local politics has been invigorated and most Cornish towns and villages are linked through twinning arrangements with more obviously Celtic Brittany. Old Cornwall Societies promote links with the Cornish diaspora, especially in Australia and the United States.

There are other distinguishing features to the West Country, not least the strength of non-conformity which created a great cleavage in many communities between "church" folk, often directly dependent on the local squire, and "chapel" folk—small farmers and weavers and other independent tradesmen. And then there is the sea, never far away, the sea that eats into people's minds and makes them restless, for this is a land of fishermen and women, of explorers, of traders and slave-traders, of smugglers, and more recently of tourism and holiday homes. Much of the most beautiful coastline in the south-west is now owned by the National Trust, and it will be obvious to the reader that I have drawn rather more on the National Trust as a protector of the countryside and coastline, than as a preserver of great country houses, which are only a fragment of our heritage.

But in the end this is not a book that has any great desire to preach to people, to define and to distinguish. It travels the byways as well as the highways of our cultural history, is interested in the environment and industry and religion, as well as art and literature and music. Much has been left out, there is much more to say, but I hope that what remains will intrigue and entertain readers in equal measure and make them want to delve further beneath the glittering beauty that is the English West Country.

ACKNOWLEDGEMENTS

Mark Adler of the *Mendip Times*

Caroline and John Birkett-Smith at Hunting Raven Bookshop in Frome

Ama Bolton for permission to use her poem "Mendip Waters"

John Boxall who escorted my wife and me to Lundy

John Channon at the National Trust Estate Office, Killerton

Nickomo and Rasullah Clarke and Frome Community Choir

Sue Clifford and Angela King of Common Ground for so often being my guides and mentors in matters of local distinctiveness

Edmund Costelloe and Viscount Raymond Asquith at Mells

James Crowden for permission to use his poem "Somerset Light – Winter"

Helen Date and Susan Wynter, voice-artists, who helped me with Coleridge and the Wordsworths

Carole Elliott, Administrator, Holnicote Estate Office

Richard Emeny of the Edward Thomas Fellowship for permission to re-use material previously published in the newsletter

Martin Graebe for his perceptive comments on an early draft

Tim Graham, Millstream Books

John Grey, Long Sutton Meeting

Martin Haggerty who encouraged me

Charlotte Hanna of Thermae Bath Spa

John Hardy, Visitor Services, Studland National Trust

Nancy Harrison for showing me the Quaker graveyard in Bath

Kate Hesketh (Netherhay Methodist Chapel) and the Purbeck Quire

Mrs W. Hillgrove, Torquay Museum Society

Satish Kumar for permission to quote from his film "Earth Pilgrim"

Mike Nelhams at Tresco Abbey Garden

The Packhorse Bookgroup, Frome

Jacqueline Peverley for talking to me about Dartington

Paul Prescott, who walked with me from Morwenstow to St. Ives in the spring of 1984

Rob Salvidge and his sister Katy at Bristol Ferry Boats

Roger Saul and Rachel Fearn at Sharpham Park

Jean Saunders at the Richard Jefferies Museum in Swindon

Chris Smaje, walker, gardener and writer

Phil and Linda Taylor for talking to me about Robin and Heather Tanner

Staff at the High Moorland Visitor Centre, Princetown, Dorset County Museum in Dorchester, Falmouth Art Gallery, Glastonbury Abbey Museum, Penlee House Art Gallery in Penzance, and Torquay Museum
My travelling companions, especially members of my own family
Staff at Frome Library and Bath Central Library. Somerset County Library service for the best inter-library loan service in England
National Trust staff and guidebooks at individual properties
Tourist Information Centres all over the place
The staff at Trebah Garden, Cornwall, for lending me an electric wheel-chair when I needed it.

The authors of all the books included in references, both living and dead; each in their own way have helped me to puzzle out why the West Country is so special.

And countless other people whose little, unremembered kindnesses helped to make my field-work such a pleasure.

John Payne
Frome, Somerset
February 2009

For Annie, John and Becky, with my love

Prologue

SECRETS OF STOURHEAD

The gardens at Stourhead in early May. Each spring I go to listen to the voices, as choirs from all over Wiltshire, Somerset and Dorset gather to celebrate an annual festival of song. The choirs sing at various settings around the landscaped gardens—the Pantheon, a fine lakeside copper beech, the Palladian Bridge, the church, the courtyard of the Spread Eagle, the Bristol Cross. There are choirs great and small, some mixed, some men or women only. There is jazz and folk and world music, Byrd and Tallis, Gershwin and Bacharach. New choirs and old choirs, choirs that have grown from adult education singing classes, choirs of friends and neighbours.

Each spring I wonder at this: the birdsong, the wind sighing and whispering in the trees, the mellow voices calling across the water, floating up from the lakeside. The greens of spring, I know this well by now, are scarcely green at all, but pink and yellow and grey, not yet the solid mass of summer greenery. The colours are reflected in the still waters of the lake, the river that is not yet allowed to be a river. This is an ornamental landscape, artificial if you like, a landscape made for pleasure. The water-meadows will come later, the mills, the flags and water-lilies and kingfishers, fine old buildings like the Minster at Wimborne, the ugly waterside marinas and apartments of Christchurch harbour. But for the moment there are sounds, reflections, musical notes like droplets of water suspended, shimmering in the atmosphere.

High above the lake, the thick woods with their tentative, shy foliage rise to the heights of Alfred's Tower. Within the gardens nature is excluded yet keeps returning. Kingcups and cuckoo flowers mass along the wild strip between the ornamented landscape and the lake, the birds fly free, squabble unmusically among the trees and shrubs; at night there are owls and bats and badgers. Songs celebrate experience, feelings, memory, everything that everyday life tries to persuade us is unnecessary. And songs celebrate places, or the experience of places: as I walked out, or up or down or along. I hear the hurrying footsteps of Richard Jefferies, of Thomas Hardy, of Dorothy Wordsworth and her companions; I hear them pause, watch them watching, listening, the many writers and artists who will be celebrated in this book. I hear too the footsteps of those who have walked beside me.

And then the noises of the day, even in the countryside: tractors and traffic, the hum of a computer, the slamming of a door, voices, music from an open window, television, radio, the distant drone of an aircraft. All the noises that stop us from listening to the music of nature, the excited beating of our own hearts.

So where does it come from, this beautiful landscape of Stourhead, the lake and woods, the temples and the grottoes, the tidied cottages and church, the grooming and the whole elaborate artifice of landscape understood in this particular English way? Centuries ago there was a house here, not the eighteenth-century mansion we see today but an earlier building, Stourton House. The ancient Spanish chestnuts at the foot of the drive to the new mansion suggest an alternative pathway. Curiously, the remains of this older house lie hidden still beneath the parkland.

From this border country flow three rivers—the Somerset Brue, the Wiltshire Wylye and the Dorset Stour. Near Stourton at Six Wells Bottom are the six fountains that were represented on the simple arms of the Stourton family. There were Stourtons here before the Norman Conquest; Sir William Stourton was MP for Somerset and Speaker of the House of Commons in 1413; but there are Stourtons no longer. The Stourtons remained royalist in the Civil War, but they also remained stubbornly Catholic. That meant punitive fines, and by the end of the seventeenth century the family was bankrupt. The house passed in two small steps to a London banker, Henry Hoare. Hoare had been lucky, making his money from the South Sea Bubble, but getting out before it burst. Stourton House disappeared beneath the turf, and in its place rose the Palladian mansion of Stourhead, with landscaped gardens to match. Hoare's Bank had been established in 1672 and still exists as a private family bank; a Hoare had been Lord Mayor of London in 1712. The money of the City, not for the first or last time, came to transform the English countryside.

The second Henry Hoare (the Magnificent) became a partner in the bank and inherited in 1725 at the age of nineteen. For the next sixty years he moulded the estate to his liking, and to the taste of the period. To these years belong the obelisk, the temple of Flora, the grottoes, the bridge. In his letters he insisted on the link between town and country, between industry and art. Without this careful watchfulness and prudence (a banker's word if ever there was one) he wrote with alarming prescience, "proud Versailles thy glory falls." Which was precisely what did happen to Versailles, or rather the French monarchy, a few years after Henry's death.

In the grotto by the lake is the recumbent figure of Ariadne. She lounges in a recess next to a cold pool fed by a cascade of constant springs and lit by an opening in the dome above. The inscription, re-carved in 1967, reads:

Nymph of the grot these sacred springs I keep
And to the murmur of these waters sleep
Ah spare my slumbers gently tread the cave
And drink in silence or in silence lave.

The words are by Alexander Pope. Sleep on she does, from one generation to the next, one breast innocently exposed to gazes poetical or lascivious.

LINES IN A LANDSCAPE

The open chalk downs of southern England provided long-distance routes for trade and other forms of human contact in ancient times. The Berkshire/Wiltshire Ridgeway formed part of a much longer route striking across England from East Anglia to Salisbury Plain. There are the many pieces of evidence of pre-historic times along this route—Barbury Castle, the White Horse at Uffington, Avebury. Especially where sheep-pasturing has been in continuous existence since the Iron Age, it is possible to imagine these ancient roads—broad open tracts of downland pasture quite different from the Roman and modern conceptions of a road as a relatively narrow, enclosed space.

If the chalk downs offered one route into the West Country, another was provided by the long seam of limestone running parallel with the chalk across England. The Roman Fosse Way, the route of which can still be followed in a car from outside Leicester down into Gloucestershire, used an earlier pre-historic route from the Humber to the Bristol Avon. The Romans, of course, continued it further south-west, linking Bath with the characterful little town of Ilchester in Somerset and the city of Exeter, which has retained its importance from Roman through medieval times into the modern world.

If many (though not all) of the ancient track-ways have been ignored by modern road-builders, this is not true of the coaching roads and turn-pikes laid out by the eighteenth century. The fanciful, often polygonal toll-houses are still a feature of many minor West Country roads. The Bath Road from London to Bath and Bristol is still the A4, though nowadays providing for much of its length a pleasant and leisurely alternative to its modern rival the M4, which takes a more northerly route across the Berk-shire Down to a point south of Swindon and then heads straight for the Cotswolds and the distant prospect of the Severn bridges and Wales.

Arguably, it was the roads in the eighteenth century rather than the railways in the nineteenth which first opened up the West Country to the rest of England. In 1760 Bath was two days' travel from London; by 1830 only one. It was the improved roads that brought Smollett, Fielding and Jane Austen to Bath. For Exeter the improvement was even more dramatic, with travel time cut from three days to one.

At the same time as fast coaches on turnpike roads were revolutioniz-ing road travel, the canals were making similar progress in relation to the transport of goods. The Kennett and Avon Canal provided a new link between two of England's great ports, London and Bristol, enabling easy trans-shipment of goods between the two cities, as well as a host of other local purposes, as witnessed by the remains of the wharves along the length of the canal. Canals are a West Country invention, rather than the product of the Industrial Revolution in Birmingham, Manchester or Leeds. England's first canal was the Exeter Canal, built by the City Council between 1564 and 1567 to allow goods to by-pass the weirs in the river between Exeter and the sea. A canal in miniature it may have been, with its three locks, three-mile length, depth of three feet and sixteen-foot width, but it was the real thing, and was easily enlarged and updated in subsequent centuries.

Canals, hugging the contours, with their elegant little bridges and canalside inns and lock-keepers' houses, fitted easily into the natural en-vironment. The same cannot be said of the railways. With their embank-ments, cuttings, bridges and viaducts, they permanently changed the look of the countryside. Indeed, so massive were the engineering works involved that where a line such as the Somerset and Dorset Railway between Bath and Bournemouth has been abandoned it is still easy to trace its route, long after the rails fell silent. The Great Western Railway, sweeping on bridges and viaducts and embankments through Bath, permanently changed the aspect of the city, as it did in numerous smaller towns, in particular Chippenham in Wiltshire, Calstock on the Devon-Cornwall border and Truro, deep into Cornwall itself.

And yet, over 150 years after the main lines of the railways of the south-west were laid down it is possible to look with some pleasure at the results. In the Limpley Stoke valley outside Bath, where the railway, River Avon and Kennett and Avon Canal share a steep-sided valley, the result is a harmonious landscape in which human and natural activities seem for once to be in balance—crowned by the splendid classical Dundas aqueduct where the canal changes course from the inhabited west bank of the Avon to its quieter eastern bank. My own mother was brought up here, in the little village of Monkton Combe. When asked later in her life why she had travelled so little, her reply was always the same: "If you are brought up in the most beautiful place on God's earth, then why travel?"

Further east, the canal and the Great Western Railway again join forces, this time in the Vale of Pewsey on the main Great Western route from London to Taunton, Exeter and beyond. Travelling generally through sparsely populated countryside, the result again is one of surprising peace and harmony, whether viewed from the window of a train carriage or from a slow-moving canal barge. In summer there are wild flowers in profusion, and in winter a landscape silent, waiting, the skeleton of a land. >dreamstime 1022257<

The bridges introduced into the landscape by the road, canal and railway builders are perhaps the most obvious and ongoing features of human disturbance of the landscape. Nowhere is this more true than west of Plymouth, where Brunel's bridge across the Tamar, proudly dated 1859, created the first permanent crossing of the Tamar, a deep and winding river valley suddenly emerging into a wide estuary that through recorded history has separated Devon from Cornwall, and in so many ways Cornwall from the rest of England. Coinciding as it did with the collapse in the world price for copper in 1866, it provided one of many routes out of Cornwall for its brightest and best young people. The other route was the sea, that constant companion that is always there when Devon and Cornwall end. Brunel's bridge, so high above the water that everything below seems in miniature, is both heroic and sad. It bridges a gap, unites two worlds, but allows the one to ebb silently into the other.

Next to it is another much newer bridge, for Cornwall at last has a

fixed road connection with England too, opened in 1961. They are two worlds, two centuries, these bridges, whether one sees the road bridge from the rail bridge or the rail bridge from the road bridge. Yet both are, after all, lines in the landscape, the marks of human cultures, like them or not. In similar fashion the motorway network has entered the West Country, with the M5 stretching now to just beyond Exeter. It links the West through trade with the rest of the country, indeed the rest of the world. It brings conformity and uniformity; it erodes local patterns of life and distinctiveness of produce. Yet ironically it also creates, as all these different landscapes lines have done, a way into the West, used by people in search of that which is different, of the very local distinctiveness it threatens. It is that balance, between the integration of the West Country into a standardized world on the one hand, and the desire of outsiders to enjoy the rich distinctiveness and variety of these western counties, that forms the raw material of this book.

FUTURE LANDSCAPES

Nature, flora and fauna, are part of landscapes. But landscapes are not just about nature. Rather they are the result of interaction over very long periods of time between people and the natural environment. It may come as a surprise to be told that England today is more thickly wooded than it was in the Middle Ages. Stretching back into pre-historic times, the clearance of forest was essential to civilization. Tree-cutting provided timber for building and fuel, as well as creating fields for growing crops. Even the landscapes of the Mendips, Exmoor, Dartmoor and Bodmin Moor are carefully induced balances between human activity and nature. The grazing of animals on these high hills prevents reforestation and creates an environment where many kinds of wild flowers can flourish.

But what of the future? There are threats, but there is hope too for West Country landscapes. Even the occupation of so many areas of the West Country by the military has its plus side. On the ungrazed areas of Dartmoor a landscape much more akin to wilderness is being created; a landscape which, in a more peaceful future age, may be opened to those who want to roam—if unexploded ordinance can be cleared to make such activity safe. On parts of Salisbury Plain, long used by the army, the long process by which grazed pasture turns to scrub and eventually back to woodland has begun.

Other changes are more about the kind of human activity that takes place on the land. Reduced loads of artificial fertilizers and chemicals dumped on the land may one day bring back the wild flowers, which writers from Chaucer and Shakespeare to W. H. Hudson and Edward Thomas tell us once decorated the downs and pastures and arable fields of England. If future generations see more sense than present ones, an end may be called to the transport of so much food around the globe. Countries like England may come to depend again for a large part of their food on local production. We may see a growth of untidy but intensely productive market-gardens again, a productive belt around each town and city. The dramatic reduction in fruit orchards in the West Country over the last half century could be quickly reversed, and add diversity to our landscapes. Nothing is impossible. Landscapes evolve, and tomorrow's landscape will not be today's.

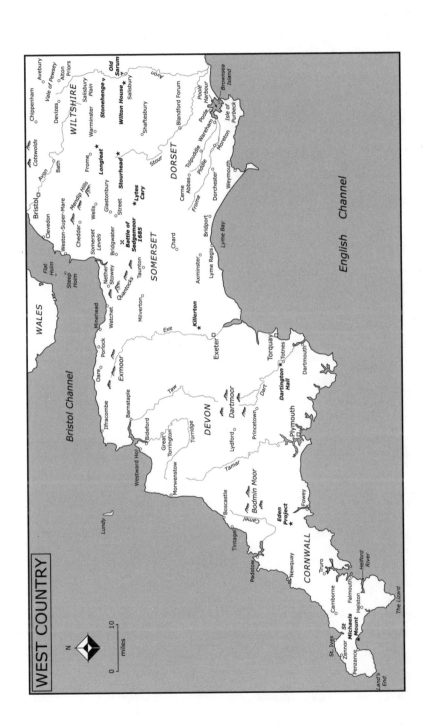

WEST COUNTRY

Chapter One

WALKING INTO WILTSHIRE

Sweet day, so cool, so calm, so bright,
The bridal of the earth and sky,
The dew shall weep thy fall tonight;
For thou must die.

Sweet rose, whose hue, angry and brave,
Bids the rash gazer wipe his eye,
Thy root is ever in its grave
And thou must die

George Herbert, "Virtue"

WILTSHIRE AND PREHISTORY

Of all the historic counties of England, Wiltshire is the one where prehistory trembles most tantalizingly. Its visual presence is all around us—the Uffington White Horse, Avebury itself, Stonehenge, the West Kennett burial chamber. Yet we know so little for sure about these peoples who lived on the downs beyond living memory and the security of written records. That the memory lingers on is sure: the extraordinary efforts made by the church to incorporate ancient belief systems into the Christian view of the cosmos is an example which we shall refer to at various points in this book. We shall see in Bath how a rational, classical architect like John Wood the Elder felt a deep need to underpin his practical work as a property developer with complex theories in which the ancient sites of prehistory, and biblical precedents such as the temple in Jerusalem, are all drawn into a single cultural melting-pot.

It was only gradually that our ancestors came to recognize the distinctiveness and the depth of mystery of prehistoric cultures. Some aspects of the material culture were easy enough to uncover. With only light ploughs, and without the technology to put in place drainage schemes, the free-draining chalk downs with their thin soils were easier places for settlement than the heavy clays of the plains and river valleys. In uneasy times, the high, breezy summits and long views of the downs made unexpected attacks less likely.

It is not just a personal preference on the part of the present author that it is Avebury rather than Stonehenge that is our focus in considering the prehistory of Wiltshire. Neither is it the happy alphabetical coincidence that the book begins at Avebury in Wiltshire and ends at Zennor in Cornwall. Stonehenge is too well-known, too controversial, for our purpose here, blighted by the roar of traffic squeezing through a single carriageway section of the A303 or avoiding it by taking the short-cut across Salisbury Plain that emerges onto the same road within yards of the stones. While there is still majesty at Stonehenge, seen in the mist of an early summer morning or glimpsed on a stormy night glistening with rain, or illuminated by a sudden shaft of moonlight between the clouds, there are few sadder sights in heritage England than visitors circling the stones in a continuous moving stream at a distance of fifty yards. Unable to touch the stones, to feel their enormous size as they stand beneath them, to lie full length upon the turf and feel the magic of the place, it is hard to know what benefit visitors derive from Stonehenge apart from the simple statement "I was there."

It is above all the continuity of human history that Avebury celebrates. At some point in the early Middle Ages, the Anglo-Saxon period of English history, there was a settlement at Avebury. The old beliefs had faded, and there was little compunction in re-using the stone from the various circles and avenues in the district. It made sense to live at Avebury. Unlike the giant megaliths at Stonehenge, the sarsens at Avebury were no great mystery in themselves. Glacial remnants, these giant lumps of sandstone are a naturally occurring and taken-for-granted part of this landscape. There are fields of them—one at Lockeridge, south-east of Avebury, and another just west of Eastbury in Berkshire. They can still be seen on Fyfield Down. Two centuries ago, the downs were littered with sarsens, but in the nineteenth century a business grew up around collecting and cutting them for a variety of uses, notably in the nearby, fast-growing railway town of Swindon, headquarters of the Great Western Railway. Fortunately the largest sarsens at Avebury were difficult, if not impossible, to move. Avebury is complex indeed, with the village lying within the circumference of the site (the henge), four modern roads passing through, a National Trust visitors' centre, a manor-house open to the public, a pub, a book-shop. We know a few things about Avebury for sure, we can conjecture other possible facts through the interpretation of historical evidence, but the scope for fantasy and fiction is quite enormous.

The rediscovery of Avebury owes much to the pioneering work of an-tiquarians such as John Aubrey in the seventeenth century and William Stukeley in the eighteenth century. Avebury could not remain concealed, since the main coach route from London to Bath and Bristol passed through the village and therefore the site (the current route of the A4, passing just to the south of Silbury Hill is both an earlier, Roman, line and a later modern line). Bristol was the second city of the kingdom, and Bath already gaining popularity as a spa city with a lively, if as yet rather anarchic, social life. Aubrey's report on Avebury to the Royal Society in 1663 is a pivotal event—the first time that an antiquarian had made a presentation to the society—but Aubrey did not publish his findings. Aubrey was a modest man, and three and a half centuries later his comment on the excavations at both Stonehenge and Avebury—"I have brought (them) from an inner darkness to a thin Mist"—continues to be an accurate description of our knowledge of the stones.

William Stukeley was a scientist first and foremost, a medical doctor who brought to antiquarianism a level of scientific rigour it had not enjoyed before. He was the first secretary of the Society of Antiquaries, es-tablished in 1717. Between them, the two scholars set out plans and alignments for the circles and associated prehistoric remains. But whereas Aubrey had only measured and mapped the site, Stukeley both recorded and published his findings. Stukeley also campaigned vigorously against the destruction of the stones. Intentional destruction that is, for local people had always found new uses such as field markers, animal shelters or bridges for stones that had fallen and shattered naturally.

Just who were these men who wanted to destroy the Avebury stones? Mark Gillings and Joshua Pollard, in their excellent book on Avebury, have suggested a link to the contested religious history of modern England. The Five Mile Act of 1665 prevented dissenting clergy from preaching within five miles of a town. Thus Avebury, equidistant between Calne, Marlborough and Devizes, was ideally suited for non-conformists. In 1670 they began to meet in a group of cottages at the centre of the henge, in 1707 built their own chapel opposite these cottages, and by 1715 had a congregation of 130 souls. Gillings and Pollard suggest, then, a combination of practical desire for land improvement and building stone with a wariness of superstition and its continued perceived influence within the established Church of England. All too often what we see in the English village is the church, the established church. What we are far less likely to see are the rather more modest non-conformist chapels, many of them converted into private homes. This clash of church and chapel, of establishment and non-conformity, the divided nature of so many rural communities in the West Country, is a theme which will accompany us on our journey west to Cornwall.

Moving closer to our time, the most important event in opening up Avebury to a wider public was the arrival in 1922 of the playboy Dundee marmalade magnate Alexander Keiller. Keiller, an amateur archaeologist, was used to having his own way, and certainly had his own way with Avebury. What we see at Avebury now is the creation of a twentieth-century Scot as well as prehistoric men and women. Where Aubrey and Stukeley had attempted to disentangle on paper, as it were, the ancient remains from the later medieval village, Keiller did the same, but with the physical relics. Fallen stones were re-erected, bedded into concrete; the position of other removed stones was marked by concrete posts and triangular markers, making the remains of the stone circles, the henge and the West Kennett Avenue easily understood by the non-specialist visitor. It is, in the perhaps unfair phrase of Gillings and Pollard, a "facsimile". But Keiller did more; inconvenient cottages were demolished (with their owners' permission), the village garage, built onto the western stone of the Cove, was torn down and rebuilt elsewhere in the village. Tree stumps were gouged out, ditches cleared of rubble that had accumulated over the centuries. This process of cleansing the site continued even after the transfer of ownership to the National Trust in 1943, and in recent years the social cost of this process has become apparent. Many villagers were resettled at Avebury Trusloe, a mile and a half west of the village, but of course facilities such as the pub, shops, post office and school did not move with them. Needless to say, sought-after houses in the original village of Avebury are now beyond the reach of local people.

It is difficult as in so many heritage locations in the West Country to balance out the gains and losses. Local people may have lost out on housing and traditional village facilities but have gained some employment in exchange. New Age followers of the Druids have acquired an accessible and impressive site at which to celebrate their beliefs. Less spiritually inclined visitors enjoy that special sense of historical continuity that comes from a well presented historical site, with its museum and café and bookshop. This is a place, unlike Stonehenge, that is about touching and feeling and lying on the earth and sensing that awe which must have come upon people many centuries ago coming to Avebury for whatever religious, ceremonial or practical purposes they may have had. Avebury, despite everything, is still a place to be experienced and enjoyed.

PREHISTORY AND MODERN HISTORY IN THE VALE OF PEWSEY
The idea of the Vale of Pewsey as a route into the West Country is a rather modern one. Low-lying, heavy clay soil was of little use in prehistoric time, and the modern visitor to the Vale will soon discover the line of prehistoric settlements and burial sites that mark the skyline to the north, the same chalk downs that lie to the south of Avebury and Silbury Hill and the West Kennett barrow. It is a stark landscape, bleak and unforgiving in winter rain and snow, bright with the green shoots of winter-sown wheat and barley in the spring, golden at high summer and harvest time. It is also an empty landscape in which people are seldom seen, especially in winter. Perhaps a tractor out spraying in spring or a combine harvester in summer, an occasional walker following an ancient pathway across the downs. Or lovers of rising hot air—hang gliders, kite-fliers and the like. Then of

course there are the originators of the crop circles, those often complex designs in fields of ripe wheat which may be a gigantic hoax, or may be something else, but which provide amusement to both those who make them and those who come to view them in their season.

The village of Alton Priors, lying beneath the white horse carved into the chalk hillside, suggests the continuity and relative peacefulness of English history. There is a carving of the white horse on a sarsen stone within the village, conveniently placed so that visitors can photograph both the horse on the hill and its image in the village. It is an open village, with no obvious centre or thickening of buildings. Alton Priors has a fine medieval church which is now in the care of the Churches Conservation Trust. This is not to suggest a lack of Anglican enthusiasm in the village, as just across the brook is another church known as Alton Barnes. This is almost certainly pre-Norman Conquest, but with later additions such as a sixteenth-century roof and a three-decker pulpit.

Slightly further away but still within walking distance, Alton Priors has spawned an industrial suburb which is perhaps better known than the village itself. Honey Street is once more a busy, thriving canalside site, thanks to the remarkable efforts of the Kennett and Avon Preservation Trust. The story of the recovery and restoration of the canal is a remarkable one. Long stretches were dry and derelict by the middle of the twentieth century, the lock gates rotten and off their hinges, the bridges crumbling. Set up by a group of enthusiasts in 1962, the trust linked volunteer effort, know-how and enthusiasm with the world of bureaucracy—in this case British Waterways, local authorities and (eventually) the National Lottery. Now the story is told as a smooth tale of success, but at many points in that story, jeremiads claimed that it could not be done. There were ferocious practical problems in restoring such feats of canal engineering as the two fine, classical aqueducts in the Limpley Stoke Valley near Bath and the spectacular straight rise of the Caen Hill Flight of sixteen locks, which lift the canal 237 feet over a distance of 2¼ miles into the town of Devizes. From Devizes, the Long Pound, a stretch of fifteen miles with no locks at all, snakes through the heart of the Vale of Pewsey, and an area in which little had happened since medieval times suddenly became the centre of a busy and often noisy industrial enterprise.

The Barge Inn at Honey Street continues to be the throbbing, social heart of the canal. Colourful barges line the canal, replete with plants, animals, flags, assorted furniture, log piles and people. The white horse can be clearly seen on the lowering, gloomy or bright, golden downs (according to season) to the north, reminding us that the horse is in fact contemporaneous with the canal. Indeed, one wonders if the canal, with its use of horse-power well into the nineteenth century, may have been the inspiration for this chalk carving. The plaque on the wall of the inn claims "circa 1810" and history for once falls neatly into place. It falls into place even more neatly a few miles to the east. The canal climbs to its summit level tunnel at Wootton Rivers, on the edge of Savernake Forest, and then begins to drop gently towards the River Kennett. But despite the best efforts of the Scottish canal builder John Rennie, who had proposed a much longer tunnel, the summit level was insufficiently long, and water supply was a problem from the beginning. The answer was the canal-side pumping station at Crofton, a highlight of any visit to this area. One engine was installed in 1809, and a second in 1812. Both had been built by the Birmingham firm of Boulton and Watt. In 1846 the first engine was replaced by one from Harvey and Co. of Hayle in Cornwall, where sophisticated steam engines had long been employed to pump water from the tin-mines.

Beautifully restored, well explained and steaming at regular intervals throughout the year, the two Crofton engines remind us that the West Country is a cradle of the Industrial Revolution as well as of British prehistory. They also remind us of the pivotal role that John Betjeman, sometime Poet Laureate, played in conservation work of various kinds in the West Country and for which, whatever one thinks of his often maudlin and sentimental poetry, we should all be grateful. It was Betjeman who in 1970 released steam into the cylinder of the Boulton and Watt engine, and set Crofton on the path to full restoration. But one object at Crofton needs special mention. It is a clock that has been brought from Honey Street. It is older than anything in the place, older than the canal, probably made originally in about 1720 for a church in Bath that was burned down. It was saved, recycled in modern jargon, moved to the timber-yard at Honey Street and has been patched up with agricultural spare parts, a "real blacksmith's job", as one of the Crofton volunteers described it. Meanwhile, the clock acts as a useful reminder that one of the key processes of the Industrial Revolution was time, the establishing of national time as opposed to local time. No longer could one look up at the village clock, or hear it strike across the fields, and bow again to labour in the surety that it was indeed twelve o'clock. Now the question of whether the clock was right or wrong could be asked.

At Crofton the canal has a new partner, of which the walker or boater heading east may have been conscious for some time—through the distant roar and growl of high-speed trains on the Great Western main line from London to Exeter and Plymouth. At Crofton you look down from the grass in front of the pumping station onto the canal and then almost immediately to the railway, which will now accompany the canal all the way into Reading. The Great Western Railway had a simple and ruthless policy when it came to canal competition: buy them up and run them down. This was what happened to the Kennett and Avon. The railway integrated local agricultural communities more firmly into national markets. Without the railways, the milk industry in lowland Wiltshire and Somerset with its complex pattern of farm collection points, local hauliers and railway sidings would not have emerged. The same might be said of winter greens, flowers and early potatoes in Cornwall. In either case, the countryside would look and feel quite different if these particular kinds of land usage had not emerged. We shall return, lightly but repeatedly, in these pages to this intimate connection between human activity and landscape. Additionally, the railway brought new labourers into the West Country. A favourite signpost (in a land of lovely signposts with outrageous names) near Trowbridge points the traveller to Scotland and Ireland, almost certainly settlements of Irish and Scottish labourers working on the Great Western Railway. The nearest houseowner, perhaps from fierce British pride, perhaps with ironic intent, flies the union flag.

OLD SARUM AND NEW SALISBURY

If the gunfire from the Larkhill army artillery ranges can be heard in the Vale of Pewsey, it can equally well be heard on the southern flanks of the Plain at Old Sarum, the settlement that eventually gave way to Salisbury. Toy swords can be purchased in the shop here, and it is really rather depressing for those of us who might hope for a more peaceful future for the English countryside. William Golding, who lived and taught in Salisbury for many years before becoming a successful novelist and eventual Nobel Prize winner, was also conscious of the military presence, though he emphasized the secret chemical warfare experiments at Porton Down rather than the more obvious firing ranges. Writing about Wiltshire, he observed of tourists:

> They will not clamber through the woods to find an orchid or a ruin. They will see Stonehenge in daylight with a guide, not at midnight with clouds scudding across a full moon… They will find us mild, and the country mild. We are not exotic or grand. We have no Yosemite, no Grand Canyon. We have kingfishers, not cardinals; sparrows, not birds of paradise. The air-fields and army camps spread. The base at Porton denies it has anything to do with germ warfare—so often that nobody believes it.

Old Sarum under the management of English Heritage tries hard, but remains in thrall to the traditions of the Ministry of Public Buildings and Works. Monuments must be safe; they may not crumble or decline gently back into the earth. So the remains of the castle walls are supplemented by over-regular courses of twentieth-century flint. The dullness of Old Sarum is complemented by the rather gaudy illustrations around the site of what elements such as the "King's privy" (more likely the bishop's cess-pit) might have looked like 800 years ago. Around the ruins carefully mown grass allows for a few buttercups and speedwell, but little of the wild profusion of species on other downland sites. There is nothing of the romantic ruin depicted by Turner in the early nineteenth century.

History has not been kind to Old Sarum. An Iron Age settlement occupied successively by Romans, Saxons and Normans, the first Norman cathedral was damaged by a storm, the second, built not long after, was abandoned within a century when the bishop determined to develop a new city on the plains below. There is even less of the cathedral than the castle, Henry VIII having granted to one of his local supporters the right to cart away stone from the site. A ground-plan remains, and little else. The thirteenth-century church was keen to emancipate itself from the firm state control exerted by the Norman kings, and there was money to be made by developing a new market town on the plain. Salisbury, with its rectilinear grid of relatively wide streets, and the vast extent of its market-place, is probably the greatest achievement in England of medieval town-planning and property development.

From the ramparts of Old Sarum the eye is carried easily across the modern housing estates to the medieval heart of Salisbury and to one building—the cathedral with its great soaring spire. Golding was to write one his greatest novels about this building. He referred to the unpublished preface to *The Spire* in a 1976 lecture in which he emphasized the varying ways it can enter the consciousness of the viewer: "…the midsummer madness of a shivering spire fevered by mirage; the floating spire when mist has severed it from the earth; the drab, factual spire of rain and cold and wind; the enchanted spire that was lit at sunset or near it by the reflection from twenty acres of open daisies."

It is all these things, but the reason that this preface remained unpublished, as he pointed out in the lecture, was because the novel came to be about something else—the human cost of building the spire:

> Only when he is dying does he [Dean Jocelin] see the spire in all its glory; and the sight reduces him to understanding that he had no understanding. Theme! What is a theme? If the reader, the critic does not understand that after all the theology, the ingenuities of craft, the failures and the sacrifices, a man is overthrown by the descent into his world of beauty's mystery and irradiation, flame, explosion, then the book has failed. The theme is not there.

Human ambition and pride may have built the spire—on shifting, boggy foundations—but the spire has held and continues to fly above the city. Dean Jocelin may consider his dying view of a kingfisher as worth more than all his building projects, but it is the cathedral spire, not the kingfisher, that visitors from all over the world come to Salisbury to see.

Salisbury is a modest and pleasant city which lives successfully from the past. It is close enough to London for commuting, but rural enough to feel as much country as town. Old Sarum was quite a different matter, sitting on the chalk downs above the present city and, as Golding suggests in *The Spire*, connecting back to earlier patterns of belief and superstition. The decision to build a new cathedral on the meadows where the various tributaries of the Hampshire Avon meet was a daring one. Yet so confident was Bishop Richard le Poore about the success of the new foundation that he also laid out between 1220 and 1225 a whole new city to the north of the cathedral. It is based on a gridiron plan, with a large market-place bor-

dered on two sides by the parish church and guildhall. The gridiron plan has, remarkably, survived to this day, as has the market.

Given the fragile, low-lying nature of Salisbury, it is unsurprising that the water-meadows have remained undeveloped, and that wandering off across the meadows from the city, it is still possible to find the view that Constable chose when he painted his well-known and iconic picture of the cathedral. A copy hangs in the cathedral tea-room, and elicits comments such as "We used to have that picture in our living-room when I was a child." In May there are fields of buttercups and daisies, ducks, geese, herons and swans on the water channels swimming among yellow flags and dark green reeds. But there is evolution as well as continuity—egrets are now a common sight on the water-meadows, while one local farmer puts a llama in with his grazing sheep "to discourage the foxes." If there is timelessness here, it is a tribute to those who planned the medieval city, and those who continue to control its waters and restrict its development.

As well as the cathedral, the water-meadows and the city of New Sarum, visitors to Salisbury also come to see the Cathedral Close, handsome, detached eighteenth-century houses with neat lawns and gardens. Edward Heath, ex-prime minister, spent his final years at Arundells, a fine Georgian house in the close; Mompesson House belongs to the National Trust; yet another is occupied by Salisbury Museum. Henry Fielding was here, as we shall see in the chapter on Bath and Bristol. Walton Canonry was leased by the painter Rex Whistler from 1938 to 1944. He settled his parents there, hoping that eventually it would be a family home for him and a future wife. As his brother Laurence wrote: "it stood in a cul-de-sac beyond the west front of the Cathedral, with a long garden running down to the Avon and the water-meadows beyond."

For many years, Laurence lived in the shadow of his elder brother. Rex was an extrovert, Laurence an introvert, Rex was a talented and fashionable painter and designer, Laurence an unsuccessful poet beginning to dabble in the ancient craft of engraving on glass. He admired, even adored, his elder brother: "No companionship was like Rex's; but in the presence of others he inhibited me and I felt like his shadow." He uses the extraordinary phrase "innate unconfidence" to describe the depth of his personal uncertainty in the 1930s. Having single-handedly re-invented the art of glass-engraving, and carved out a creative artistic life for himself independent of his brother, Laurence engraved, over a long career, many of the scenes which will be described in the pages of this book. He engraved Stonehenge on a goblet in 1955, "imagined at the moment of midwinter sunset, probably its hour of sacred climax," a fine conceit. Yet the most moving of all his work remains the memorial in Salisbury Cathedral to his brother Rex, killed in Normandy in 1944. A slowly revolving prism is engraved on one side only, but each face of the prism shows different aspects of the cathedral: the nave, the spire, the chapter-house, the birds that dive and float around the spire, the family home at Walton Canonry. It is especially moving to the visitor who has descended from Old Sarum and heard the guns pounding on the Plain, much as they must have sounded in Normandy on the day of Rex's death.

Walton Canonry takes its name from Isaac Walton, son of Isaak, the fisherman who knew and loved the clear streams flowing down from Salisbury Plain and merging in and around Salisbury to form the Hampshire Avon. Less well known is the fact that Isaak Walton was the first biographer of George Herbert, poet and hymn-writer. At nearby Lower Bemerton the Wilts and Dorset bus heading for the "City Centre" squeezes between the church and the rectory. The church is a tiny flint-built building with a tiled roof, a porch and a curious little wooden, tile-hung belfry with stone mouldings round the windows. Opposite, the rectory is flint with stone mouldings, and some chequerboard work (where the white squares are stone and the black squares flint), an altogether grander building. So that we can be in no doubt, there is a plaque stating "George Herbert was rector here from 1630-33." He had been married in 1629 at Edington, on the northern edge of Salisbury Plain, where an annual Festival of Music in Liturgy takes place in August. Herbert wrote most of his religious poetry and many of his hymns at Bemerton. He died here and is buried in the churchyard opposite. He left a young wife and three adopted teenage nieces. George Herbert, dead from consumption a few days before his fortieth birthday—such an end to one of the brightest young men of his generation, Public Orator of the University of Cambridge at the age of 27. But such a life he made of it, making a virtue out of ordinariness, the humdrum, the daily round, the transient beauty of nature and the certainty of death.

The church that John Aubrey, the Wiltshire antiquarian, called "a pitiful little chapel of ease" is gay with flowers for Easter. Such were the things that delighted Herbert, for in everything he saw the creator at work.

The west window, with the handsome figures of Herbert and his friend Nicholas Ferrar, shows Salisbury Cathedral and its spire behind Herbert, for it was in Salisbury that he was ordained a priest. He carries a fiddle, a reminder that he was an accomplished musician who saw poetry and music conjoined, just as his words and the familiar hymn tunes have always been in the popular imagination. He comforted his parishioners—perhaps himself, the humble parish priest too?—with the thought that

> A servant with this clause
> Makes drudgery divine
> Who sweeps a room, as for Thy laws,
> Makes that and the action fine.

But much of his poetry, lost for centuries and rediscovered by Coleridge, is powerful and speaks to doubt and frailty as well as to faith and joy:

> Love bade me welcome: yet my soul drew back,
> Guilty of dust and sin.
> But quick-eyed Love, observing me grow slack
> From my first entrance in,
> Drew nearer to me, sweetly questioning,
> If I lacked anything. [spelling modernized]

Coleridge knew all about guilt.

Since Herbert's friend and biographer, Isaak Walton, was more famous for his fishing than his religious sentiment, it seems appropriate then that the garden behind the rectory slopes down to the clear, chalk stream of the Nadder. Upstream past Quidhampton, within the sanitized grounds of Wilton House, the Nadder is joined by the Wylye, and it is this stream which forms this most enchanting and unlikely of entries into the West Country.

THE WYLYE VALLEY

The modern traveller will probably cross to the eastern side of the river at the stone bridge at Stoford, just beyond Wilton, and proceed along the causeway across the water-meadows to Great Wishford, one of the most attractive of the many attractive villages of the Wylye Valley. The village shows the valley's characteristic mixed use of stone and flint, here laid in layers rather than in chequerboard. Some walls within the village are of brick and flint, others of stone. Into the retaining wall of the churchyard are placed the bread stones which mark the increasing price of bread down the centuries. Wiltshire people may be famous as "moonrakers", drunken yokels trying to dredge the silver reflections of the moon from the village pond, but here they celebrate their sound practical sense and their desire to get value for their money.

This is only the beginning in Great Wishford. An announcement on the village notice-board calls attention to the Oak Apple Club. But the celebration of King Charles II's escape from capture by hiding in an oak tree, which is the core of the 29 May celebration of Oak Apple Day, has little to do with Great Wishford. Here, the celebration is of common rights—rights to graze animals and collect firewood in Grovely Wood, the vast wood that stretches between Wylye and Nadder. The right to collect wood is registered under the Commons Preservation Act of 1965, and enacted on 29 May each year with the physical dragging of timber from wood to village, dancing, eating, drinking, high jinks and all sorts of fun. "Grovely, Grovely, Grovely and all Grovely" is inscribed on the inn sign of the Royal Oak pub, together with four women dancing in a circle bearing bundles of firewood ("nitches"). William Golding attempts to mystify what Grovely is about:

> I could take you to Grovely Wood, to a spot known only to three or four people, where you can pick Roman coins out of the mould if you care to take the trouble. In the middle of that wood is a block of sand-stone that must have come a long way—and not surprisingly, since it is all that is left above ground of a Roman temple. Yet perhaps the temple has left something behind that is even more enduring than sandstone; for once a year, the young people of the nearby parish go to the woods to have fun and gather green boughs, and come back in procession shouting "Grovely! Grovely! Grovely!" Nobody knows why, or what "Grovely" means, but if they had a voice, I think the burnt bones in the buried pots could tell us.

Grovely is not as obscure as that. The banner which is carried to Salisbury

Cathedral each 29 May makes this clear with its slogan "Unity is Strength". Four women dance solemnly with their nitches on the cathedral lawn to the music of a melodeon, watched by local people wearing oak apples in their lapels, and schoolchildren from the village carrying boughs of oak. All this takes place in the shadow of the great spire, with the wind, the birds, the gay fluffy clouds of early summer. As the clock strikes 10 a.m., the crowd forms into a loose procession which winds its way into the cathedral and right up to the high altar. They are welcomed by one of the cathedral priests, who rather surprisingly reminds them that their "charming" ceremony is also about "human dignity and human rights". (Quite how such an obvious spring fertility celebration became confused with the rights of medieval peasants, and then the celebration by royalists of the escape of the future Charles II from England during the English Civil War is beyond the scope of this book to tell.) He mentions the Prisoners of Conscience chapel in the cathedral and the fact that Salisbury is home to one copy of the Magna Carta. The rector of Great Wishford then reads out relevant sections of a 1603 charter, and the people's "claim", to which the villagers, led by the Oak Apple Club Chairman, respond with the cry "Grovely, Grovely, Grovely! And all Grovely!"

In the afternoon, the dancers, still holding their nitches aloft, process round the village with the Amesbury Town Band, the Bourne River Morris dancers, the Oak Apple Queen (and her predecessor from 1926 in a wheelchair) and several carnival floats. The beer tent does good business, there is jollity and feasting and dancing, the children wind and unwind the maypole, and join in other dances with the Morris men. And Great Wishford goes on being, well, Great Wishford. In this eccentric village, it is not surprising to find in the church a Victorian fire engine, a rather ornate funeral bier bearing an enormous pot of Easter lilies and a memorial to a priest who after landing his wife with twins abstained from sex for seven years before returning to the marital bed and producing septuplets—according to John Aubrey and subsequent tellers of tales.

Farther up the valley, thatch follows thatch, flint follows flint and stone follows stone, the stone and flint often jumbled into the same buildings with repairs carried out in red brick. There are some modern brick houses and sturdy rendered council houses looking not at all out of place in this mixed economy of building styles, the old and the new, the picturesque and the workaday. These are not picture-postcard villages but living communities, with their farms and village halls and welcoming pubs. At Langford, really a collection of villages, one of which is alarmingly named Hanging Langford, is a nature reserve and education centre run by the Wiltshire Wildlife Trust. A full month before the May celebrations at Wishford, a swan sits quietly on its nest enjoying the abnormal April warmth, ignoring a passing train. The flint, the stone, the bricks and the thatch continue. But shops are thin on the ground and these must be difficult places to live if you do not have a car. At Wylye there is a post office, but it is closed. A stone cottage shares its thatch with a splendid example of the chequerboard style—both cottages have smart cars in front of them. There is wealth in the valley, and perhaps some of it comes from the nearby presence on Salisbury Plain of the army. The post office may be shut, but the splendid Bell Inn is open, with next door the even more splendid mill, the ground floor in stone, two more floors of brick and a fine tiled roof with modern skylight windows. More splendid still are the giant cherries in the orchard behind, snowy with blossom, sending their fragrant message of peace across the militarized zones of Salisbury Plain east of the river.

At Stockton a school bus weaving its way between parked cars marks a certain moment in the long spring day. And there is half-timber to add to the medley of building styles and materials. A modern thatcher wearing nothing but a pair of pink shorts (this is April) looks to have enough work to last him well into summer, by which time he will probably have weathered just like the dark mature thatch on other houses. There is a large and very modern dairy just outside the village, as the road climbs towards higher, barer pastures. Until Boyton, that is, where the rural economy asserts itself at the Ginger Piggery, where a ginger pig lolling outside clearly pines for the cool mud of winter. This is all very recent, the main run of piggeries converted into craft workshops, a farm shop and associated restaurant and tea-room boasting that everything which is sold is produced within forty miles (what supermarket could make this claim?). A superb black, weather-boarded barn rests on 24 mushroom-shaped staddle stones. Previously, Boyton had not been much more than a large farm, and an interesting church tucked away in the grounds of the "big house". Farming has been around for a long time in this area. As in other places in the West Country, the Romans were here and there are indications that the medieval lynchets, or farm strips, alongside the road into Boyton from the south were once terraces for growing vines. There is talk of an olive tree once used as a boundary mark, though no indication of whether a crop was harvested. The new local food economy is beginning to fall into place, though on the chalk downs, industrial crops of rape continue to meld their yellow with the spring green of vast fields of autumn-sown wheat and barley.

An easy footpath (in summer at least) leads across the fields to the lost hamlet of Sherrington, population 72 in 1990 as against 179 in 1831, though one suspects the number of houses is probably much the same. It is not a place to come to by car—a few narrow, winding lanes leading down to the river, the ponds with their kingcups and weeping willows, and the church. There is a wooden bridge on stone piers, swans and ducks. Despite the absence of people, except a United Kingdom Independence Party lady in a long skirt and black stockings delivering election leaflets (does she know the Ginger Piggery is partly financed by European Union money?), the church is wide open, protected only by a mesh screen to exclude the birds. The dedication is to Saints Cosmas and Damian, Middle Eastern saints from Crusader times. It is a dedication which may or may not appeal to local army officers struggling once more with the politics of the Middle East. Outside is nicely weathered stone and a simple open belfry. The position of an orchid self-seeded into the grassy churchyard has been carefully marked, and two dandelions flower in anticipation of their grander neighbour. But the real surprise is the partial internal re-construction of 1624. Why a small country church should have had a costly restoration at this difficult time in English history is unclear, indeed obscure, but in recent years the church has been carefully restored back to its 1624 condition, a finely proportioned hall with beautifully semi-circular carved bench-ends on the pews, and an almost magical sense of space opening up in what from the outside is a tiny building.

On the walls, framed by pillar and scroll decoration, are texts such as the creed. The world had moved on from the Latin and the wall paintings of the medieval period. Here is good plain English, and one assumes some effort at least to teach the people of rural England to read and write. Later and more strongly the farther west we go, they would thank their masters by turning to Puritanism, Methodism, agricultural trade unionism. Herbert's domestic drudges were finding other ways to God. A large and well thumbed bible on the lectern is open at Ecclesiastes, Chapter One: "One generation passeth away and another generation cometh: but the earth abideth for ever." It is good to be reminded sometimes of the old truths.

We are now in more open country, though within a very few miles the Wylye will peter out among the chalk downs of Brimsdown Hill, Little Knoll, Long Knoll and Whitesheet Hill. Sutton Veny is quite large, almost a suburb of military Warminster, but has an old church at the far end of the village, replaced in Victorian times. Its chancel is still lovingly pre-served and tended, the rest of the church only a few walls. The key is lodged in a flowery cottage down the lane. You will find it if you are meant to find it. In Victorian times, the church must have seemed absurdly small for a large village in which the Church of England was resurgent in the face of non-conformity. There was little sentiment in the war for souls. At Longbridge Deverill, the first of the four Deverill villages, the busy A350 road down to Poole and Dorset crosses the Wylye and begins its climb up across the chalk downs past Pertwood Farm, one of England's largest organic farms. Longleat and Center Parcs are a mile or two away through the woods, but in a different world. At Monkton Deverill locals take pet goats for walks along the lane; there is an ancient standing stone in the paddock next to the church, usually patrolled by a goat too, and a useful reminder that there are continuities as well as ruptures in the history of rural England. Herbert's certainty of a kind and loving God is only one version of the search for meaning in life.

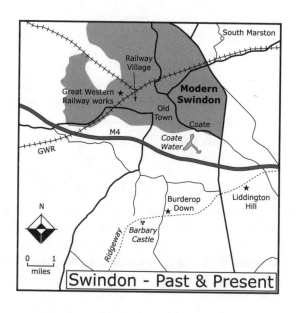

Swindon - Past & Present

Chapter Two
WILTSHIRE: A HOLLOW LANDSCAPE

Green grows the holly, so doth the ivy;
though winter blasts blow ne'er so high,
green growth the holly.

Gay are the flowers, hedgerows and ploughlands;
the days grow longer in the sun,
soft fall the showers.

Full gold the harvest, grain for thy labour;
with God must work for daily bread,
else, man, thou starvest.

Fast fall the shed leaves, russet and yellow;
but resting buds are snug and safe
where swung the dead leaves.

Green growth the holly, so doth the ivy;
the God of life can never die,
Hope! saith the holly.

English Christmas carol, traditional

THE VIEW FROM THE DOWNS

Today the chalk downs stretching down from Berkshire into Wiltshire and Dorset, so busy in prehistory, are lonely places, and have been so for some time. There is still some grazing, but also much arable farming, attractive in its own way, especially at harvest time, but requiring little input from the farmer—apart from occasional environmentally damaging inputs of fertilizers and pesticides. Hedgerows, flowers and wild life are a rarity in many parts of the downs. Most people flash past in motor-cars or trains and do not miss them. A few people care.

At Burderop Down above Swindon, stands a memorial to two men, Richard Jefferies (1848-87) and Alfred Williams (1877-1930). They both cared intensely about the natural world and they both wrote about this part of the world, although there is no evidence that they ever met. Indeed, Alfred Williams would only have been a boy when Jefferies died. Though both men were brought up in villages near Swindon, Williams at South Marston and Jefferies at Coate, Williams wrote about industry—the brave new world of the Great Western Railway workshops at Swindon—while Jefferies throughout his life continued to write about rural life, about farming and about nature. Both men have their supporters: the Friends of Alfred Williams and the Richard Jefferies Society.

Near Burderop is Barbury Castle, another prehistoric settlement with imposing earthwork ramparts. Here at least people come to admire the view and exercise their legs, their children and their dogs. Here the downs are well managed and access is encouraged. In autumn and winter they are grazed by sheep to keep the grass short; in spring and summer the sheep are removed and the result is a riot of wild flowers throughout the summer months. All is as it should be.

At Barbury Castle, the ramparts plunge, the skies are wide, the earth is broad. Cloud shadows chase one another across a great open landscape: the Vale of the White Horse, the smudge of greater Swindon, the flatter, more sombre distant line of the Cotswolds from where the weather is coming. The Cotswolds act as horizon, linking shades of grey from earth to sky. Kite-flying in blue and red takes place against a sky of complex blue and white and a million shades of grey. The kites stand out like splashes of paint on the canvas of the sky. On an autumn afternoon, the sky is by turns blue, white, black, grey, complex, volatile, impermanent; the earth green and deep, mysterious and still. We move on earth's surface, trying to belong, as the birds, flowers, animals, insects belong; seeking meaning, finding happiness or not, puzzled by beauty and violence, creation and destruction, frightened of our own mortality. The birds wheel and plunge and call above us. Welcome to the world of Richard Jefferies.

JEFFERIES ON THE DOWNS

Richard Jefferies was not easy as a man, is not easy as a writer. Like a later author who did much to establish the reputation of Jefferies, Edward Thomas, Jefferies wrote to order. He was a journalist, a good one, but writing within certain limitations. Like Thomas he was prone to depression and pessimism. Writing in 1884, three years before his death, Jefferies penned these words: "When I look in the glass I see that every line in my face means pessimism; but in spite of my face—that is my experience—I remain an optimist." "Three giants," he claimed, "are against me—disease, despair, and poverty."

On the Jefferies face of the Burderop Down sarsen, which commemorates both Jefferies and Williams, are the following words: "It is eternity now. I am in the midst of it. It is about me in the sunshine." Like most mysticism, like Herbert and the lines about cleaning a room, it seems at one level banal and incontrovertible, at another level profound, at a third simply contradictory. "Eternity" and the "now" are opposite concepts in most people's minds, and the notion of each moment as full of whatever life force sustains an infinitely vast universe is a difficult one. It is a case of where to start with Jefferies. First of all, he is one of the great English nature writers. Perhaps only Richard Mabey in modern times has come near to equalling Jefferies as detailed observer of the richness and variety of plant life. This is how he describes wood sorrel in the collection *Field and Hedgerow* (1887), published two years after his death:

> ...wood sorrel had taken root, and flower and leaf covered the space within, white flower and green leaf flourishing on old age. The wood sorrel leaf is perhaps more lovely even than the flower, like a more deli-

cately shaped clover of a tenderer green, and it lasts far on into the autumn… At its coming it is folded almost like a green flower; at mid-summer, when you are gathering ferns, you find its trefoil deep under the boughs; it grows, too, in the crevices of the rock over the spring.

Jefferies understands nature through the seasons, one of the most diffi-cult gifts for those who write about it. He also understood that this re-quired some effort, insisting that we need to know one locality very deeply, and in all seasons, rather than trying to extend ourselves over a wider area: "But you should know the place in winter as well as in tempting summer, when song and shade and colour attract everyone to the field. You should face the mire and slippery path. Nature yields nothing to the sybarite." He emphasized, in a way closer to modern ecology than nineteenth-century romanticism, the independence of nature from human kind. He wrote of flowers: "Beautiful though they are, they are bloodless, not sensitive; we have given them our feelings, they do not share our pain or pleasure."

Another place to start is the modest little farmhouse in Coate, on the outskirts of Swindon, where Jefferies was born and raised. This is now a small museum dedicated to his life and work, run by a dedicated little group of volunteers. They are replanting the orchard with traditional English varieties, and a young mulberry to replace, eventually, the old gnarled tree that Jefferies knew and loved. As Swindon extends south towards the M4, the farmhouse finds itself crowded in by the Sun Inn, the new Great Western Hospital, and opposite a Texaco garage. The young Jefferies slept in an attic bedroom, his immediate companions the birds twittering and squabbling around the gutters and eaves of the house. Another attic was the cheese and lumber room. The bookcase of books read by Jefferies as a child and young man springs no surprises: the Bible, Shakespeare, the great story-tellers—Rabelais, Chaucer, Bunyan—and the Romantics: Scott, Byron. In 1860 the farmhouse was complemented by dairy, pigsties, a well, a summerhouse, cow-houses. Now it has the Coate Country Park on one side, the new hospital on the other and the threat of a vast new housing development stretching down to the M4 and domi-nating Coate Water, which the Richard Jefferies Society opposes. The di-nosaur currently rising above the lake is the 1936 art deco three-stage diving board, last used in the mid-1950s before the polio scare put paid to swimming at Coate.

Jefferies made his living as a journalist, beginning work on the *North Wilts Herald* at the age of seventeen. There was something "driven" about him—a daytime job and all those books in a short life—two or even three every year. He began as a novelist (disarmingly the early novels are described in the museum as "mediocre") but he discovered his true vocation as a nature writer and also as a children's author. In the latter he used directly his experience of a lively rural boyhood on the farm, in the woods, and playing by the side of Coate Water. *Wood Magic* (1881) is a fable about a child who can speak to animals and birds, but the most direct reflection of Jefferies' magical childhood comes in the 1882 book, *Bevis: the Story of a Boy*. Many of the features of the farm and the lake described in the book are still recognizable at Coate today, and it is quite apparent why the Society opposes further development on the land surrounding Coate Water. But the "Council Oak" which features in *Bevis* lost its crown to disease in the 1990s. It survives, but in a reduced state. It is still possible, though, to imagine Jefferies' boyhood as that of "The School Boy" in William Blake's poem:

> I love to rise in a summer morn
> When the birds sing on every tree;
> The distant huntsman winds his horn,
> And the sky-lark sings with me.
> O! what sweet company.

If school, work, perhaps even marriage were to be his "cage", writing was to be his continuing link across time with the liberty of an idyllic childhood.

While *Bevis* and *Wood Magic* mark out one side of Jefferies' legacy as a writer and a man, another side of his importance and originality as a writer must centre on *The Story of My Heart* (1883). It is an intense, almost mystical book. As suggested above, he refuses to see nature as in any way expressing human emotions. Indeed, he switches the argument in a very "modern" ecological way by stressing repeatedly that human beings are part of the whole cosmos, equally important, equally unimportant, as everything else in the universe. Thus "prayer" for Jefferies is a process of immersing the self in this cosmic arena of which nature is merely the most immediate aspect:

> I was utterly alone with the sun and the earth. Lying down on the grass,
> I spoke in my soul to the earth, the sun, the air, and the distant sea
> beyond sight. I thought of the earth's firmness—I felt it bear me up;
> through the grassy couch there came an influence as if I could feel the
> great earth speaking to me.

He then goes on to treat the air and the sun in similar vein. There is a literature of this sensibility: the St. Francis of Brother Sun and Sister Moon, Emerson and Thoreau in North America, Edward Carpenter in praise of the simple life, perhaps Dorothy Wordsworth, or her brother William at his best.

The disconcerting feature of *The Story of My Heart* for those who enjoy Jefferies as a nature writer is that he turns his back here on the detailed description of plants and flowers, of animals and birds. He is asking instead important questions about a very personal experience of landscape and the meanings that might be ascribed to it. Indeed, the issue of meaning comes to dominate the later pages of this short book, and again he comes to some conclusions that must have surprised his contemporaries but which are close to the positions adopted by many modern "green" writers and enthusiasts. He contrasts, for example, the wealth of the earth and the energy of the sun with the inability of human beings to use wisely and share equitably these resources. In twenty-first century terms, think the inequalities of economic globalization that condemns the majority of people in the world to a life of poverty; or think solar power.

If Edward Thomas was one of the first to recognize the importance of Richard Jefferies and promote his work, a second disciple was Henry Williamson. We shall meet up with Williamson in North Devon in Chapter Nine, but a few preliminary remarks may be made here and now. Williamson was a man of the 1930s, bearing such double-edged swords as back to nature, the cult of the body, sun-bathing and sun-worship. He visited Coate at the time of the opening of the splendid new lido, and wrote:

> Thousands of people were swimming, boating, walking about. It was
> August. A tier of ferro-concrete diving platforms arose out of Bevis' lake.
> Also there was a new, special swimming pool, which was reached by the
> bathers only by way of a chloride of lime footbath. Within the enclosure

about a hundred youths and girls were water-playing, idling, sun-bathing. Was Jefferies near in spirit, I wondered to myself, as I reclined in the heat of the sun, my half-closed eyes warm-dazzled by the broken ripple-reflections.

What Jefferies found in solitude on Liddington Hill, Williamson found in a crowd at Coate Water.

For Williamson, Jefferies was (with capital letters) "The English Genius". He expands: "He was a genius, a visionary whose thought and feeling were wide as the human world, prophet of an age not yet come into being—the age of sun, of harmony." In a marvellously funny and blasphemous piece of Williamson over-writing, Jefferies of Wiltshire becomes a saint, a prophet: "The affinity of Jefferies with Jesus of Nazareth is patent in nearly all his work. If Francis of Assisi is a little brother of the birds, Jefferies of Wiltshire is a little brother of Jesus, of the sun, of clarity, of all things fine and natural and designed and efficient. Jefferies saw with paradise-clearness."

It is instructive to compare, as Jean Saunders, Secretary of the Richard Jefferies Society has done (in personal communication to the author) the selection from the writings of Richard Jefferies made by Williamson with that made by the poet Jeremy Hooker (*At Home on the Earth*). She confirmed that Williamson had left out one aspect of Jefferies: the concern for social justice in his later writings—precisely the texts to which Raymond Williams drew attention in *The Country and the City* (1973). He contrasts the myth of Jefferies as the writer of an unchanging, eternal countryside with the actual reality of what was happening on Jefferies' doorstep:

> This is the countryside of North Wiltshire and South Gloucestershire, where a portable threshing-machine had been invented and where rioting labourers, soon after Jefferies' father moved to Coate, had fought pitched battles with the local Yeomanry; where at Swindon, just down the road, a railway workshop was being built, and the town expanded rapidly as a junction and repair centre; where in Jefferies' time as a young reporter, the long depression of agriculture was beginning.

Bearing in mind that Jefferies wrote for conservative papers, it is hardly surprising that his views on rural discontent (he was born only a decade after the Swing Riots, which were especially violent in Wiltshire, and the beginnings of agricultural trade unionism) were relatively conservative too. Yet in a number of late essays there is evolution in his opinions. Here is Jefferies on the beauties of a wheat-field: "Behind these beautiful aspects comes the reality of human labour—hours upon hours of heat and strain; there comes the reality of a rude life, and in the end little enough of gain. The wheat is beautiful but human life is labour." In "Thoughts on the Labour Question" he criticizes the "divine right of capital" to exploit human beings worried over where their next meal was coming from. He argues for parish councils that would make decisions "irrespective of parson, squire, tenant or guardian".

Jefferies changed then, however reluctantly, and recognized a world changing around him, very different from his remembered childhood idyll at Coate. It is to that new industrial world of Swindon that we now turn, to consider the career of Swindon's second great author, Alfred Williams.

WILLIAMS ON THE PLAIN
On the Alfred Williams face of the sarsen on Burderop Down, we find the words:

> Still to find and still to follow
> Joy in every hill and hollow
> Company in solitude.

This is immediately easier than Jefferies. Obstinate, argumentative, opinionated Williams may have been. But there is something straightforward about him, even if he, like Jefferies, was prone to "disease, despair, and poverty".

Williams walked. The influence of the older man, Jefferies, came as a revelation and went with him where he walked: "The world, and especially this corner of it, has not been quite the same to me since; it is fuller and richer, more wildly and riotously beautiful than ever." Like Jefferies, he walked up on to the downs for pleasure. Williams also walked in search of Wiltshire and its traditions and its folk-songs. But above all he walked to work. And when he did not walk to work, he cycled. Jefferies certainly thought that he had a hard life, but Williams equally certainly had a hard life. Williams is the complete autodidact, often rising several hours before dawn to read and study before breakfast. Many of the writers whose works we shall refer to in these pages write obliquely of the changes that were coming over the face of the countryside in the nineteenth century. Alfred Williams confronts these changes head on. Born in the little village of South Marston, north-east of Swindon, to a mother whose husband deserted her with eight children, he worked in the fields from the age of eight, and when fifteen, in 1892, he joined the exodus from the land and two of his elder brothers in the Great Western Railway factory at Swindon. Eventually Williams would write poetry, stories, scenes of rural life. But no apology is made here for referring first and foremost to his book *Life in a Railway Factory* (1915), one of the first and best accounts of the realities of industrial time and discipline.

That part of Wiltshire was very quiet—very quiet. Life went on as it had always gone on. People were born, were married, worked the land, had children, died, had their funeral at the church or the chapel according to their family. But the railway changed all that, and not just in the town either. At a time of rural hardship it offered an alternative source of employment, with regular hours, winter and summer. The Great Western Railway was a stern but compassionate employer, with its model workers' housing, its social centre, its Mechanics' Institute for education, social contact and concerts, its baths and its own health centre well in advance of the coming of the National Health Service. Alfred Williams documented how its influence spread into all the villages around, like South Marston:

At an early hour the whole neighbourhood within a radius of five or six miles of the factory is astir; there is a general preparation for the coming day's work. The activity will first begin in the villages furthest from the town. Soon after four o'clock, in the quiet hamlets amidst the woods and lanes, the workmen will leave their beds and get ready for the long tramp to the sheds, or to the nearest station touched by the trains proceeding to the railway town. Many of their younger men have bicycles and will pedal their way to work. They will not be forced to rise quite as early as the rest, unless they live at a very great distance. A few workmen I know have, for the past twenty years, resided at not less than twelve miles from the town and have made the journey all through the year, wet and dry together. The only time at which they cannot get backwards and forwards is when there are deep floods, or after a heavy snow-storm. Then, if the fall has been severe and the water or snow lies to any depth on the roads, they will be compelled to walk or to lodge in the town. Sometimes the fall of snow has taken place in the night and the workman, under these circumstances, will be forced to take a holiday until it melts and he is able to journey along the road again.

Yet something was lost, and much of Williams' later work seeks to pin-point those losses. Sunsets are lovely throughout the West Country, but for Williams they brought something new, unnatural and dreadful into people's lives—the night shift:

The time of day fills you with a sweet sadness. The summer sun enter-ing into the broad, gold-flooded west, the soft, autumn twilight, or the gathering shades of the winter evening, all tell the same story. It is drawing towards night; night that was made for man, when very nature reposes; night for pleasure and rest, for peace, joy and compensations, while you—here are you off to sweat and slave for twelve dreary hours in a modern inferno, in the Cyclops' den, with the everlasting wheels, the smoke and steam, the flaring furnace and piles of blazing hot metal all around you.

While he worked he studied, beginning a Ruskin Hall correspondence course in literature. He belonged to the Swindon branch of the Workers' Educational Association (WEA), he lectured at the Mechanics' Institute; he taught himself Greek and Latin (later he was to learn Sanskrit too). And still he worked, and walked and cycled. *Life in a Railway Factory* was written at speed, while he was still employed at the works. He realized that to publish the book, with its frank appraisal of factory life, was incom-patible with his continued employment. In 1914 his health broke down, he left the works, and the book was published the following year. As he ex-pected, the company reacted with incandescent fury. A review in the company magazine referred to his "soured view of life", his "bitter preju-dices", his "unwholesome jibes". To give the company its due, it did allow Williams the right of reply, of which he took full advantage, claiming that "the life of the factory is forced, artificial, and unnatural."

The careful reader might assume, then, that Williams was a socialist, but this was far from the case. Despite his membership of the WEA, he felt ill-at-ease with the trade union and socialist politics which were coming to dominate the town, notably in the person of his old friend Reuben George. One of a number of unpublished books by Williams which exist in manuscript is called *A Worker's Letter to Workers*. He mistrusts trade unionists and socialists, preferring self-improvement, the kind of self-improvement he had demonstrated himself. Turning aside from industrial conflict and struggle, he proposed in one of his published works (*A Wiltshire Village*, 1912) other aims that the working class might pursue:

> The aim of the working classes should be not altogether for the highest wages, which must often be procured with terrific effort, but more leisure, more rest, more time for study and thought, more time to live; a greater freedom, good health, a clear conception of themselves and things, and a truer sense of the real independence with it.

Rather to his surprise, Williams was passed fit for military service in 1916. He did not have a distinguished military career, ending up in the backwater of India, where during long months of inactivity he was able to observe Indian life at close quarters, and begin to familiarize himself with Indian beliefs and stories. Especially at Ranikhet, within sight of Mount Everest, Williams found a new landscape to excite his imagination. Eventually in 1930 he was to publish *Tales from the Panchatantra*, a translation from Sanskrit, but most of his writings about India, his descriptions of landscape and customs, his rejection of the distinction between colonials and natives, his belief in the unity of all spiritual insight, remain in manuscript form. This author, at least, has seen them, and believes that they should be published. Back home in Wiltshire, Williams and his wife Mary called their new house Ranikhet.

Williams' scenes of rural life, published in his lifetime, bear witness to the continuing liveliness of life in rural Wiltshire in the interwar years of the last century. He described local characters of the villages of Swindon's downland fringe. There is acute social comment here. Like Flora Thomson in *Lark Rise to Candleford*, he observed in his portrait of Granny Bowles, a six-foot Amazon of a woman, the continuing commitment of some women to independent work in the fields:

After she married Bowles… she still went out to work, and while she had infant children, too. As soon as these were big enough she took them out in the fields with her, wrapped them in a shawl, and set them down under the hedge while she worked away, as they did in olden times… It was not until middle age that she adopted the profession of midwife. Jacky Bridge's mother fulfilled the office before her. They had no certificates in those days, nor were doctors often called in to attend at births in country places, and accidents were rare.

He is less sure of himself when rendering Granny Bowles in dialect ("Lar, what wonderful things they moticas and cycicels be! Oonder who fust pervented them"). Dialect literature has an uneasy history in the West Country, perhaps because regional dialects are so local, so varied, and so baffling to the outsider. In the same chapter, Williams refers, indirectly, to the agricultural riots of the 1840s which had so infected Wiltshire:

"'Tis main dull yer this marnin', chaps. Bistn't agwain to seng us a bit of a song to liven us up narn a bit, Jimmy?" the old man said one day in the hayfield. So Jimmy, the boy, struck up with lines from an old agricultural song, used in the time of the riots, and handed down to that generation:

> O you working men of England,
> Take heed to what I say,
> And have no rest, but do your best
> To get a fair day's pay.

"Yer, that 'ull do, that 'ull do. Dwun want to yer no more o' that. Casn't thenk o' nothin' else no different to that?" Jimmy thought a minute, then broke out again:

> O you big-bellied farmers, you pot-bellied farmers,
> Your pride and ambition shall soon be brought low.

"Damn tha, shet up! Tha's ten times wuss than ever…"

Fortunately, Williams chose not to use dialect in his folk-song collection

Folk Songs of the Upper Thames. This is a large and rich volume, for the purpose of which Williams claimed to have cycled some 13,000 miles between leaving the railway in 1914 and joining the army in 1916, straying into the border-country of Wiltshire, Gloucestershire, Berkshire and Oxfordshire. Little wonder he was declared fit to serve.

ROBIN AND HEATHER TANNER: LANDSCAPE AS A WAY OF LIFE

Landscape in the English West Country is a way of life. What we see can tell us much about both past and present. The trick is not to confuse the two, but at the same time to recognize elements of continuity as well as rupture. Parts of the great railway works at Swindon still stand. They do not build and repair railway locomotives and carriages. Instead there is Steam—in all but name the Great Western museum—a designer outlet village, the National Monuments Record Centre and a swathe of land awaiting redevelopment. The villages north and west of Swindon may look very pretty, but who lives behind the freshly painted front doors, the carefully tied back curtains? Indeed, the question we might well ask in some villages on the Cotswold fringe of Wiltshire is whether anyone is actually living there. So many of the cottages have gone to holiday rental or have been bought as second homes by rich Londoners. Even those who do live here on a year-round basis are more often than not dependent on jobs in Chippenham, Swindon, Bath, Bristol or even London. The hollowing out of life on the Wiltshire Downs is matched by the hollowing out of life in the thickly strewn villages of the Avon and its tributaries. Life has lost a certain texture, a certain denseness. There is less poverty, but less sociability too.

The countryside fights back, as it has done periodically since the days of William Langland's fourteenth-century *Piers Plowman* and the 1381 Peasants' Revolt. There are signs to look for: children going to school in the morning or being collected in the afternoon, a well maintained village hall with advertisements for forthcoming events outside, a general stores cum post office, perhaps run by a group of village residents, a pub that is still more than a restaurant and does not have signs up banning would-be drinkers "in working clothes" or "muddy boots", a farm shop selling local produce to local people. Arrive by bus or on foot, and a village can seem a different place. Langland emphasized the contrast of the peasant's life in winter and summer—the drudgery of winter replaced by the bright, shining summer's morning, just as toil and misery on earth might one day be replaced by joy in heaven. It remains true that these Wiltshire villages, golden and bright with flowers in summer, can retreat into a certain grey nothingness on a cheerless, sunless winter's day. It is impossible to ignore the seasons.

Alfred Williams stands astride the great divide between agricultural and industrial England and wrote about both. A generation later, Heather and Robin Tanner made their home at Kingston Langley, near Chippenham. *Double Harness* is the touching title of Robin Tanner's autobiography. It is subtitled "teacher and etcher", and these are the two activities for which he is remembered. Firstly, as a great art teacher, in schools in Deptford and in Wiltshire villages, later as an inspector, organizer of in-service courses, and one of the profoundest influences on the great flowering of primary education that took place in the years following the Second World War. Tanner believed in children, in their powers of creativity, their boundless potential, and their "astounding resilience". He wrote that "they inhabit an inner world which adults cannot enter or meddle in." Of course, we no longer believe these things. The edifice that Tanner and his colleagues created is now denounced as "progressive", for the purpose of education is to feed the voracious appetite of the global economy. Tanner blamed Margaret Thatcher in particular for this change, but now we can see that the backlash against child-centred education had been a long time coming and has gone deeper than even he might have guessed.

Secondly, and in some ways more potently, Tanner was the most gifted etcher of his generation, in a career that began in the 1930s and then resumed on his retirement from education in 1964. Heather wrote and Robin etched, rather as Eve had spun while Adam delved, in the medieval rhyme so often quoted by their hero William Morris. It was a formula for some wonderful art and a happy marriage, which lasted more than fifty years from 1931 until their deaths in the late 1980s. Together, they chronicled the survival of traditional agricultural communities well into the twentieth century. *Wiltshire Village* is loosely based on Kington Langley— which becomes Kington Borel in the book. This fiction allowed author and etcher to create a world very close to reality, but not unduly constrained by it, bringing in elements from various villages in the vicinity. For example, the engraving of harvest festival at the church is a 1931 engraving based on Draycott Cerne, with details of Langley Burrell and Biddestone churches.

The Tanners lived in an Arts and Crafts house they had built for themselves, the Old Chapel Field. They were Quakers too, part of that long West Country tradition of non-conformity in religion and social liberalism that has upheld much of the best of the region's life for 350 years, and will crop up like hard, weather-beaten rock at various points in this narrative. In a lecture in 1963, republished in 1989 by the Craft Studies Centre Robin Tanner helped to found at the Holburne of Menstrie Museum in Bath, he set down "What I believe." God is not mentioned, people are: "I believe in the powers of ordinary men and women; in their immense potentialities; in their capacity to rise higher than themselves; in their essential creativeness; in them as artists." To deny the mystery of life, its spirituality, as reflected in the created world, is to downgrade the human experience, to see only "through a glass darkly". This sense of something beyond that is intuited in love, in nature, in the cycle of the seasons, comes in the mysterious, other worldly glow that illuminates the best of his etchings, for example "February" in which the earliest flowers—snowdrops, aconites, coltsfoot, the first primroses—push through the debris of winter, beech mast and skeletal holly leaves.

There is sadness in the work of Robin and Heather Tanner, caused by the gradual disappearance of a world they knew and loved, by question marks over the future (the nuclear bomb, materialism and acquisitiveness). *Wiltshire Village* was completed in 1939; many of the changes came in the aftermath of war. Tanner wrote in his autobiography in the 1980s:

> We mourned for a lost Eden. Farming was becoming a noisy, mechanised, stinking business. Wagons, ploughs, and the horses that drew them were all disappearing. Wood and stone were giving place to asbestos and corrugated iron. Care and grace, and the old slow pace and the old thoroughness and craft were all abandoned. The farm-tractor was now king, and speed was all important.

If such changes were driven by human agency, the other disaster to strike the lowland Wiltshire landscape in the second half of the last century was Dutch elm disease in the 1970s. It began slowly enough but its progress was inexorable. In Wiltshire, at least, few elms survived. They still grow up from suckers in the hedgerows, but after ten years of growth again inevitably succumb. A tree that for many defined this kind of landscape has to all intents and purposes disappeared from our lives. The Tanners had their twelve giant elms injected with fungicide, but still they died, leaving great gaps in their daily lives, as trees, just like people, do. They planted small-leaved limes to replace the elms, to assert that the power of life, of living nature goes on, whatever happens. All is not lost: now once more farmers are being urged (and paid) to act as custodians, as trustees of the land. Young and enthusiastic people are looking for a life on the land, their attitudes very different from those whose outlook has been undermined by subsidies, over-production, foot-and-mouth, and all the other ills that have afflicted English farming in the last sixty years.

The Tanners had a wide circle of friends in the West Country, and were respected and admired wherever they went. Robin Tanner had taught for the WEA in Swindon, and known Alfred Williams' sparring partner, its secretary, Reuben George: "a ragged-looking visionary and true social-ist". George was an unlikely but much loved Mayor of Swindon too. The Tanners also knew Helen Thomas. She lived in yet another village near Chippenham, waking every morning afresh to the reality of the death in action, in 1917, of her husband Edward Thomas. Hers was a lifelong grief eventually to be assuaged only in her passionate, stirring prose. Thomas is part of this long march into Somerset, of people who knew one another as creative writers, as artists, and who have come to influence so heavily the way in which we perceive the world around us.

EDWARD THOMAS HEADING FOR SOMERSET

In 1913 Edward Thomas researched and wrote a book called *Journey into Spring*. His life was about to change—he was about to become one of our greatest poets. The world was about to change—the First World War was at hand. The two went together: Thomas enlisted and died at the front in 1917. He left us his poetry. Like Jefferies, Thomas was a depressive. It was not just a love of nature, an appreciation of Jefferies' qualities as a nature writer, that led him to write a biography of Jefferies. There is a meeting of minds too, of natures, a divine discontent. If the gleaming surface of the world is so beautiful, so varied, then why is so much of life routine, dull and devoid of meaning? Moving around was one way of avoiding the issue. If Thomas left us his poetry, he also left a widow, children, a tradition, a myth. Helen Thomas wrote of their life together in later years, and specif-ically about Thomas' discontent:

[Edward] had a fair amount of work, but never enough to keep him from anxiety, and never enough to free him from the hateful hack-work books written to the order of publishers, which although he did them well did not at all satisfy his own creative impulse, the damming up of which contributed largely to his melancholy. Yet against this has to be put that he was untrammelled by routine. He loved the life he lived away from towns, his own master, though in a freedom that perhaps gave him too much opportunity for brooding and for introspective doubts and hatreds [*sic*] of himself.

In his wanderings Thomas visited Broughton Gifford and enjoyed hospitality and cricket matches with Clifford Bax, the playwright, and his later-to-be much more famous composer brother, Arnold. Here he met Eleanor Farjeon on a number of occasions. Eleanor was to become famous as the author of that favourite children's hymn "Morning Has Broken":

Morning has broken
Like the first morning,
Blackbird has spoken
Like the first bird.

Whether they had anything that the modern world would recognize as an "affair" is hard to say. They certainly loved one another, a love which Helen Thomas acknowledged and embraced.

Thomas also stayed at Dillybrook Farm, Rudge, just into Somerset or maybe still in Wiltshire, and thus discovered Tellisford, a tiny hamlet on the Somerset bank of the River Frome. Part of *In Pursuit of Spring* was written on a return visit to Dillybrook. The book recounts the author's March cycle tour from London to Nether Stowey. On his way to Tellisford he visited the Richard Jefferies memorial in Salisbury Cathedral and deplored the way that it had been felt necessary "to drag in Almighty God." He was more tolerant of George Herbert at Bemerton. He lingered with his friends at Dillybrook.

West Country rain, as Thomas discovered (if he did not already know it for fact), can be insistent and unforgiving. In winter, the River Frome is often dark brown and swollen, swirling along at breakneck speed, tugging angrily at the willows and alders on its bank. At Tellisford itself, where the

valley widens slightly and the track from Dillybrook reaches the river, the water-meadow floods, which is after all its function. There is a stone bridge, a ruined mill which is ruined no longer, and a pretty cottage attached to it. There is an ancient flight of stone steps, and a hamlet—a few more stone cottages, a church and the crossroads.

All this, then, was well known to Thomas. His predilection for Tellisford is recounted through his alter ego, the Other Man, in Chapter Seven of *In Pursuit of Spring*:

> Away from this farm a beautiful meadow slopes between the river and the woods above. The grass, which becomes level for a few yards nearest the bank, was the best possible place, said the Other Man, for running in the sun after bathing at the weir—we could see its white wall of foam half a mile higher up the river, which was concealed by alders beyond.

Who is this Other Man who appears at various points in the journey? Conscience, desire, the sum of roads not taken, of how life might have been different, better in some obscure way? Who knows? As the travellers ascend the stone steps on the Somerset bank of the river, Thomas notes the "walls that were lovely with humid moneywort, and saxifrage like filigree, and ivy-leaved toadflax." So are they still, these walls. It is at this point that the Other Man refers to the problem of writing about nature, "the impossible task of reducing undigested notes about all sorts of details to a grammatical, continuous narrative" and the way that this could blind the writer to the spirit of nature itself. He wonders whether by taking no notes at all, he might render his detailed observations more accurately, "arranged not perhaps as they were in Nature, but at least according to the tendencies of his own spirit." Surely this is Thomas feeling his way towards poetry? The discussion is of such intensity that the two men, the soon-to-be poet and his alter ego, manage to miss the lane to Norton St. Philip. Nowadays it is easy, unless some local joker has changed the signpost around, a common rural sport in the West Country. In any case, a splendid wooden bench with the date 2000 carved on its back also marks the way to Norton St. Philip and the pleasures of the George Inn and the Fleur-de-Lys public house.

That night, Thomas reflects on his day on the road, "dwelling chiefly on Tellisford, its white bridge over the Frome, the ruined mill and cottage, the round tower of Vaggs Hill Farm, and the distinct green valley which enclosed them …" Come and see for yourself, arriving on foot if you possibly can, or by bicycle, as Thomas did. It is all there, nothing added and nothing taken away, certainly including his thrush and probably his nightingale too. Thomas omitted only the kingfisher, that glorious blue bringer of good luck and enlightenment. The Tellisford kingfisher is no shy bird, here one moment and gone the next. Up and down the river he sped when I was last there. On the Wiltshire bank he entertained the bathers, lying on the green meadow or splashing happily and noisily in the Frome. On the Somerset bank he caught the attention of an earnest bunch of adults who had come to inspect the weir, as part of a visit to the newly restored mill which now generates electricity for the national grid. This is a serious project, generating enough electricity for forty houses—more houses, indeed, than there are in the hamlet—but at least one of the party wished he was in the Other Group …

Thomas's predilection for river swimming is well known. And river swimming is alive and well in the River Frome. The weir above the mill creates a good depth of water, which is clean and soft, although opaque because of the tiny soil particles floating in it. There is an old Second World War pill-box, crumbling and grass-topped, which makes a good place to sit and watch the light, dissolved by the overhanging willows, playing on the silver waters. At nearby Farleigh Hungerford, with its beckoning romantic ruin of a castle, a water-meadow on the Somerset side of the Frome is the headquarters of the Farleigh Hungerford Swimming Club. There are simple changing rooms, and there were diving-boards before they were ruled unsafe. There are yellow water-lilies in season, and more willows to float beneath in the cool, dark, deep waters of the Frome.

Tellisford's other claim to fame, a curious one of which its inhabitants are reluctant to boast, is being a Thankful Village, one of only a handful in Somerset. The three men who served in the First World War came home safely. It is doubly thankful because the seven local men (out of a population reckoned to be about forty) who served in the Second World War came home safely too. Only a handful of villages in England can make this double claim, which makes the Edward Thomas connection that much more poignant.

Chapter Three

TRADITIONAL DORSET

Only a man harrowing clods
In a slow silent walk
With an old horse that stumbles and nods
    Half asleep as they stalk.

Only thin smoke without flame
    From the heaps of couch-grass;
Yet this will go onward the same
    Though Dynasties pass

Yonder a maid and her wight
    Come whispering by:
War's annals will cloud into night
    Ere their story die
        Thomas Hardy, "In Time of 'The Breaking of Nations'", 1917

A Quick Tour

Dorset has a northern fringe that scarcely seems to belong to it at all, a chalky, dusty hinterland that gathers itself suddenly in a wild surge up to the heights of Shaftesbury. Shaftesbury betrays its age by its position; unusually it stands upon a hill top, a high ridge that drops steeply on every side. Alfred the Great founded a nunnery here in 888, which housed the bones of Edward the Martyr, and for a time Shaftesbury was known as St. Edwardstow. Cnut or Canute, tired of the sea, died here in 1035. The houses of Gold Hill tumble towards the green and watery fields and hedges of Blackmoor Vale. They are famous as the setting for the Hovis bread advertisements made in 1973, and infamous because in 2003 a Sunday newspaper revealed that a brothel was operating from a house at the top of the hill. Common Ground, which campaigns on behalf of local particularities, have their headquarters here. Angela King and Sue Clifford, the authors of Common Ground's *England in Particular*, are modest and kindly neighbours and do not mention the brothel. They do, however, note the mists that lie across the Vale on winter mornings and above which Shaftesbury soars majestic and untroubled. It is a fine town.

Two roads head south out of Shaftesbury in the direction of Blandford. The lower route is an A-road that struggles to merit that category, sneaking through villages and suffering from disconcerting right-angle bends, no doubt to please a local landlord of years gone by. The other road is unclassified, but once Melbury Abbas—Melbury belonging to the abbess of Shaftesbury—is past, the road strikes upward onto the downs and the National Trust lands at Fontmell Down with their rich flora, especially cowslips in spring, and panoramic view of the Blackmoor Vale and weather rolling slowly in from the west.

Blandford Forum, where the Upper and Lower Blandford Roads meet up again, was lucky. Almost completely destroyed by fire in 1731, it was rebuilt methodically in handsome Georgian brick. Not that the locals thought themselves especially lucky. There were thirteen deaths, with many more dying in the outbreak of cholera that followed. In all, 480 buildings were destroyed. Whereas Bath, which we shall reach in Chapter Seven, was built in stone in a rather heavy classical style out-of-sympathy with human scale, Georgian Blandford retains that human scale, with the domestic feeling of a busy market town, which is what it is, sustained by a busy army camp just over the hill. Many of the rebuilt houses contain dormer windows, now a rarity in Bath, although common in the towns round about. Blandford was well supported in its recovery, whether from insurance payments or state subsidy is unclear. On the London-Exeter stage-coach route, it was a lively, go-ahead place and worth the investment. The main beneficiaries of the post-fire payments were the Bastard brothers, architects, builders and busy entrepreneurs who owned most of the town centre properties. The pump in the Market Place reads honestly: "John Bastard, a considerable sharer in the general calamity." He shared in the calamity of loss but also in the very profitable re-building. Both Bastards, John and William, are engraved with suitable ambiguity into the pavement outside the handsome Town Hall:

> Recipe for regeneration:
> take one careless
> tallow chandler and
> two ingenious Bastards.

West Country black humour at its best.

Like so many small towns in the region, Blandford is in the process of remaking itself, and its role as a market town. People still come in from the surrounding villages to shop and visit banks and building societies. In that sense it is still the Blandford Cheaping of Saxon times, as well as the Blandford Forum of more recent times. But the animals that formed such a large part of most West Country markets are a thing of the past. The chief memory in Blandford of these long-gone creatures is the delightfully named The Plocks, the place where sheep rested for the night before being sold at market. Unsurprisingly, local children memorialized this in their own version of the Christmas carol: "While shepherds watched their plocks by night."

The smart new trend is the farmers' market, held on the second Friday of each month. Here, local producers sell directly to the public, as indeed they have done for centuries, without the need for wholesalers and other intermediaries. This is not so much new as the reinvention of tradition. It is not just a question of bringing the countryside into the town, but of understanding the countryside in a different way. For nearly a century now, farming has been an industry, providing staple foods to a food manufacturing industry, initially very cheaply indeed, but for the sixty years following the outbreak of the Second World War at prices subsidized by the state (initially the UK government, later the European Union through the common agricultural policy). Now most of the subsidies have gone and the supermarkets drive down prices relentlessly. Many small farms have been driven out of business, while others, the clever ones, have diversified. In the West Country, this means not only holiday cottages, but also bed-and-breakfast, rural study centres and a return to older ways: meat and vegetables sold directly to the customer either through a farm shop or a farmers' market, home production adding value to good quality home-grown ingredients—farmhouse cheeses, wines and ciders, pies and cakes. All of these can be bought at Blandford if you get there on the correct Friday morning.

Blandford, like Dorset more generally and indeed the whole West Country, is a hot-bed of non-conformity. The Methodist church is not only still open, but is greatly enlarged in recent years, a social centre as well as a place of worship. Here young offenders serve lunches to the elderly, and some like it so much they stay on after their probation ends. The Wesleys' grandfather was a Dorset man and a non-conformist. He suffered prison and fines for his refusal to support the established church after the restoration of the monarchy in 1660. The parish church of Blandford, St. Peter's, despite its dominant position overlooking East Street and Market Place, seems less lively, and is closed to visitors in the afternoon. Its Georgian simplicity was rather spoiled when the apse was moved back thirty feet in late Victorian times to make room for a chancel. There is some remaining Georgian plain glass but rather more coloured Victorian glass. The tower is a later addition too.

And so on to the sea at Poole. The harbour is a vast natural feature that eventually converges on the narrow gap between Sandbanks and Studland. A busy chain ferry fills the gap. Most yachts and other small craft simply dodge the ferry. Only the larger container ships and the ferries across to France cause it to pause in its constant movement.

There are a number of islands in the harbour, the largest of which is Brownsea Island. Now it is owned by the National Trust and boasts a nature reserve. It is one of the last strongholds of the pretty red squirrel, an animal that seems to always raise a lump in English throats as it struggles for survival against its more aggressive imported cousin, the grey squirrel. Three hundred years ago, when that redoubtable traveller Celia Fiennes passed this way, the island was almost completely given over to industry—the extraction of copperas (ferrous sulphate), a most unpleasant green mineral which was used in dyes, to make ink, and in tanning. In the nineteenth century there was an attempt to set up a pottery here to rival that of Poole itself, but that failed and Brownsea's fate as a leisure island was sealed in the early twentieth century when Baden Powell discovered it and brought his nascent Scout movement to camp on the island in 1907. Brownsea survived the Second World War, despite being used as a decoy for Poole, and Scouts and Guides still use the campsite on the island. From here there are fine views across the sombre Purbeck Hills, across the heathland to Studland Bay and the Old Harry Rocks, and back towards Poole and the security of the mainland.

Copperas and clay are not the only minerals that lie beneath Poole Harbour. There is oil too, and a small site at Wytch Farm offers an incongruous view of camel-like oil derricks more familiar to most people from films set in Texas. Much of the oil operation is screened by carefully planted tree belts, but the derricks are linked by an underground pipeline to Southampton and their own rail terminal, so perhaps some people think they see an oil-well, blink and decide they must have imagined it. The ever-observant Celia Fiennes knew about the oil, though she spotted it in Swanage. Here, she observed, "they take stones by the shores that are so oyly as the poor burn it for fire, and its so light a fire it serves for candle too, but it has a strong offensive smell."

The chain ferry across the narrow neck of Poole Harbour gives access to Studland Bay and to the hills of the Isle of Purbeck (not of course a real island) beyond. Owned by the National Trust, the bay is home to an interesting experimentation in coastline management that will eventually change the whole prospect of the place. A National Trust strategy study concluded that "any option to protect property from coastal erosion would entail adverse effects on the landscape, earth science and nature conservation value of the area, as well as the quality of the visitor's experience." Erosion and deposition are both allowed, so to the south the coast is being eroded, while to the north the dunes, an important nature reserve, are growing. Some beach-huts south of the café on Knoll Beach have already been relocated; eventually the visitor centre will also need to retreat from the busy sea. If the weather is good, it is hard to drag yourself away from the beach at Studland, with its views north towards Bournemouth, south to the shaggy white pinnacles of Old Harry Rocks and across the sea to the gleaming cliffs of the Isle of Wight and the Needles. If Wight is not visible, then it is probably no day for the beach, and indeed it is behind the beach that much of the interest of Studland lies, especially around the Little Sea, a large lake formed as recently as 1880 by dune development, loud with wintering birds, surrounded by purple heather in late summer. The heathland is home to all six English reptiles—the rare smooth snake and sand lizard, the more common adders, grass-snakes, slow-worms and common lizards. Most shun visitors—to see an adder is extreme good fortune, while to be bitten by one is extreme misfortune.

From Studland, the road curls dramatically upwards and over towards Corfe Castle, with panoramic views of the joys of Poole Harbour, oil rigs and all. Corfe is a romantic and unlikely ruin, a fortified house built on a dramatic outcrop that dominates a narrow route from Wareham towards the sea at Swanage. Like other romantic ruins in the West Country, it owes its ruined state to the obstinate defiance of royalists during the English Civil War. These are matters that still arouse passions in the West. The Bankes family were well rewarded for their stubborn support of the king: on the Restoration of 1660 they received the splendid estate at Kingston Lacey, including Badbury Rings, one of the finest of Dorset's many prehistoric hilltop sites. Since 1982, all of this has been the property of the National Trust, including Studland for which Mr J. H. R. Bankes is reputed to have once turned down an offer of £2 million from Billy Butlin, who wanted to build a large holiday camp there.

Back across the hills, Dorchester is still the thriving county town that William Barnes and Thomas Hardy knew. North of Dorchester, the countryside climbs rapidly up the valleys of the Piddle, the Cerne and the Frome towards the chalk heights again. Queen Victoria was reputedly not amused by the lavatorial humour of the place-names hereabouts, and this has been posthumously used to explain why the villages of the lower Piddle (Affpuddle, Tolpuddle) through which she might pass on her way to Weymouth have changed the vowel in their names, while the more remote villages (Piddlehinton, Piddletrenthide) have retained the offending sound. Dorset tries hard to be respectable, and William Barnes, the dialect poet, did his best to persuade visitors that Dorset folk were friendly, decent folk, but the county never quite manages to be respectable. Which brings us neatly to Cerne Abbas and the giant figure with his club and his permanent erection, as fixed as the smile on the Mona Lisa, on the hillside above it. Even those who have seen photos of it marvel at both the size and the sexual explicitness of this rather unique monument. Ancient it possibly is (a Roman Hercules the most likely explanation), but no-one knows for sure, and sensible viewers prefer to enjoy rather than to puzzle. Cerne's history is well documented and it does seem surprising that there is no mention of the "giant" until the eighteenth century. It may just have been a giant practical joke executed in more recent times, but still long enough ago for the modest cloak of antiquity to be drawn across it in this obscure corner of England.

LYME REGIS

Westwards, Dorset goes on, and on, until it eventually becomes Devon. The coast has always attracted visitors. Chesil Beach, with its churning, straining pebbles, stretches for mile after lonely mile westwards from gentle Weymouth and savage Portland. Bridport, with its Arts Centre and its Local Food Centre, is a phoenix rising from centuries of decline. At Charmouth the cliffs are crumbling into the sea, making this a favourite haunt of fossil-collectors and more serious scientists. The coiled ammonite is one of the most common fossils here, but occasionally much larger fossils of prehistoric sea-creatures have been found. It was a local girl, Mary Anning, born in Lyme in 1811, who began the process. On her walks along the coast she found bones sticking out of the crumbly blue lyass, and persuaded some men to help her excavate. To their astonishment, they found a thirty foot-long skeleton, eventually named *ichthyosaurus* and deposited in the British Museum. *Plesiosaurus* and *pterodactylus* followed, and Mary Anning became famous among townspeople and visitors alike. Eventually a window in the local church celebrated her work, even though it did, of course, constitute another indication of the wild inaccuracies of biblical accounts of creation. Each winter storm continues the process of uncovering inch by inch the processes that once went into forming the land.

Lyme Regis and its Cobb continue to draw on their Jane Austen associations to attract visitors, while more recently the town became the home of the novelist John Fowles. Fowles contributed much to Lyme Regis, in particular to its museum. Ironically, his modest pamphlets about local history and museum guides now exchange hands for figures far in excess of their cover prices. Fowles would probably have been much more pleased that his beloved Undercliff, the secluded landslip area of crumbled cliffs and woodland west of Lyme (and in Devon—this is one of a number of points at which we shall play fast and loose with county boundaries) is a well protected part of this World Heritage coastline. It is the setting, of course, for key episodes from Fowles' 1969 novel *The French Lieutenant's Woman*, made into a film in 1981.

The initial meeting between Charles, the Darwinian fossil-hunter and the melancholic "French Lieutenant's Woman", Sarah, takes place on a storm-tossed Cobb at Lyme with the waves breaking over the pier. No doubt Fowles was conscious of the Austen allusions here, and in particular Louisa Musgrove's fall in *Persuasion* (1818). For Austen, there is something wrong about the visit from the start—it is horribly out of season, "too late in the year for any amusement or variety which Lyme, as a public place, might offer." That leaves the mighty two-tier breakwater, the Cobb, as the main attraction: "its old wonders and new improvements, with the very beautiful line of cliffs stretching out to the east of the town." For Fowles, it is not the coming out of season nor Louisa's carelessness, but the Undercliff itself that constitutes the problem. Charles is a methodical Victorian scientist and the Undercliff is the home of nature in riotous, promiscuous confusion and, by imaginative extension, of irregular sexual encounters. It leads to the portentous conclusion: "Charles did not know it, but in those brief poised seconds above the waiting sea, in that luminous evening silence broken only by the waves' quiet wash, the whole Victorian Age was lost. And I do not mean he had taken the wrong path." Where Charles had walked, Louisa Musgrove had already prepared the way. There is still something unsettling about nature around Lyme; we are used to a well-formed land, we like to think of landscape as unchanging or at least time-honoured, but here all is young and provisional, and change is of the essence of things. Perhaps, the breeze whispers, we are merely an infinitesimally small and insignificant corner of a universe we cannot even begin to comprehend. The Undercliff is an unsettling place.

In the Austen novel, the "fall" (like Adam's in the Garden of Eden story that leads eventually to the salvation of mankind) is a "happy" one, leading by a series of happy coincidences to a successful courtship and marriage. In Fowles it takes us into darker areas of human relations, despite the eventual reconciliation and happy ending on Lake Windermere. This darker side of human life is embodied in the story and film by the Un-

Charmouth Beach

dercliff, where the lovers' second (unintended) and subsequent (deliberate) meetings take place. Sarah's employer (she is a governess) identifies the Undercliff as a place where respectable people simply do not go. "Do I make myself clear?" she screams at Sarah, at least in the film. It is an ambiguous place, of great natural beauty but because of the cliff falls, nature in disorder with fallen trees and boulders all jumbled. The sky very distantly peeping through the lush foliage of the trees makes this seem a private, separate kind of place. Only occasionally are there glimpses of the sea far below. And as Sarah emerges from the Undercliff to return to Lyme in the film, there is a stunning view across to Golden Cap shining golden in the sun. One wonders how long the director had to wait for that shot? Patricia Beer, in her very amusing and even better book about the National Trust properties in Wessex (a word we shall turn to shortly), is very funny and pessimistic about the Golden Cap. She comments especially on the mists and fogs that can arrive without warning from the sea and envelop the visitor in impenetrable swathes of white. This accords with the experience of the present author, who spent his fortieth birthday ascending the Golden Cap in rain and fog, to be rewarded by nothing more than cold, wet, swirling mists at the top. Experiences in a landscape can be less than sublime or pastoral.

HARDY'S WESSEX

Thomas Hardy was not the first writer to "discover" Dorset. That honour must surely go to William Barnes, born in 1801 at Sturminster Newton, a handsome old town on the River Stour. There are aspects of Barnes that recall Alfred Williams. Like Williams, Barnes was largely self-taught but did acquire sufficient schooling to become a solicitor's clerk, first in Sturminster, then at Dorchester. Like Williams, he was a proficient linguist, eventually claiming a knowledge of twenty languages. Unlike Williams, he was supported by an ambitious wife. In 1823 he set up a school in Mere, in the far north of the county. The school prospered and eventually relocated to Dorchester. Later, Barnes took holy orders and a degree in Divinity. His wife died in 1853, the school declined, and Barnes ended his life as a much-loved parish priest, dying in 1886. The much younger Thomas Hardy (born 1840) knew Barnes and liked him. With that eye for a quick character-sketch in which physical and moral traits combine, Hardy described him as "attired in caped cloak, knee-breeches, and buckled shoes, with a leather satchel slung over his shoulders, and a stout staff in his hand." It is much like the statue of him outside St. Peter's Church (though carrying a book rather than a satchel), next door to the delightful museum he helped to found.

Barnes wrote much of his work in dialect. He aimed to replace foreign loan words in the language with more authentic Saxon terms. This was a serious project, not mere whimsy. In 1863 he published *A grammar and glossary of the Dorset dialect*. Now few speak it. Hardy chose and edited the "Selected poems of William Barnes", many of them in dialect. Yet Hardy himself makes only limited use of dialect. Dialect is part of the scene-setting, the general atmosphere of his stories, used mainly for minor characters. In general the central characters speak standard English, though Gabriel Oak in *Far from the Madding Crowd* uses some dialect expressions in speaking to the farm labourers. Hardy knew how to package and present rural Dorset to a wider, and mainly urban, audience. His readers would tolerate quaintness, indeed enjoy it, but to transliterate regional ways of speaking too literally would be, he judged, too much of an imposition on his audience. Already we have the first important shift of position in Hardy.

It took Hardy a great deal of time to admit the central fiction of his fictions, that the world he created in his novels no longer existed. The subject of his novels was the world of his childhood in the pretty cottage at Bockhampton on the edge of the heath, the stories he heard from his parents, not the world of the ugly urban villa that the established writer had built at Max Gate in Dorchester. And that world went beyond Dorset, as the map so often inserted in his novels, and helpfully provided by Hardy for the first collected edition of his novels, makes clear. He chose Wessex as the name of this world—the fictional becoming the mythical. Wessex is Dorset but also borders over into neighbouring counties from Toneborough (Taunton) in the west to Aldbrickham (Reading) in the east and Christminster (Oxford) in the north. In a preface to *Far from the Madding Crowd* (the novel is 1874; the preface is dated 1895-1902) Hardy wrote of the anachronistic view of "Wessex" which his early novels promoted:

> ...the press and the public were kind enough to welcome the fanciful plan, and willingly joined me in the anachronism of imagining a Wessex population living under Queen Victoria;—a modern Wessex of railways,

the penny post, mowing and reaping machines, union workhouses, Lucifer matches, labourers who could read and write, and National School children...

Hardy referred to the material changes in the countryside and the cultural results of those changes:

The change at the root of this has been the recent supplanting of the class of stationary cottagers, who carried on the local traditions and humours, by a population of more or less migratory labourers, which has led to a break of continuity in local history, more fatal than any other thing to the preservation of legend, folklore, close inter-social relations, and eccentric individualities. For these the indispensable conditions of existence are attachment to the soil of one particular spot by generation after generation.

And yet, and yet. The very attraction of Hardy's novels to an urban, novel-reading public was that they might be taken to be a description of the countryside of late Victorian, rather than early Victorian, times. Church music is a prime example. Hardy's father and grandfather both played in "West gallery" bands. We can admit that the very term was first used by Hardy the novelist. We can also admit that Hardy's grandfather served 35 years as bass viol in the Stinsford church band. Yet that group of players was disbanded when Hardy was only one year old. Who would believe this reading *Under the Greenwood Tree* (1872)? Its sub-title, *The Mellstock Quire*, which Hardy in retrospect preferred to the original title, suggests the importance to the novel of the singers and musicians. There are lively discussions of the advisability of using the clarinet, especially when carol-singing on cold December nights—"An icicle o' spet hung down from the end of every man's clar'net a span long", remembers their leader about a Christmas long past—and the pernicious actions of vicars who preferred the barrel-organ to the band. Hardy describes them assembling for a long Christmas Eve of carol-singing:

Shortly after ten o'clock the singing boys arrived at the tranter's house, which was invariably the place of meeting, and preparations were made for the start. The older men and musicians wore thick coats with stiff perpendicular collars, and coloured handkerchiefs wound round and round the neck till the end came to hand, over all which they just showed their ears and noses, like people looking over a wall. The remainder, stalwart ruddy men and boys, were dressed mainly in snow-white smock-frocks, embroidered upon the shoulders and breasts, in ornamental forms of hearts, diamonds, and zig-zags. The cider-mug was emptied for the ninth time, the music-books were arranged, and the pieces finally decided upon.

As an evocation of the past, this is fine writing indeed, and forty years later, in the 1912 preface, Hardy was to bemoan his light treatment of the Mellstock Quire and to reflect that they deserved perhaps "another kind of study", aiming at "a deeper, more essential, more transcendent handling" of the material. Such are the regrets of elderly writers, but the truth is that *Under the Greenwood Tree* has little to do with that "changing and struggling rural society" Raymond Williams identified as Hardy's milieu. Yet the notion that Hardy only memorialized the music, the culture, but not the poverty and the discontent, seems unfair. Williams, born on the borders of England and Wales, between the rural and the urban, identified strongly with Hardy:

> ...the real Hardy country, we soon come to see, is that border country so many of us have been living in; between custom and education, between work and ideas, between love of place and an experience of change.

An experience of change: Williams was one of the first to recognize in Hardy's output the importance of the later novels, of *Tess of the d'Urbevilles* (1891) and *Jude the Obscure* (1896). The dislocated lives of Hardy's later characters, Tess and Jude, are examples of a wider social dislocation, and the realities of rural life and social change go on being important for Hardy. *Tess of the d'Urbervilles* is significant in this light. We meet Tess and her young friends initially in the context of traditional May revelries. They are dressed in white, "a gay survival from Old Style days, when cheerfulness and May-time were synonyms—days before the habit of taking long views had reduced emotions to a monotonous average." There is no confusion here; Hardy is writing of the past, even allowing his own sullen pessimism about the modern world to intrude. His touch is light, making much of the many shades of white in the dresses of indeterminate age. Then we come to the core of the matter:

> In addition to the distinction of a white frock, every woman and girl carried in her right hand a peeled willow wand, and in her left a bunch of white flowers. The peeling of the former and the selection of the latter, had been an operation of personal care.

The language is very precise. The women take "personal care" because they believe in what they are doing, believe it has some meaning, some significance, however obscure that meaning may be to them. At the other extreme of experience, there is the description of Tess at work on the threshing-machine with its "despotic demand upon the endurance of their muscles and nerves". By the end of the day, she is reduced to "a stupefied reverie in which her arms worked on independently of her consciousness." Not work, but labour. Not care, but discipline.

That Tess is between worlds is beyond doubt. The second time we meet her in the novel is in the context of her own home. Hardy notes, in parenthesis, that Tess spoke two languages: "the dialect at home, more or less; ordinary English abroad." No doubt this had been the experience of Hardy himself, upwardly mobile from the little cottage in Bockhampton, reluctant to acknowledge in public his many relations in the area.

Hardy's own personal world stretched beyond Dorset. It encompassed London, as did that of Richard Jefferies—Jefferies in arguably romantic Sydenham, Hardy in less-than-romantic Tooting. We shall meet Hardy again towards the end of this book, in and around the village of St. Juliot in North Cornwall, where he met his first wife while working on the restoration of the church. The full measure of the Hardy tragedy may then become a little clearer.

CHAPELS IN THE LANDSCAPE

The borders between Dorset, Devon and Somerset, as already observed, are uncertain. Some towns and villages have regularly changed their county affiliations over the centuries, and this makes it easier for the writer to sometimes ignore county boundaries, as the thematic thread demands it. Non-conformity was important all over the West Country. But there is

one perfect place to savour just what non-conformity meant in its historical context. That is the Loughwood Meeting House, situated just off the A35 road and west of Axminster, so already in Devonshire. It is in the hands of the National Trust, but also cared for by the present-day Baptist congregation in nearby Kilmington. Even under the Commonwealth, life was not easy for Baptists, who were seen as religious extremists, unprepared to compromise with even an established church shorn of its statues and crosses and rood screens and other "Catholic" decoration. Indeed, two early members may well have been disillusioned soldiers from Cromwell's army who settled in the district. The decision to build a chapel, or meeting house, at this isolated spot reflects the social and religious isolation felt by the 219 members of the congregation who sought refuge there in 1653. It was 1832 before they moved back to the village of Kilmington.

They were Particular Baptists who followed Calvin's doctrine that only a chosen few were to be saved. This led to a complicated series of disputes and fissures that belie the simplicity of the building. According to the early record books, worship was demanding: during the summer season, activities began at seven o'clock in the morning, and continued until three in the afternoon. At that point, and "after the dismission of those that are nott members", the remaining congregation (of certain faith, if uncertain spelling) would "spend one hower or 2 in communicatinge their experiences; inquiring after persons absent; trying the things heard and dutys neglected"—in other words, maintaining discipline. Almost the first entry in the record book records 105 members "in good standing" but 28 members "since cast out and withdrawn from for sin and disorder." It was a hard, demanding religion, not least in the distances members travelled to worship at Loughwood. This explains the kitchen and rest-room facilities in the building. Eventually Loughwood was to become the mother church for Baptists meeting at Chard in Somerset, Lyme Regis in Dorset and Honiton in Devon.

The building is one of the earliest Baptist churches in England. Under the Clarendon Code Acts of 1661-65, the Baptists suffered badly. (The main target were Presbyterians, who shared with Particular Baptists many Calvinistic doctrines.) Their worship remained illegal throughout the reigns of Charles II and James II. The National Trust booklet available at the chapel notes that persecution was especially harsh in the years 1684-88, when "men and women were ostracised, ridiculed, imprisoned, transported and sometimes killed." It was a moving reminder of their bravery to find the Bible open at Psalm 27: "The Lord is my light and my salvation, whom shall I fear? The Lord is the strength of my life; of whom shall I be afraid?" The situation of the chapel near the county boundaries of Devon, Dorset and Somerset supports the theory that it was built there to make escape from constables across the county borders easy. The congregation included Huguenot refugees, given the nickname of "French". This later stuck as a surname in the area, and recurs in membership lists. Not until 1688, when William of Orange was invited to take over from James II in the so-called Glorious (and bloodless) Revolution, were acts passed by parliament granting freedom of worship to non-conformists (but not to Roman Catholics). But the tradition of meeting in the seclusion of the countryside remained for a further 150 years.

The building itself is a sturdy stone structure, lodged neatly into the hillside, with massive buttresses at the east end, organic, like giant legs taking the strain of its being. The thatched roof fits snugly; it replaced a tiled roof that had in turn replaced the original thatch, since the view of those responsible for the restoration was that thatch would place less of a strain on the building than tiles. It sits there among may blossom, it endures the winter rains, a place of refuge, of pilgrimage almost. For all the religious incongruity involved, the ark-like pilgrimage chapel designed by Le Corbusier at Ronchamp comes to mind. Inside, the emphasis is all on simplicity, with white-painted walls and plain box pews filling most of the available space. There is a raised preaching pulpit at one end, and below it the baptismal pool, carefully concealed beneath a trap-door. Continuing the theme of sustainability, this pool was fed from a local spring. The rest-room has a brick floor, a fireplace, simple wooden chairs. The gallery was used by musicians and singers, that same tradition memorialized by Hardy in *Under the Greenwood Tree*.

West Gallery music is alive and well in the West Country. Its history is a curious one, its temporary demise a contradictory result of nineteenth-century religiosity. Bands of musicians playing string and woodwind instruments would play, while a four-part harmony singing style was developed which drew on both folk-song and classical music (Haydn and Handel both wrote West Gallery tunes; music by Tallis and Purcell was borrowed as required). The religious revival of the nineteenth century chased this style of music from the churches, replacing it with the solemn tones of the organ, and a choir placed in the chancel under the approving eye of the priest. Within two generations, it had disappeared. In non-conformist chapels the tradition of part (as opposed to unison) singing continued longer, but as we have seen at Loughwood, the organ, however simple, came to be seen as a statement of both musical and religious seriousness.

The revival of West Gallery music owes something to the continuing popularity of Thomas Hardy's novels, and something to the folk music revival of the twentieth century. In 2007 the bicentenary of the birth of John Wesley was celebrated around Dorset by performances by the Purbeck Quire of a musical life of the founder of Methodism. At Netherhay they performed to a large and appreciative audience of local Methodists. Netherhay is scarcely a village even, more a tiny hamlet on the outskirts of a larger village called Drimpton. The few houses straggle along a minor road; the village notice-board is a telegraph pole next to the post-box. The chapel comes as a surprise, neat and tidy, freshly decorated in green paint. It doubles as religious and social centre, and has a well-equipped kitchen, meeting-room and toilet facilities to one side, almost a modern equivalent of Loughwood.

The Purbeck Quire (the revival of the older spelling is, of course, Hardy again) are a cheerful band, based in Wareham. Like the musicians whose tradition they follow, many are engaged more broadly in music-making—folk-music and barn dances. There is also a serious programme of musicological research and involvement in the national West Gallery Music Association. They dress for the part, as it were: there is a lot of lace and shawls and floral bonnets. The men have red kerchiefs and smocks or leather jerkins with britches and white woolly socks. Most are past the first flush of youth. There is much commentary and good humour, including warm appreciation for the congregational singing—not only do they know their words (many by Charles Wesley, John's brother) but also the part settings and the repetitions that the Quire are using.

Methodism, although not by that name (Charles remained within the Church of England until his death), was a family business. John Wesley believed in singing; "lift up your hearts with strength," he declared. His brother wrote nine thousand poems, including three thousand hymns. Two hundred and forty out of 984 songs in the 1933 Methodist Hymn Book, published in connection with the reunification of the various strands of Methodism (Wesleyan, Primitive and Free), are by Charles Wesley. This hymn book also reprinted John Wesley's 1779 preface to "A collection of Hymns for use of the People called Methodists".

The hymns were originally sung unaccompanied or with a band. Words and music were published separately, so congregations could choose their own tunes taking account of metre and the musical tastes of the musicians. Men predominated, with the tenors frequently carrying the tune. John Wesley appreciated neither children nor women, describing the latter as "a feeble mind in a feeble body". Neither women nor children at Netherhay seemed much bothered. The evening sun slanted in across happy, smiling, singing faces, the ash leaves waved against a determinedly blue sky. It was the First of July after the wettest June on record, and before the equally wet July and August had had time to gather their strength. They sang "Come let us renew", the hymn sung at the annual Covenant service at the beginning of the year, and something of the moral seriousness of Methodism, diluted with music and good company shone out:

I have fought my way through
I have finished the work
Thou didst give me to do.

Somehow it seemed wrong not to be a believer.

THE TOLPUDDLE MARTYRS

Every year, trade union and other banners descend on the tiny village of
Tolpuddle, east of Dorchester, and process up and down the long village
street. It is all easier now that the new by-pass strikes off around the village.
The leader of the Trades Union Congress usually comes, Tony Benn is a
regular, as is Billy Bragg who now lives along the coast at Burton Bradstock
near Bridport. A leading Labour Party politician is usually detailed to
attend, and greeted with waning enthusiasm. There is a beer tent, trade
union stalls, children's activities, bands and choirs. Of the six martyrs, five
were Methodists, two of them lay-preachers. This is significant, as it meant
that they were already exposed to suspicion and criticism, if not down-
right hostility, from the representatives of the established church. It was
one thing for independent craftsmen to be non-conformists; for landless
labourers, dependent on the goodwill of conservative-minded farmers, it
was quite a different matter. George Loveless and his comrades were
serious, god-fearing men, driven by their conscience to do what they felt
to be right. James Hammett returned to Tolpuddle (the martyrs were transported in 1834, and pardoned in 1836). A lifelong Methodist, he is buried
in the village churchyard, and as part of the annual commemoration, a
Methodist minister leads a small party to his grave, with its headstone el-
egantly carved by Eric Gill and paid for by the TUC.

Did the men of Tolpuddle form a trade union? It is doubtful. True,
they consulted Robert Owen, pioneer socialist and trade unionist, but the
main result of this was the setting up of the Tolpuddle Grand Lodge of the
Agricultural Labourers Friendly Society. The only crime they could be
accused of was swearing an oath of loyalty to each other, and in order to
prosecute, the nervous authorities used the 1797 Unlawful Oaths Act, designed to deal with the naval mutinies of the 1790s, not half-starved farm
labourers. The memory of the 1830 agricultural riots—rick-burning and
machine-breaking under the cover of the name of Captain Swing—was
still alive. It is sad that the names of the twelve labourers transported to

Australia after the Swing Riots in Dorset have not been kept in the general memory, while those of the men of Tolpuddle have been kept in the public consciousness ever since. James Brine, James Hammett, George Loveless, James Loveless, Thomas Standfield and John Standfield: their names endure. Those of the rioters of 1830 do not.

Chapter Four

MODERN DORSET

The little house, so harmless and demure …
I am glad to think that on its last day it wore
Its laundered garden, its look, as when in love we were there.

Sylvia Townsend Warner

ROLF GARDINER AT SPRINGHEAD

In the 1920s and 1930s, Dorset became very crowded. Exactly why is unclear. Perhaps because it had tried to keep itself so remote, so unsullied, more likely because Thomas Hardy had persuaded the world against his own better judgement that such was the case. The First World War had something to do with it. Even before 1914, as Hardy made clear, the railway, the post and telephones had drawn Dorset into the modern world with scarcely a murmur of dissent. The 1914-18 war seemed to focus minds on what was being lost, had been lost already. Some wanted to turn their back once more on the modern world, others wanted to embrace it. Rolf Gardiner is in many ways typical of the Janus face of the times.

We are all indebted to Patrick Wright's splendid researches into twentieth-century Dorset for uncovering a few less than sweet-smelling and dubious activities in this usually fragrant county. Some of these took place on Springhead Farm at Fontmell Magna, neatly placed at the foot of the flowered downs, just south of Shaftesbury. Here in the 1920s Rolf Gardiner set himself two tasks: one was the desirable and achievable aim of running a farm along co-operative and organic lines; the other was the rather more daunting mission of national renewal. This was to be achieved by bringing young men down from the slums of London and instilling in them new respect for their own bodies, for the land and for England. There was a good deal of running around in very skimpy shorts, or less. And there was to be music too, animating and reflecting the new order which was itself a recreation of an older order, "folding people into their land and its seasons" in David Matless' memorable phrase. Gardiner viewed Cecil Sharp (we shall meet him in Somerset in Chapter Six) as an urbanite folklorist; his own view of folk music was more deeply rooted into the land and physical work: "Discussion divides men, ideas confuse and confound men; but song and work unite men and clarify their minds." It sounds ominously familiar, and it should. Gardiner's youth movement fits all too neatly into the ideology and practice of organizations such as the Hitler Youth Movement and the various youth bodies being set up in Soviet Russia at the time. Perhaps there is something of the Boy Scouts and the Woodcraft Folk here too? Gardiner drew on the German and English roots of sword-dancing and took parties around the county to dance: in Blandford, in Dorchester, Cerne (a good place to take young men), Sherborne, Shaftesbury. The young men hiked too, twenty-five mile route marches to the accompaniment of marching songs. It is strange and disturbing stuff. Yet Gardiner felt confident enough about what he was doing to publish an account of it during the Second World War (*England Herself*, 1943).

While Patrick Wright is at some pains to assert Gardiner's independence from mainstream fascism in either Germany or England, he also paints a distressing picture of how Gardiner "stumbled through the 1930s, a morris-dancing boy scout who had dreamed of healing the industrial nation, but who now found himself overtaken by storm troopers." Gardiner was sensible enough to retreat in the 1930s from some of the more extreme political conclusions that might have been drawn from his youth movement. This left music, which became a family business: musical events continued and continue at Springhead. Rolf's son, John Eliot Gardiner, is a distinguished and well-respected conductor of classical music. At the 2007 Proms in London's Albert Hall he gave perhaps the outstanding, certainly most challenging, concert of the series, conducting his own English Baroque Soloists and the Buskaid Soweto String Ensemble from South Africa. It felt as if one or two family ghosts were being laid to rest. The withdrawal from the politics of national renewal also left organic farming methods, still the chosen way of working with nature, rather than against her, at Springhead.

There is an interesting comparison with another leading organicist of the period, H. V. Massingham, who had some very strange ideas indeed about the people who once inhabited the Stone Age hilltop settlements in Dorset. In his imagination, they become small, self-sufficient, communities, trading between one another in a sustainable way. Massingham had an almost limitless ability to wander off down the by-ways of early twentieth-century life and thought, but an almost equally uncanny knack of finding his way back. And what linked everything together was respect for nature, for the land, for the food we grow and eat. Dying in 1952, he lived long enough to condemn stubble-burning and conifers and to extol the virtues of mixed farming, compost, wormeries, hedges, organic pest control and English apples. He also condemned the use of artificial fertilizers and insecticides at a time (just after the Second World War) when they were becoming big business in the brave new world of state-subsidized agriculture. But with Massingham in this mood there is always a better path, a better role model to follow. Of one fellow organic gardener, he writes:

> He made one reflect that the modern system of supplying massed populations with cheap devitalised foods, cheap synthetic medicines and cheap clothing as ephemeral as the houses they live in is more expensive and impractical than any the world has ever seen.

He is as economical with commas as with the rest of creation. The next paragraph begins with a remarkable and simple definition of ecology: "the organic relation of things to their environment", which makes this particular author wish that science had treated of such matters at school half a century ago.

But there is always an absolutism about Massingham. In contrasting industrialized food production and the organic way, he writes: "The one philosophy is dominant and possesses all the power but the other is in possession of *the truth*." Perhaps the experience of organicists in the 1930s, and the whole sad tale of the twentieth century, should lead us to be cautious of anyone who makes rash italicized claims about truth. Yet certainly Massingham would recognize the world of farmers' markets, of small independent organic producers, of farm-shops and vegetable box schemes. He would feel at home at the fine Bridport Food Centre, or exchanging experiences with the growers at Blandford farmers' market. Massingham at his best represents a link between an earlier generation of organic farmers, gardeners and consumers, and those of our own day.

A DEN OF WRITERS AT EAST CHALDON

While murky clouds block out the stars of night,
Flaming afar I stand a tower of light
  Llewelyn Powys, translation of seventh-century Latin riddle by St.
  Aldhelm

While Gardiner was flirting with fascism and Massingham with megalithic culture, elsewhere in Dorset a community of a rather different kind was growing up. East Chaldon, or Chaldon Herring, lies in that contested area of dry stone walls, rounded chalk downs and isolated farmhouses and tiny valleys between the Wareham to Dorchester and Weymouth road and the coast with its chalk cliffs and outcrops of limestone and Purbeck marble. Theodore Francis Powys was the first. He moved to the little village of Chaldon Herring in 1905. Here he eked out a living from his garden and from writing short stories and novels, interspersed with the study of philosophy and the Christian mystics. He had farmed for a time in Suffolk, with little success, but at least he understood the basic facts of agricultural life. Success as a writer became him, the garden became more and more untidy, and his novels became mellower and kinder with age. The allegorical *Mr Weston's Good Wine* (1927), in which Mr. Weston sells bottles of Love and Death from his old van in the village of Folly Down, still bears a read. His house, Beth Car, stands today, a red-brick villa as ugly as Hardy's own Max Gate in nearby Dorchester in a village of stone cottages, many of them white-washed, rose-decorated and capped with clinging thatch. Theodore chose not only the village, but its people, marrying a local beauty, Violet Dodds. It was Dodds who tied Powys to the village and its people, Dodds who worried about money, and Dodds who insistently pulled him away from the more introspective and speculative aspects of his complex character.

Disentangling the Powys family is a hard task. Their father was the vicar of Montacute, just across the border (that border again!) in Somerset. There were six brothers, sisters too. Three of the brothers became writers. Theodore, for reasons which are unclear, was sent away to school in East Anglia, his elder brother John Cowper Powys and younger brother Llewelyn Powys both attended Sherborne, just one of a number of public schools littering the countryside of Dorset. Quite how the three sons of a Somerset churchman became radical iconoclasts is unclear. John Bunyan was certainly a major influence, perhaps John Milton too or even William Blake. It is the extraordinary mixture of speculative religion, allegory and brilliant story-telling that binds them together. (And also sex, a good deal of which seems to have been going on in Chaldon Herring in the 1920s and 1930s.)

John Cowper we shall meet again in Glastonbury in Somerset in Chapter Five, since he based an extraordinary and bizarre novel there which both drew on and contributed to the Glastonbury myth. More than any other Chaldon writer, he linked past and present. Like Hardy in the famous Fifth of November bonfire scene in *The Return of the Native*, he saw in fire the elemental streak that linked old and new civilizations, noting in his diary of the crowds outlined against the 1935 Silver Jubilee bonfire at Poundbury outside Dorchester: "they might have been the Neolithics under the Crescent Moon." They might have been, but were not. In the end, it is social condescension, as it is in the T. S. Eliot of "East Coker":

Round and round the fire
Leaping through the flames, or joined in circles,
Rustically solemn or in rustic laughter
Lifting heavy feet in clumsy shoes,
...

Llewelyn Powys was an essayist and journalist. Although his early life took him far and wide, he was the brother whose work most evokes the Dorset landscape and its characters. His *Dorset Essays* include an essay on St. Aldhelm's Head, which mentions the use of the chapel there as an early marker for shipping on this dangerous coast, and quotes the riddling saint himself in translation—the lines used as a preface to this section. Powys' ashes are buried deep in the chalk on the cliffs above Chaldon, marked by a lichen-covered stone. In the United States he met Alyse Gregory, feminist, poet and the editor of the distinguished literary journal *The Dial*. She is one of a number of "modern" women who were to add lustre to the life of Chaldon Herring in the inter-war years and beyond. Llewelyn was sickly, suffering from tuberculosis throughout his life, but loved the open air life, and women too. Returning with his bride to Dorset, he lived at the coastguards' cottages at White Nothe (known familiarly to the locals as White Nose from the resemblance of one feature of the chalk cliffs). In 1931 they moved to Chydyok, next door to Llewelyn's sisters and protectors, Gertrude and Katie.

Both Alyse and Llewelyn had determined on an open marriage. Unfortunately in this case the open marriage soon became a *ménage à trois*, with the also American Gamel Woolsey forming the third angle. There were pregnancies, abortions (Gamel too had had TB and was not the strongest of young women). When Gerald Brenan arrived in Chaldon in 1930, the affair had already reached end-game—Brenan married Woolsey and after a brief period at East Lulworth they settled in La Alpujarra in the mountains "south from Granada"—the title of one of Brenan's many fine books about Spain. Of course, it was not quite as straightforward as that, but for further details the reader may be referred safely to Judith Stinton's splendid book on the village and its characters. Woolsey also deserves a very large footnote in the history of British censorship: her semi-autobiographical novel *One Way of Love* was pulled by the publisher, Victor Gollancz, in 1930 at the page-proof stage for fear of legal action—not so much over its explicit dealing with sex, but because of its frankness about contraception and abortion. Cue Virago to the rescue in 1987.

The enigmatic words on the stone that lies above Llewelyn Powys' ashes—"The living The living He shall praise thee"—were carved by the sculptor Elizabeth Muntz. The carving was done *in situ*, there on the cliffs, exposed to the winds and weather. Born in Canada, Muntz bought a cottage at Chaldon in 1929 and lived there until her death in 1977. She is remembered with affection in the village, especially by those who knew her as children. The Children's Corner in St. Nicholas East Chaldon is still watched over by the fabric nativity scene which Muntz worked on during the Second World War with the children themselves. The landscape is memorialized in the outline of the Five Marys, the five ancient burial mounds, overrun by furze and wild flowers and dog-walkers, which still dominate the skyline north of the village. The animals were worked from those known to the children, such as Sammy the chestnut horse and Benny, a black-and-white collie. The gifts laid before the baby are those the children would have liked to have given themselves, while the frame was made from driftwood by the local carpenter.

The church is a haven of embroidery: three interlocked herrings for the village, a boat for St. Nicholas, the patron of sailors, in this land-locked marine landscape. Muntz and her French partner and handyman André Bonnamy are buried next to one another in the churchyard. If her inscription is conventional—"I will lift up mine eyes unto the hills"—his might well have applied to both: "L'humanité refait son âme plus avec ses mains qu'avec sa pensée" (Humanity refreshes its soul through its hands more than its intellect.)

Two other women are quietly remembered in the grassy graveyard at Chaldon: the poet Sylvia Townsend Warner and her lifetime partner Valentine Ackland. Warner is one of the most engaging of the many "special" people of Chaldon, people who specialized in being their own persons at all times. She wrote a lovely book about Somerset to which we shall refer later, poetry, novels and short stories; she also contributed to *The New Yorker* for nearly forty years. Initially her great love was music; she might have been a student of Arnold Schönberg had it not been for the First World War, and through the 1920s she worked on the ten volumes of *Tudor Church Music*. She met Valentine Ackland at Theodore Powys' house and when she bought a cottage opposite the pub, The Sailor's Return, in 1930, Ackland joined her there. They fell in love and shared their lives, in Chaldon, in Norfolk, and at Frome Vauchurch near Maiden Newton, for the next 39 years. They shared politics too, joining the Communist Party in 1935 and actively campaigning on behalf of the Spanish Republic during the Civil War (1936-39). Theodore and John Cowper Powys were engaged as unlikely allies, John Cowper speaking alongside Warner at a

Cottage at East Chaldon

Left Book Club meeting in Dorchester. Even closer to home, Warner wrote a series of articles for the *Left Review* exposing conditions in rural England, and the poverty and squalor that lay behind the picturesque façade of villages such as Chaldon Herring.

Sadly their little cottage opposite The Sailor's Return did not survive the war they had hoped to avert. In 1944 it was destroyed by a random German bomb. Warner wrote those lovely lines quoted at the head of this chapter:

> The little house, so harmless and demure …
> I am glad to think that on its last day it wore
> Its laundered garden, its look, as when in love we were there.

A village in Dorset, for all these writers and artists was not just a place to live, but a place to love, and to experience to the full the uniqueness of a human life, lived out in a chosen place.

LAURENCE WHISTLER AT MORETON

Several artists and writers recur in this book. Both John Cowper Powys and Sylvia Townsend Warner will appear again in Somerset, since both wrote major works about that county—a novel the former and a work of non-fiction the latter. Thomas Hardy visited Cornwall to plan the restoration of the church at St. Juliot's, and found love, of a kind, there. Laurence Whistler, however, merits three entries in the book, two of them in pursuit of love. His difficult relationship with his man-about-town brother Rex, ultimately a relationship of love, was mentioned in Chapter One at Salisbury Cathedral. His passionate but tragically short first marriage will find its place in the North Devon chapter. And here in Dorset, where he eventually settled at Lyme Regis, is his greatest public work, the church of St. Nicholas at Moreton, near Dorchester, on the lovely, graceful, winding Dorset River Frome.

Moreton is neither the greatest not the least of Dorset villages, with its pretty thatched cottages—cob protected now by cement rendering, some brick, a little stone. Moreton has a tea-room that is more than a summer tea-room, a year-round delight located in the old Victorian school of brick, slates and lattice windows. Now what children there are must travel into Dorchester to school. At least its thatch and brick post office is still open. Down the lane past the post office is the river, crossed by a long pedestrian causeway. In summer it attracts children to play safely in its shallow, dappled backwaters. Dragonflies float overhead and the modern world seems a long way away. It is not. In winter the river is deeper, more purposeful, swifter-flowing, searching out Wareham Harbour and the sea.

The little grey church would probably be little visited were it not for the bad luck of having been destroyed by a bomb dumped by a fleeing German plane during the Second World War. There were plenty of military targets in the county, not least the busy naval dockyards at Portland, and it is difficult to understand why this village church should have been singled out by chance in this way. The church was rebuilt, after a fashion, but over the years has become a place of pilgrimage for the engraved glass that has gradually filled up all the available windows—fourteen in total. The very few local people who remember the church before the bomb fell speak of its colourful scheme of stained glass decoration, and indeed there is a picture on the wall supporting this view. But St. Nicholas Moreton now is about light rather than colour. On a dull winter's day, with the first snowdrops pushing up their white heads in the churchyard and a single shy purple violet already in flower, the church manages, with no artificial lighting, to seem brighter than the world outside. It is a quite unique church, in which every picture tells a story both ancient and modern.

The parish might have opted for modern coloured glass, but Moreton chose engraved glass, which meant Lawrence Whistler. There is no overall scheme—how could there have been? The first windows, which date from 1955, were paid for from war damage money, but the rest have been financed by private donors. There is something quite magical about engraved glass in windows, especially in this kind of rural setting. We do not see the glass, but only the design engraved into it, yet it is the light passing through which creates the illusion of the image. We also see beyond the world outside, trees and flowers and birds and clouds. In Whistler's work there is a constant play on this duality. Nature is represented in both engraving and in reality, and always there is a sense of spiritual yearning, of longing, for a greater reality of which we know nothing and of which our beautiful world may be an intimation.

The first windows were the five in the apse, and have a consistency of design. Each has three lights, and the two side lights are filled by giant candles, each bearing a scroll with a conventional Christian message: "Out of darkness into light", "A light that shineth in a dark place"—appropriate but still conventional. Each phrase refers in some way to light, the light coming from God, or reflected in the human spirit. The central lights are dealt with differently. In the middle window is the cross, with emblems of the passion (the spear, the crown of thorns); a grape vine climbs up the cross, and wheat sprouts from the ground beneath, to symbolize the mystery of the communion service. On the north (left) side of the apse, the central light is occupied by a Christmas tree, remembering that St. Nicholas was forever re-inventing himself. If he is the patron of sailors at Chaldon, here he is the kindly old man who brings children their presents. The south window has an ash-tree, the pre-Christian "tree of life", springing up as it does wherever living water comes from the earth. The remaining two central lights have a pair of medallions each. In one, the church as bombed and as restored, in the other harvest by land and sea (the good saint again). Above are Christmas lanterns of evergreens, candles and apples, all decorations that preceded the Christmas tree and now exist in parallel with it.

The years went by, and it was not until 1974 that new windows began to be added. The Seasons window is a memorial to the Findlay family in the north aisle. In the centre is the sun, the origin of all light and sustainer of life on earth. Four linked roundels, like large bubbles, represent both the seasons and their transience, and indeed the transience of all life on earth. Here Whistler introduces a new "place"—Loch Lomond and Ben Lomond in spring for the Findlays' Scottish home. Whistler is at the peak of his abilities here: Moreton Hall, the big house in the grounds of which the church lies, is portrayed in a snowstorm with the flakes swirling about the house like a shower of bright meteorites. For summer and autumn, Whistler produces favourite motifs: bright butterflies as if straining to escape their glass bubble; the lazy curling smoke of a bonfire.

In 1975 the Light and Darkness windows were added, also in the north aisle. The Light engraving shows candles blazing ("Truly the light is sweet") while the snuffed out candles of Darkness remind us again of the

terrible 1940 bomb ("Remember the days of darkness"). In the same year the Dream of the Rood window was added, to commemorate another Findlay. Noel Findlay lived in Kent, and the oast-houses and his cottage are introduced into the design. It is not, Whistler seems to be saying, that any one place—Dorset or Kent or Scotland—is better, more important than another. What matters is the significance of place, of landscape in our lives, that it should matter to us, that where we are is an integral part of who we are. Likewise in the Trinity Chapel window Salisbury Cathedral appears, for this window celebrates the life of an RAF pilot, stationed near there in the war. Two owls fly high and free above the cathedral as if mocking human ambition, while in the right-hand panel a magnolia in bloom reaches towards the sky both celebrating and mourning the life ended in the crashed plane below. Finally there are the swirling, spiral galaxies of the west windows, where the mystery of life on earth is repeated infinitely throughout the universe.

T. E. LAWRENCE AT CLOUDS HILL

Of course, many visitors to St. Nicholas Moreton know nothing of Laurence Whistler. If they are patient and not pressed for time, they may discover him for the first time; but equally they may not even go inside the church at all. The other man who draws visitors to Moreton is T. E. Lawrence (Lawrence of Arabia), who is buried in the new churchyard on the other side of the Wool road, and whose grave seems seldom without a visitor and even more seldom without a flower. The grave itself is relatively modest, but a vaguely classical and rather pretentious portico has been erected over the entrance gate. It is a curious graveyard, apparently suffering an outbreak of plastic flowers as well as snowdrops and a friendly tabby cat. The headstone speaks neither of Lawrence the war hero, nor of Lawrence the hope of the political right. It refers rather to the fact that he was a Fellow of All Souls College, Oxford. A few remembrance crosses remain from the previous 11 November. Back in the village, the tea-room has a lot of Lawrence memorabilia, enough at least to keep alive the hubbub of debate about Lawrence's life and death. But it does not mention Whistler.

The facts are well enough known at one level, but still disputed. Lawrence felt that his mission to reconcile England and its allies to the Arab cause had failed. His protégé, Faisal Hussein, had declared himself King of Palestine and Syria at the Paris Peace Conference in 1920, a bold bid to establish the strong Arab state in the region that Lawrence felt would secure future regional stability (subsequent events suggest he may have been right). But Faisal had lasted only a few months, and thanks in part to Lawrence's influence at the Foreign Office, became King of Iraq, then a British protectorate. Lawrence thought this a failure. During 1920-22, he wrote his great masterpiece, *Seven Pillars of Wisdom*, not published in a general edition until after his death. (He brought out only a shortened version, called *Revolt in the Desert*.) Angus Calder, in a sympathetic modern edition of the *Seven Pillars*, refers to the man's "guilt and self-loathing". He sees the root of this as the war of which Lawrence did not speak or write—the Western Front in the First World War, where two of his brothers and many of his Oxford contemporaries died. The heroics, the romance, that Lawrence found in the desert were in very short supply in Flanders. There was also a different attitude to men and fighting. In *Seven Pillars* he contrasts his own attitude to casualties to that of the professional English soldiers attached to his rebel army: "To me an unnecessary action, or shot, or casualty, was not only waste but sin… Our rebels were not materials, like soldiers, but friends of ours, trusting our leadership. We were not in command nationally, but by invitation; and our men were volunteers, individuals, local men, relatives, so that a death was a personal sorrow to many in the army." This is a local rather than global world-view.

Lawrence eventually seems to have opted for some kind of fresh start. Under an assumed name he joined up as a private in the Tank Regiment. This brought him, of course, to Bovington Camp, another precious corner of Hardy's Egdon Heath. Even as a private, Lawrence was not just an ordinary soldier. Through his connections with the Frampton family, local landowners, he was able to take a lease on Clouds Hill, a small cottage hard by the Camp. From Moreton, the footpath to Clouds Hill leads across that picturesque causeway over the River Frome. Lawrence was happy at Clouds Hill. The exterior is nondescript, but inside the cottage has the denseness, the compactness of a Bedouin tent. Preserved by the National Trust much as it was when Lawrence lived here, the cottage has no electric light, and is surrounded by woods, and even during the visiting months (March-October) visitors are warned that it may have to close earlier in poor weather conditions. All this makes one concentrate the better on the austere furnishings, the books, the many pictures reflecting Lawrence's life and interests.

And so it was that on a certain day in 1935, Lawrence set out on his motorbike to send a telegram from the local post office. It was an accident, they said, as he swerved to avoid an oncoming vehicle and hit a tree, dying instantly. Two boys who observed the crash were sure that it was indeed an accident. They sang in the choir at Moreton and sang at his funeral. In the tea-rooms at Moreton there is a picture of them, as well as other photos of the funeral cortege. The mourners included Sir Winston Churchill and his wife. Not everyone believed the story then, and many still doubt it. Lawrence had good friends, but some of them had vivid imaginations. Not least Henry Williamson.

There is another, finer Williamson, the author of *Tarka the Otter*, one of the best works of natural history in this or any other language. But the darker Williamson, the active fascist and admirer of Hitler, concerns us here. In England, Williamson hankered (rather at a distance, it is true) for a comparable leader. After the abdication, he wrote "T. E. Lawrence gone; now the Prince of Wales. These men *knew*." But what did they know? Williamson, such a detailed observer of natural reality, was a fantasist when it came to both personal relationships and politics. It was largely Williamson who was responsible for keeping alive and passing down to later generations of right-wing conspiracy theorists the notion that there was something badly wrong about the "accident". Lawrence was on his way to post a telegram to Williamson when he crashed and died. For some time Williamson had been attempting to persuade Lawrence to meet Hitler. According to Williamson, this telegram was simply to confirm that he (Lawrence) would be at home if Williamson called while in Dorset to discuss a possible meeting. The rather more alarming idea that has come down in fascist circles is that the subject of the telegram was to confirm that Lawrence consented to meet Hitler.

Like Williamson, like Rolf Gardiner, Lawrence, as we have seen, deeply deplored the loss of life in the First World War, massive by any scale of the imagination. Few families had remained unaffected, in either Britain or for that matter in France or Germany or Russia. England had been let down by its leadership, at one level by the politicians, at another by their generals ("But he did for them both by his plan of attack," wrote Siegfried Sassoon in his poem "The General"). It is a relief to return from this kind of historical speculation to Lawrence as a writer, as an artist, a man who appreciated a sunset as fervently as any Arab leader:

Jizil was a deep gorge some two hundred yards in width, full of tamarisk sprouting from the bed of drifting sand, as well as from the soft twenty-foot banks, heaped up wherever an eddy in flood or wind had laid the heavier dust under the returns of cliffs. The walls each side were of regular bands of sandstone, streaked red in many shades. The union of dark cliffs, pink floors, and pale green shrubbery was beautiful to eyes sated with months of sunlight and sooty shadow. When evening came, the declining sun crimsoned one side of the valley with its glow, leaving the other in purple gloom.

For Lawrence, difficult, restless, unfulfilled, the direct sensual perception of nature was a relief from thought, from the torment of a mind that weaved visions that would never come true in reality—"the sounds, scents and colours of the world struck man individually," he wrote, "and the lack of design and of carefulness in creation no longer irritated."

Occupied Territory

There is an order in the geology of Purbeck, yet it is not immediately apparent. The same might be said of the social order, containing as it does a great swathe of Ministry of Defence land used as tank and firing ranges, the deserted village of Tyneham (of which more later) and a major centre of nuclear research at Winfrith. The latter is described as "unattractive buildings that sometimes steam" in one guidebook—slight but ominous words. Winfrith and nearby Bovington Camp occupy what Hardy knew as Egdon Heath. Clouds Hill is within this same landscape, squeezed tightly between the rivers Frome and Piddle. There is still a good population of reptiles here, as at Studland, and Winfrith recently sold several hundred acres of land to the Dorset Wildlife Trust. Once an important centre for the production of nuclear power, it competed in the 1960s for the heavy water reactor eventually sited as Dounreay in distant Caithness, no doubt considered to be politically less sensitive than South Dorset with its hundreds of thousands of visiting tourists each year. Now Winfrith's main research is into the difficult and controversial subject of decommissioning nuclear sites, beginning with itself. It is hoped that the clean-up will be over by 2020, and that economic activity on the site, to be designated a "business park", will be in private hands.

All this was well in the future when the first tanks arrived at Bovington during the First World War, rolling up the hill from Wool station. It was all meant to be very hush-hush, villagers being advised to stay indoors with the curtains drawn. But as Patrick White describes in his monumental account of military activities in Dorset (*The Village that Died for England*) the secret was hard to keep. One tank broke down and a local farmer used his horses to tow it into his farm-yard, where it remained for the next several days. The future of the Tank Regiment was in some doubt after the end of the First World War, some military commentators even proposing bringing back the cavalry. But survive it did, and it strengthened its hand in Dorset, at least. A large tract of land was acquired on lease from the Weld family using the threat of compulsory purchase to develop a firing range at Bindon Heath, just to the east of Lulworth Cove and the Weld family home of Lulworth Castle. The military took possession with several conditions attached: restrictions on firing (for example, not on Saturdays and Sundays) and some access to the coastal path.

It was in 1943 that the military authorities moved to greatly extend the ranges by taking over the village of Tyneham. It had begun gradually, with army personnel taking over empty cottages in what had become a very run-down rural village. Then, in 1943, the evacuation of the village and its immediate environs was decreed; some 225 Dorset people left the area. Lilian Bond, who was later to write a book about Tyneham, left this sad message pinned to the church door:

> Please treat the Church and houses with care. We have given up our homes where many of us have lived for generations, to help win the war to keep men free. We shall return one day and thank you for treating the village kindly.

The wartime takeover at Tyneham produced the conditions after the war for one of the great set-pieces in the battle not just for the land of rural England (walkers, environmentalists, farmers and landowners on one side, the military and the state on the other) but for its very soul. The battle may be followed closely in Wright's book, but what of the outcome, of this extraordinary blend of military activity and tourism that now graces the Isle of Purbeck?

Tyneham has never been re-settled. And yet it has still become a symbol of a certain rural way of life. A particular version of rural life, that is, because the conflict has never been a clear-cut one. The arrival of the military in Dorset brought work and jobs to a poor part of the country—cue Sylvia Townsend Warner again. The Frome Valley may have been full of flourishing green farms, but the heath was covered in gorse and bracken, and broken-down cottages. Local businesses thrived to meet the requirements of army personnel, who rented houses, bought food and clothing, drank in village pubs. Then there is the unholy but nevertheless real alliance between the tourist industry and the military. The ruined schoolhouse at Tyneham was re-opened in the 1980s as a museum and gallery. It makes the well-known claims that the military presence is good for the environment, preventing the despoliation of the land by deep-ploughing, fertilizers and pesticides. Wright points to the ultimate irony of the military blasting out dragonfly pools in the wet heathland. The unresolved and probably irresolvable arguments about Tyneham continued in the passages of the first visitors' book, a document that seems to have disappeared in 1990. Was it morally wrong for the villagers who left Tyneham for the sake of the common good in wartime to be excluded from their village in peacetime? Do the claims of the military to be the custodians of the environment hold water? And just how much does this protection cost the taxpayers in comparison with the "single farm payments" which now take account of such important environmental issues as care of hedgerows or sites of special scientific interest?

At one point, about 1970, those pressing for a review of the MoD's occupation of the Lulworth ranges seemed to be in a dominant position. Rolf Gardiner was back on the scene, speaking at a public meeting in Wareham in November 1968 as the Tyneham Action Group launched a renewed campaign. Gardiner had long since cast off the fascist overtones, but was now firmly and deeply in the personal and psychological grip of Thomas Traherne's spirituality, a spirituality that urged that the creative force that had given birth to and sustained the universe was everywhere present, in a grain of sand as much as in the Milky Way (or the nuclear processes under investigation at Winfrith). "It is only by belonging to a place," Gardiner claimed, "that we are really in harmony with our surroundings, with nature, with all God's creation." Yet right from the start there were issues that were to tear the campaign apart, and lose its members the high moral ground they had so carefully staked out. Above all, who did or should the land belong to? Many of the traditional land-owning families of Dorset asserted that the land should ideally be returned to its previous owners. Others, wary of turning over this unique stretch of countryside to the risks of private ownership, proposed placing it in the hands of the National Trust

So the Ministry of Defence, with its growing interest in public relations and its ability to plan a series of strategic concessions worthy of military planning at its most subtle and comprehensive, was able to repeatedly divide, confuse and de-motivate the protesters. A complex system of range wardens, telephones, warning and information boards and flags developed. The ranges are "open" to the public every weekend, except the six weekends when they are closed, plus all public holidays and the school summer holidays. The issue is the meaning of the word "open". The Lulworth ranges, like any other site where tanks and guns have been fired, is littered with unexploded ordnance. The only parts that are routinely cleared of unexploded shells are the paths marked by yellow markers. It is scarcely surprising, then, that walkers' websites report that this stretch of the coastal path is usually quite quiet. The South West Coastal Path official website, otherwise complimentary of the MoD's efforts to provide public access, reports a large cliff fall at Mupe Bay, "probably partly the result of firing". Also, and in parenthesis: "there were many rusting tanks when I walked this part of the path." Perhaps they have been cleared by now.

Visitor figures at Tyneham Museum are modest: perhaps 60,000 per year. To put this into perspective, it compares with one million at the National Trust's Studland Estate or the 200,000 who travel on the busy steam railway between Corfe Castle and Swanage or the 200,000 plus who visit the nearby Durlston Country Park. Bovington Tank Museum manages 120,000, and is expanding year by year. We might speculate on exactly what the attraction of a tank is. Perhaps it goes all the way back to the wooden horse of Troy. Certainly, visitors to historic castles are always excited by displays of armour. It would be nice to think that we are invincible and safe from attack. The shattered remains on the tank ranges, and in pictures of real warfare (especially the two Gulf wars) suggest otherwise.

Yet even a brief visit by the present author on a day when the museum was officially closed suggested more personal motives. An Australian in search of family roots had travelled down from London and been allowed to go round the museum. The man on duty explained that in the past the

Second World War galleries had received organized visits by veterans' groups and British Legion branches. But now it was mainly single men, or small groups, ex-soldiers in their eighties. That generation was passing. He said the same had happened with the First World War displays—now there were no veterans left to come and remember; those ugly, insect-like early tanks were simply objects, had become, as he put it starkly, "history".

Chapter Five

SOMERSET: ROMANCE AND REALITY

Love can't be cured, but it can change its course
like spring-waters that, swallowed by the ground
splash hollowly and disappear. Earthbound
their flow is charged with subterranean force.

Pouring headlong pent in a narrow vein
they pound and tumble in their bed of rock
and carve a labyrinth into the dark.
They percolate through centuries of stone

and ooze and gather, drip and drip again,
and seep through porous to impermeable
leaving their solute burden as they fall,
passion and power laid by, a chalky stain.

Out of earth's darkness dancing bright they run
into the light of the absolving sun.

Ama Bolton, "Mendip Waters"

GLASTONBURY: A THORN IN THE FLESH OF SOMERSET

For many people, Glastonbury is the heart of Somerset, if not of the whole West Country. It needs to be approached slowly, carefully, with patience, a sense of humour and some scepticism, which is to say much like life itself, which is to say that all life is here in Glastonbury if you care to search for it. Glastonbury Tor insinuates itself rather than imposes itself upon the surrounding landscape. Looking south from the summits of the Mendip Hills, it is often there, rising above the low-lying ground of the Somerset Levels. But equally often there is mist and cloud, and the tor seems to float above the land, rather detached, rather forbidding. In the gloaming of a winter's afternoon it sinks slowly back into earth-bound darkness as Venus begins to glimmer in the western sky. From the lower flatter lands, the profile of the tor is gentler than its height, over five hundred feet above sea level (and most of the Somerset Levels are at sea level) might lead one to expect. There is something about the gentleness of the landscape hereabouts, the green tor seen through pink and white apple blossom or red and green fruit in the orchards east of Glastonbury, or with a foreground of rhynes (drainage channels) and willows and sleepy cows on the levels themselves, or rising above the waving heads of a field of spelt. Something too about the way the hill burns red and brown and purple in the sunset, the stormier the better, like a sparkling jewel set into the green landscape. Something finally about the terracing of the hill, taming its abruptness. These terraces have been variously interpreted down the centuries, sometimes as military fortifications, sometimes as a giant labyrinth dedicated to the ancient British goddess, although modern secular historians now prefer to explain them as having had a purely agricultural function.

The monks of Glastonbury had plenty of land, but much of it was under water, or at least under water for several months each winter. Thus the hills that rise around Glastonbury—the tor, Chalice Hill and Wearyall Hill—were intensively cultivated for crops that could not be safely entrusted to the lower ground, and hence the sculptural terracing of the tor. Well, that is what the historians say. There are plenty of websites to argue the contrary, the most comprehensive of which boldly states: "Glastonbury Tor is home to Gwyn ap Nudd, King of the Fairies. In the human realm it is managed by the National Trust."

On the top of the tor is St. Michael's Tower, the remains of a small chapel placed here in medieval times, destroyed in an earthquake of 1275, and rebuilt in 1300. On one wall is a small relief carving of St. Anne milking a cow—she is the patron of milkmaids—and often the cows that graze the tor as part of the National Trust's land management scheme will shelter here from the heat of a summer's afternoon. People gather here too, and often there is music. An enterprising person has laid out a discreet plastic tray with sweets and bottles of water. Needless to say, payment is by trust. This is, after all, Glastonbury. Whatever we believe, it is a special place, with the even line of the Mendips to the north, the levels to the south and west, often glittering with standing water after heavy rain, the squalls that blow up from nowhere and seem to concentrate all their force on this little hill with its lonely stone tower. It is hard not to be moved by Glastonbury Tor.

Below Chalice Hill and a little closer to the town lies a spring that flows summer and winter, and which used to be the one sure supply of pure water in Glastonbury during a drought. Little wonder then that it has acquired a sacred reputation. The spring is now in the hands of a private religious trust—the Chalice Well Trust—that charges for admission (except on Christmas Day and Boxing Day). There is, however, an over-flow outside from which local people can collect water. Formerly this was known as the Chalk Well, or sometimes the Blood Well, because of the iron content of the water that stains the outflow dark red. It is somehow typical of Glastonbury that the two quite separate names have become confused, so that Chalk has become Chalice with its association with the legend of the Holy Grail, and the blessed wine that becomes the blood of Christ. The street outside retains the name of Chilkwell Street. The Well Trust is comprehensive in its pattern of activities and celebrations. There are many opportunities to simply be quiet and contemplative, but there are also celebrations for the major Christian festivals (Christmas, Easter) as well as for the solstices, the equinoxes, and the Celtic festivals of Imbolc (1 February), Beltane (May Day), Lughnasadh (1 August) and Samhain (Halloween).

The third hill of Glastonbury is Wearyall Hill, south of the town, and here the visitor's eye is immediately captured by a gnarled old thorn tree leaning against the prevailing wind. It is often decorated with coloured ribbons. The story is much loved and much repeated, of the visit of Joseph of Arimathea with the boy Jesus (the source of Blake's "Jerusalem": "And did those feet in ancient times…"), and his return with the Holy Grail, linking back into older Celtic myths. On one of those visits he struck the ground with his staff when he landed from his boat (Avalon was truly an island until the Middle Ages), it took root, and with it the thorn that flowers at both major Christian festivals of Christmas and Easter. Descending the hill, much as medieval pilgrims must have done, brings us to the town. Here, a few days before Christmas, a young child cuts a flowering shoot from another Glastonbury thorn in the churchyard at St. John's church, which is then sent to the Queen in London. What she does with it is unsure, but a modern story has it upon her breakfast table on Christmas Day. The good stories are like that, with a life of their own, demanding not belief, but simply a suspension of disbelief.

Glastonbury was a very large and wealthy abbey indeed. The western boundary runs along Silver Street, at the back of the High Street, to the north runs Chilkwell Street, to the south Magdalen Street, and to the east Bere Lane. Just across Bere Lane, at the corner of Chilkwell Street, lies the Abbey Barn, Somerset's delightful rural life museum, where eager staff and volunteers will induct you into the mysteries of cheese and cider and mistletoe and peat and willow. Beyond the town, the monks owned manors at Mells, Leigh-on-Mendip and Nunney, far up on the eastern fringes of the Mendips. Across the marshes, and to complement their monastic fish pond, they held a much larger "pond" at Meare, recorded in Domesday as holding three fisheries and ten fishermen. Sylvia Townsend Warner in her recently republished *Somerset* (1949), which she describes as an "err-and-stray-book" rather than a "travel guide", refers to the "heron-grey Fish House, so sober and purposeful" and points out that it now belongs to "the best of owners, the National Trust".

The exhibition area at the abbey ruins treads carefully around the history of the place. The community was self-sufficient: grains for flour, beer and fodder, peas and beans, milk, fish, poultry, vegetables, honey, eggs and herbs. Oil and wine were the main imports. Besides the tithe barn at Glastonbury, there was another at Doulting; at Doulting too were the quarries which provided much of the finest stone for both Glastonbury and Wells. The monks continued to live well right to the end: in the last three months of 1539 they consumed 27,000 bundles of firewood in the abbot's kitchen, the catering centre of the establishment. Yet, as we have indicated, its extensive holdings beyond the town went somewhat beyond the carefully drawn Benedictine rules:

The monastery should be organised so that all its needs, that is to say things such as water, a mill, a garden, and various crafts, may be met within its premises, so that the monks have no need to wander round outside it, for that does not profit their souls at all.

But wander they did—and made enemies.

Others wandered purposefully in their direction. Pilgrimage was important to Glastonbury, and essential to pilgrimage was a shrine, and stories. Glastonbury had both, abundantly. The Joseph of Arimathea story climaxed in the late Middle Ages, when a chapel was built below the Lady Chapel. As for shrines, there was St. Patrick, "borrowed" from Ireland and claimed to be abbot here in 443, and to be buried at the right of the altar. And there was England's most important Saxon saint, Dunstan, abbot here from 940 to 957. The official shrine of Dunstan is at Canterbury, but Glastonbury disputed this for 400 years in the name of tourism (pilgrimage, that is). Seven years after a disastrous fire in 1184, which threatened the monastery's economic success, the bones of Arthur and Guinevere were very conveniently discovered here. The volume of pilgrims increased, and the increased revenues were put to good use. Glastonbury received official support too, Edward I and Queen Eleanor visiting in 1278 to see "King Arthur" transferred to a holier place in the choir. Building continued, right up to the dissolution. The abbey church is vast, presumably to hold all those pilgrims.

When Henry VIII issued his Act of Supremacy by which power over the church passed from the hands of the pope into those of the king, there was little sign of what was to come. Some monasteries were certainly in decline and had never recovered from plague and depopulation. But Glastonbury was successful as, to coin a phrase, an ecclesiastical business. Abbot Whiting was elderly and benign and happily (or unhappily, because in truth we do not know) took the oath to uphold the Act of Supremacy. But in 1539, just three years later, in one of the most barbarous events of the dissolution, the frail old man in his eighties was summarily tried, carried to the top of Glastonbury Tor on a hurdle and executed with two of his monks. His head was displayed on the abbey gatehouse, his body quartered and displayed at Bridgwater, Ilchester, Wells and Bath. Glastonbury decayed, stone was taken and re-used, trees and flowers invaded the site. Some buildings found new uses, including the use of the abbot's kitchen by Quakers in the 1680s. Finally the site was sold back to the Church of England in 1907. Queen Mary came for a great pageant in 1909. In 1924 the Christian church reclaimed the abbey as a site of pilgrimage, though Anglicans and Roman Catholics honour old wounds by gathering on different days. The followers of the old beliefs prefer the Chalice Well.

Still people come to Glastonbury, as tourists, as pilgrims, or just the idle and curious; and go away believing what they will. Patricia Beer's verdict of "a plague of conflicting and mindless legends and superstitions" is forthright, if unsympathetic. One such visitor in the interwar years was John Cowper Powys, who did his own level best to promote as many legends and superstitions as he could lay his hands on. Powys is a difficult man to come to grips with—philosopher, anarchist, gifted story-teller. Perhaps the difficulty is in knowing sometimes where one ends and the others begin. *A Glastonbury Romance* (1932) comes as near to unreadable as it is fascinating, a vast, sprawling, repetitious novel, full of politics, religion, sex and generous doses of dialect and exclamation marks. The characters, a cast of 45 from all walks of life, dispute the legacy of Glastonbury by their words and actions. Everything has some basis in fact—the development of the Wookey Hole caves as a tourist attraction, the Celtic vision of Owen Evans, the "mystical realism" of John Geard—but Powys weaves and elaborates a tangled web upon his canvas, including a communist "Glastonbury Commune" making tourist souvenirs.

There are a number of dramatic set-pieces in the book. The first is the pageant, which rapidly turns into a riot. A second is the great flood, in which capitalists, communists and grail-seekers are all caught up together by the force of nature. These are not the usual floods on the Somerset Levels, where nature and people co-operate to control and order the water, but a dreaded combination of tide and moon, of rain and wind, that carries all before it. No doubt Powys had read of the great flood of January 1607, when a tidal wave swept across the levels and killed 2,000 people. At the end of well over 1,000 pages he attempts a summary, referring back again to Stonehenge:

> The builders of Stonehenge have perished; but there are those who worship in stones still. The builders of Glastonbury have perished; but there are people, yet living among us, whose eyes have seen the Grail. The ribs of our ancient earth are riddled with desperate pieties; her

hollow caves are scooped out with frantic asseverations; and the end is not yet.

The novel could only have been set in Glastonbury.

THE WATER IN THE WELLS

As Sylvia Warner Townsend suggests, any city where the bishop's main task appears to be feeding the swans in the palace moat when they ring the bell at the gate-house, has to be a special place. As recently as 2007, new swans were granted to Wells by the queen and have been taught the bell-ringing trick. In 2008 cygnets followed, but only after a marital squabble in which both parents ended up in the Market Place. In medieval times the bishops were princes of the church but also important political figures, and both the present bishop (Peter Price) and his predecessor (Jim Thompson) have followed this tradition by speaking out on issues of war and peace, of wealth and poverty, as well as the cares of church governance. Thomas Bekynton was Bishop of Bath and Wells from 1443 to 1464 and a civil servant—at various times described as secretary to the king, Secretary of State, Treasurer and Keeper of the Privy Seal. Back in Wells, he argued with the Abbot of Glastonbury, who disliked episcopal visits. Above all he organized the water supply for the town, for the church owned St. Andrew's Well in the palace gardens, to the north-east of the cathedral. The actual springs are located beneath the wall that divides the palace gardens from the cathedral garden and can thus be viewed from either side. The Well House in the palace garden dates from 1451, but was rebuilt in Victorian times and topped by a talbot, a favourite hunting dog of the bishops. The flow of water from deep beneath the Mendips is constant and used to power mills in Wells, including one on the site of what is now the pond. The overflow fills the moat and then drains into the River Sheppey, at the entrance to Palace Fields.

Bekynton secured public use of the springs by running lead pipes under the cathedral to a public conduit with four taps in the Market Place, south-east of the cathedral. This fountain was in a ruinous state by the end of the eighteenth century and was replaced by the current "picturesque" neo-Gothic structure. Bekynton was a shrewd politician as well as a philanthropist. Once the Peasants' Revolt in 1381 had been bloodily put down, it made sense to do something to improve the general living con-

The Bishop's Palace, Wells

ditions in both town and country, and to deflect the increasing criticism aimed at the church's wealth and love of luxury. Bekynton's gift is remembered each January in a service of thanksgiving attended by the City Council, a custom revived in 1985. Two candles gleam in Bishop Bekynton's chantry, the flickering light dwelling on a small bowl of water from the well and a little posy of winter flowers from the gardens. The words of the Magnificat seem appropriate to a man determined to not simply enjoy the fruits and riches of office, but to live a life of service to others: "He hath put down the mighty from their seat: and hath exalted the humble and meek." Now Wells, where water is always abundant, works closely with the tribal people of the Indian desert state of Rajasthan to develop ways to harvest and use what little water there is.

Bekynton was not the only bishop to think of the people of Wells. In Victorian times Bishop George Low allocated sixty acres of land to poor labourers to be used as allotments. Land was also allocated to a park and bandstand—perhaps to rival the new Royal Victoria Park in Bath at the other end of the diocese? Further land was made available for allotments in the Second World War, and remarkably these have survived and thrived. Entrance is through a discreet wooden door in the high stone wall in Tor Street, but they are best seen just to the east of St. Andrew's Well in the palace gardens. They are very mature, colourful on a grey October afternoon with yellow chrysanthemums, red and purple dahlias, cheerful with red apples alongside the crystal-clear waters of the well pond. Development continues to the north of the springs and allotments, where a further garden site with old greenhouses, currently rather neglected, is to be developed as public space.

REFORM AND DISSENT

Just beyond Wearyall Hill lies industrial Somerset, or what is left of. Even the name Street conjures an everyday sort of place. Edward Thomas, fresh from flowering thorns of Glastonbury, hated it: "It is a mostly new conglomeration of houses dominated by the chimney and the squat tower of Clark's Boot Factory; and since it is both flat and riverless, it sprawls about with a dullness approaching the sordid."

On the contrary, Street is one of the more interesting towns in Somerset. Hard by the factory and the chimney is decent grey-stone workers' housing of a standard that puts both the private philanthropy of estate cottages and the public benevolence of council housing to shame. There is a recently restored heated lido in purest 1930s art deco, surrounded by lawns and trees. There is a quietly classical Quaker meeting house that sits comfortably in the shade of an enormous London plane tree. The burial ground is a monument in itself to Quaker ideals of equality and personal dignity, row after row of identical stones marking the final resting-places of Clarks and workers alike. Clark's has moved seamlessly into the modern world of global capitalism; shoes are no longer made here but imported from wherever shoes may be cheaply made, and there is a giant, gleaming steel-and-glass distribution centre to the south of the town, where research and development are still carried on. And as if cocking a snook at the abstemious Quakers, there is a fine cider and perry-maker called Heck's where you can watch the apples and pears arriving and their juicing, taste from the barrel and buy by the bottle or the flagon.

Somerset, like Dorset, is a county of dissent. For every soaring, decorated tower or spire of a parish church, there are probably two or three chapels belonging to dissenters. Gradually these are closed and converted into private residences—a whole slice of West Country history is disappearing from the landscape. At the other end of the county, between Wiveliscombe and Milverton is another Quaker burial ground. Sylvia Warner Townsend found it up a lane, signposted "Fry's Burial Ground":

> The land is narrow as an eel, and at first it runs between banks that wear a thick sighing fleece of rough grass, and then it winds and tunnels among trees, and the sigh of grass is exchanged for the rustle and creak of branches.

Others have taken the same route since, although not all have found it, for the sign "Friends' Burial Ground 1681" lurks demurely at the roadside. Like north-east Somerset, this was a land of independent-minded weavers. Indeed, such was the strength of Quakers here in the west of the county that Milverton had a street called Quaker Street. Now the burial ground is maintained jointly by Wellington and Taunton meetings. There are large yew trees (a symbol of everlasting life until the Victorians made them synonymous with death) at the entrance, a small beech hanger beyond the banks on two sides, ground cover of cyclamen and ivy and the grave markers. At Street Meeting House, the stones stand up; here they lie flat, but there is that same modesty, that same dignity. It would be a good place to lie.

Architecturally, Long Sutton near Taunton, dating from 1717 is the finest of the Somerset Quaker Meeting Houses, its interior still lined with bare wood, for the Quakers believed that neither people not their buildings should be showy. Like the Arts and Crafts, and indeed the modernists, fitness for purpose was all. The contrast, for example, between the austere plain pew-ends and the intricately carved bench-ends so typical of the Anglican churches of the moors and levels could not be more telling. Initially the women sat separately in a "preparatory" meeting, on a screened balcony. Later this was used by children, until a more recent Children's Room, a separate building like a smaller clone of the original, ensured that the children are occupied while their elders sit and listen to the silence and their souls. Despite the terrible defeat of the Monmouth Rebellion in 1685, which we shall come to in a moment, the 1689 Act of Toleration allowed a great flourishing of chapel-building in the west. In the great weaving centre of Frome, the proud classicism of Rook Lane chapel (built 1707, now an Arts Centre) proclaims the wealth of the newly liberated dissenters. Taunton's 1721 Unitarian church is wood-panelled and dominated by a rich chandelier. Dissent had arrived and was a power in the land. Congregational, Unitarian, Methodist, Baptist, Moravian—the sects multiplied and bifurcated. Yet still there is the very recent story told by Roger Thorne of a tiny chapel in North Devon: no sect this, for "we belongs to ourselves," he was told. By the time of the ecclesiastical census of 1851, of 1,129 places of worship in Somerset, 49 per cent were Anglican, 28 per cent Methodists, 10 per cent Congregational, 8 per cent Baptist and 5 per cent merely "others". Many people had ceased to attend church, but that is another story.

THE MOORS AND LEVELS, FROM ALFRED TO MONMOUTH

Somerset light	murky in the mist brooding
Sullen and damp	winter's mantle
The shroud	its invisible spell cast
A shawl	binding moors and levels
A solitary fastness	a thick blanket
Within which people move	slow and sluggish

Tarnished by its vapour	seeping into their joints
Struggling	the rising damp
To meet the midday sun	to penetrate the veil
A faint halo	half-hovering over ditches
Rivers, rhynes and runnels	islands
Connected by thin causeways	thin slices of cattle-breeding land
Fuelling the flatness	uneasy and unrepentant
The ghosts of withy trees	caught between water and mist
Marsh-memory lingering still	a quirkiness settling in

The solemn grey pulse… out of which only the heron rises
James Crowden, "Somerset Light—Winter"

The attraction of the moors and levels is that they are more broken, more manageable to the eye than the sweeping monotony of the East Anglian fens. There are always hills to frame the picture—the long flat line of the Mendips to the north, Glastonbury and its tor, the bulk of Brent Knoll, the Poldens heading west and then changing their mind and turning south through the heart of the picture, the misty Blackdowns to the south, Exmoor and the Quantocks where the weather comes from, over on the western horizon. Then there are the islands—Athelney, where Alfred burned a good woman's cakes and ruminated on the future of England and how to move from contemplation to action (did the anger of the good woman assist him in this?). There is Muchelney, an abbey like Glastonbury, but because of its isolated position there has been less stone-raiding here and there is much to see. In the tiny village the priest's house still stands, one of the smallest of all National Trust properties, and nearby John Leach's pottery where the customer is provided with water to test the pouring properties of a jug. Some islands are so tiny, perhaps enough to sustain a farm or a church, that their significance only appears in time of flood.

Burrow Mump (rather confusingly, both words mean hill) lies above the little village of Burrow Bridge with its Victorian church a decorative mix of grey local stone and honey-coloured Ham stone mouldings, as in other levels churches such as Westonzoyland. This is a significant point on the levels, where the waters of the Tone, draining through Taunton from the Quantocks, meet the Parrett, which has already gathered the waters of the Isle and Yeo from the Blackdowns. Together they will flow, with considerable help from human ingenuity and pumping stations, through Bridgwater to the muddy Bristol Channel. The Mump is a little grey ruin on a green mound, yet clearly visible from the trains speeding westwards on the Great Western main line from London to Taunton. There is a discreet car-park, and a National Trust information board, but these are the only signs of heritage hereabouts.

The Anglo-Saxons used Burrow Mump and its strategic position to serve as a defensive outrider to the larger "island" of Athelney. Alfred's Athelney can now be only an imagined landscape of lakes and marshes, compared with the present human landscape of rectilinear rhynes, rich pasture and withy beds. A thirteenth-century chapel dedicated to St. Michael stood on Burrow Mump, but proved difficult to maintain. An attempt to rebuild it as a smaller parish church ended in failure in 1793, and the Victorians in 1838 then built the church in the village at the foot of the hill, among the now drained lowlands. Burrow Mump was garrisoned by the royalists in the Civil War and also used by the royalist army during the Monmouth rebellion.

Somerset had been largely parliamentarian during the Civil War. The picturesque ruined parts of the Bishop's Palace in Wells are a direct result of the conflict. At different times, both royalists and parliamentarians held the palace, while the other side subjected it to bombardment. It was ransacked and looted by both sides, and left in a state of neglect for 200 years. The restoration of the monarchy in 1660 made little difference to deeply held social and religious views in Somerset; groups like the Quakers thrived on identifying themselves as martyrs to a cause. That cause became a military campaign in 1685 when the Duke of Monmouth attempted to contest the succession of James II, an acknowledged Roman Catholic. That he landed at Lyme Regis implied that he expected support from the West Country. Up to 10,000 men did indeed join him. Despite the name of Pitchfork Rebellion, the majority of the rebels were not farm labourers but rather independent craftsmen and weavers motivated by religious sentiment. Among them was Daniel Defoe. The officer-in-charge, Nathaniel Wade, was a Bristol lawyer, a non-conformist and the son of a senior officer in Cromwell's Civil War army. The record book of the Chard and Axminster Congregational church tells us that "A great number of sober and pious men marched forth with the army... Both the pastor, the Ruling Elder and several of the brethren were with the army." Yet an ill-equipped rag-tag army it was, and the march east fizzled out after skirmishes with royalist troops in the Bristol area. The rump of the rebel army—no more than 3-4,000 men—retired to Bridgwater, closely followed by the royalist army; the rebels attempted to surprise the royalist soldiers camped on dry ground by a night-time march across the marshes, and the rebellion fell apart among the ditches and drainage channels on the outskirts of Westonzoyland. Sedgemoor was the last military battle on English soil. Defoe became an important witness, noting the shots fired "either by accident or by treachery" which alerted the royal army to the rebels advancing through the watery darkness.

The merciless persecution of the rebels almost defies belief. Many were butchered in cold blood. Prisoners were kept in appalling conditions in Westonzoyland church. Later, frankincense, pitch and resin had to be used to disinfect the church. Other prisoners were taken to the ruined palace at Wells, and held pending trial. There they found a friend in Bishop Thomas Ken, who despite differences of religious opinion ministered to them, and took messages to their families. He also wrote to the king, appealing for mercy for his people. But Lord Justice Jeffreys was on his way, determined at his Bloody Assizes to make an example of the rebels. Some 330 were executed, while 849 were transported to the slave plantations of Barbados. There was a good profit to be made from human traffic, as Sylvia Townsend Warner reminds us: "Mary of Modena, that virtuous queen-consort, complained furiously at being allotted only 98 Somerset prisoners to make her profit on by selling them as slaves to the plantations, and demanded 100 more." Those who had given practical help or moral support to the rebels did not escape punishment. The families of some schoolgirls in Taunton (the Maids of Taunton) who had made and presented a banner to Monmouth had to pay heavy fines to secure their release from prison.

Thomas Ken provides a moving footnote to the story. When William and Mary came to the throne in 1689—the Glorious Revolution that was to secure England for Protestantism and, eventually, parliamentary democracy—he was deprived of his see. He had sworn an oath of allegiance to James, and was not prepared to now make a similar oath to a new king while the old king lived. A non-juror, he went into "exile" at Longleat under the protection of the Thynne family, and remained there. There is something of George Herbert in Ken, perhaps something of what Herbert might have become had ill-health not intervened. Indeed, Ken had been brought up by his half-sister Anne, second wife of Izaak Walton, the well-known angler and biographer of Herbert. Another twist to this story is that as a young priest Ken had spent a year at The Hague as chaplain to Princess Mary, daughter of the future James II, and future queen alongside her husband, William of Orange. Ken had disapproved of William both for his Calvinism and for his treatment of Mary, so there were reasons in plenty for tensions between Ken and the new monarchs. Ken ordered in his will that he was to be buried in the church in the diocese of Bath and Wells closest to Longleat. This is how he comes to be buried in a strange stone dog-kennel at the east end of St. John's Church in Frome, outside the church that is, for the diocese would not permit him to be buried inside. There he stays and, some would say, rebukes a church that dealt so cruelly with the conscience of a caring priest.

EARNING A LIVING
The unique landscape of the Somerset Levels sustains and is maintained by a unique economy. Westonzoyland is not only the starting-off point for the memorial to the battle of Sedgemoor but also for the old family firm of Musgrove Willows, down the long straight drove that leads to the Museum of Steam Power and Land Drainage. It is a strange sight, the neat stacks of orange willow sticks (withies) stacked in long lines to dry in this otherwise green countryside. Musgrove's supplied the willow for Serena de la Hey's giant Willow Man, which haunts the M5 as it crosses the levels. Originally a metal sculptor, she now uses mainly welded metal frames covered with basket weave. Yet willow is also a very practical material. Apart from basket-weaving, once more a thriving trade in Somerset, there is a strong demand for willow for making coffins for environmentally friendly burials (willow is harvested annually), and also for baskets for the popular Bristol-based sport of ballooning. The Somerset Willow Company at Bridgwater is the world's largest maker of balloon baskets. There is no surer sign of a warm summer's evening in North Somerset than the appearance of a brightly coloured balloon over the horizon with the characteristic hissing of the gas jets below it. At Coates Willow and Wetlands Visitor Centre, very close to Athelney, a Lithuanian basket-weaver has learned the Somerset art of weaving while seated on the floor, which he now finds very

comfortable. As long as everything is in reach there is no strain or pull on the back.

Kate Lynch is a local painter and community artist who has linked her own atmospheric pictures of the willow industry (from growing through stripping and drying to weaving) with the words of the men and women who keep alive these ancient arts. Men like Eddie Barnard from Middlezoy whose earliest memories are of coming home from school to help two aunties who were basket-weavers strip the new crop of withies. Lynch's book *Willow* has a series of paintings and drawings, each one linked to an extract from a sound recording, often the person pictured at work. In her afterword she refers to the "foreign country" she found moving just sixteen miles away from North Cadbury:

> I sat and painted the unfamiliar landscape but the pictures lacked passion. I needed to find out whose landscape this was, so I began to ask and took my sketchbook with me.
>
> In getting to know the land, I met the willow growers and basket-makers whose families have farmed this flat, often wet, landscape and hand-crafted its harvest for generations. It's been a three-year journey. Reg took me to see George boiling, men harvesting willow at Stathe sent me to Pete, the basketmaker, Alf introduced me to the Denhams, the Denhams sell withies to Aubrey, Aubrey makes shrimp 'reaps' for Brendan and so on.

Yet there is more to her pictures than just a documentary recording of reality. There is always the light, coming from the sky, through a window, from a lamp, catching the burnished gold of the willows, the glow of people's faces. Here craft is more than just a job; a way of life, something that gives meaning to a life, and suggests there may indeed be hope and sense in life itself. Much the same kind of ethereal vision is present in the work of her artist-husband James Lynch. Sometimes there is just the landscape, in all its size and majesty, but just as often there are the little touches that remind us that this landscape is a lived-in and human-created world—a land of dairy-farmers, of a tractor ploughing, a neighbour cycling home from work in the twilight, a dairyman milking on a moonlit evening, a neighbour's green caravan behind an ornamental gate. It is a peopled world, a human-scale world, but always with that suggestion too of something wider, deeper, a feeling for landscape to which we shall return in the next chapter when we look at the lives of William and Dorothy Wordsworth in Somerset.

James Lynch has also painted one of the cider farms that cluster round the drier, firmer fringes of the levels, or on one of the islands. Like the willow, cider is a deep and ancient craft which persists whatever the pessimists may have to say about the disappearing orchards of the West Country. Celia Fiennes wrote of cider. A non-conformist like Defoe, she took the same keen interest in the details of life, in how people live and how they earn a living. She wrote in exciting times—her diaries span the years of the Monmouth Rebellion, and the Glorious Revolution when William and Mary achieved the Protestant ascendancy that Monmouth had failed to win. She described the "cheese process" of cider-making, extracting the juice with alternate layers of apple pulp and straw, a ceremony re-enacted each year at the Museum of Rural Life in Glastonbury. Fiennes was not impressed:

> In most parts of Sommer-setshire it is very fruitful for orchards, plenty of apples and peares, but they are not curious in the planting the best sort of fruite, which is a great pitty; being so soone produced, and such quantetyes, they are likewise as careless when they make cider, they press all sorts of apples together, else they might have as good cider as in any other parts, even as good as the Herriffordshire...

Well! Somerset cider apples, both sweet and sour, are carefully selected varieties that have stood the test of time. It is indeed possible to make cider of a sort from any apples, but that is not the Somerset way, whatever they do elsewhere. When *The Independent* claimed that a particular variety of Somerset cider apple had disappeared, the response in the Letters column was swift and succinct:

> Sir: In your "A-Z of apples" (19 Oct) you state that the cider apple "Slack-ma-girdle" is now extinct. I am happy to report that I have enjoyed singe-variety Slack-ma-Girdle cider produced by the Hecks family in Street, Somerset, within the last year.
> Brian Jefferson, Glastonbury, Somerset

Woodbines, Rice's Jerseys, Redskins, Black Vallis, Red Vallis—the same apples with different names, different apples with the same name; apples still confound the wary, and compound the joy of life in Somerset.

Parsonage Farm at West Lyng, just down the road from Athelney and the handsome monument to King Alfred, is my own favourite Somerset cider farm, bright with blossom in spring, bright in autumn, too, with apples that shine alternately deep red and luminous yellow on the trees. There are also walnuts, and as summers warm, the walnuts become plumper and new trees are planted. The seasons are marked here by the swallows, nervous and agitated in early summer, in autumn equally agitated as they swoop and whistle in search of insects, keen to use every moment to fatten themselves for the long flight south to Africa.

PUTTING ON A SHOW

It is not just the birds in Somerset that like putting on a show. Somerset is addicted to shows, big, medium-sized, small, quiet, rowdy, discreet. The largest of them, if we except for a moment the Glastonbury Festival, is the Bath and West Show, the history of which we shall trace in the Bath and Bristol chapter to the great enthusiasm for science and the uses of science in eighteenth-century Bath. It is, to be frank, a rather staid and proper affair, full of giant agricultural machinery and, when foot-and-mouth outbreaks permit, giant specimens of farm animals. It inspires loyalty and enthusiasm on the part of the farming community, but is of less interest to the general public.

The Bath and West Show used to be peripatetic, but now has a permanent show site lies south of Shepton Mallet. This means that it is a near neighbour of a very different sort of festival – the Glastonbury Festival held at Michael Eavis' Worthy Farm at Pilton. Glastonbury—an inspired choice of name for a festival that is not actually in Glastonbury—has a short but interesting history, beginning in 1970. It became an annual event in the 1980s, and in recent years has attracted considerable media interest with highlights and live broadcasting from the site. Its popularity was nearly its downfall, with problems involving gatecrashers and overcrowding. In 2001 it was cancelled. Its survival owes much to another festival man, Martin Bax (a relation of Arnold Bax the composer who played cricket with his brother Clifford and with Edward Thomas at Broughton Gifford in Wiltshire). Bax, founder and unpaid director of a lively annual cultural festival in Frome, was also a Mendip district councillor. In 2002, he happened to be chair of the relevant licensing committee that was charged with making a decision about the future of the Festival. He was able to thrash out a deal on security with the police, Michael Eavis and local residents, and thus was born the Great Wall of Pilton that encircles Worthy Farm each June. Now everyone, well nearly everyone, loves the Glastonbury Festival.

At the other end of the agricultural spectrum from the Bath and West and of the cultural spectrum from the Glastonbury Festival lie the village shows with their competitions for growing flowers, fruit and vegetables and making jam and cakes, their cream teas and whatever else is going— majorettes, perhaps Morris men and fund-raising stalls selling (or should it be recycling) unwanted household junk. Then there are Christmas Fairs, and Easter Fairs, and Summer Fairs and any number of other excuses to get together, to organize, to review the pecking order of local busybodies. And between the village shows and the Bath and West come the middling size shows such as Frome Cheese Show. It is nearly a decade now since the Frome Show moved out of Frome, although the field where it took place is still called the Cheese Show Field. In those days the Cheese Show was on a weekday and the local schools all shut for the day. Remarkably, and despite some interesting "goings-on" in the meantime, the show has retained its traditional mixture of soft, community and hard, farming interests, despite the move to a new farmland site several miles out of town.

Even more remarkably, the sun always shines for the Frome Show—

splendid mid-September summer days—the hedgerows turning red with hips and haws, the trees showing the first brown and yellow hints of autumn to come. There are teasels, once used in the cloth industry in Frome, at the field-edges, while brown cows rest in deep shade under hedgerow trees. The show continues to revolve around the Cheese tent, a massive marquee with table after table of yellow cheeses laid out in long lines. Most of these are the products of large-scale farming and industrial manufacturing processes, but there also stalls from smaller cheese-makers such as Keen's, Montgomery's and Westcombe who continue to make cheddar cheese in the traditional way. Keen's has been at Moorhayes Farm in Wincanton, Somerset, since 1899. It wins prizes at Frome, and indeed at the Bath and West, and is sold at specialist shops such as the delightful Sagebury Cheese in Frome. In recent years, Somerset has learned to make brie as good as any French brie, suitable retribution for the theft of the name cheddar by the whole world of cheese-makers. The camembert is coming on too, and there are fine goat and sheep-cheeses.

In the Frome calendar, the September Cheese Show was always closely linked with Carnival, one of a number of excuses Frome finds to close off its town centre to traffic each year. Carnival is about light, and it seems a little early in the year to worry about the disappearing sun when it is scarcely the autumn equinox. But worry they do, and the brightly illuminated floats rumble slowly through the streets of Frome accompanied by interminable processions of majorettes, brass bands and walking figures in highly decorated costumes. So Carnival will grind on through the streets of Somerset: Wincanton, Castle Cary, Glastonbury, Wells, Shepton Mallet, Weston-Super-Mare. Each will have its own character, its own special features, although the large, brilliantly illuminated floats will normally appear at every carnival in their "circuit". The whole phenomenon comes to a climax at Bridgwater in November, where Carnival has become hopelessly and spectacularly muddled with Fifth of November Guy Fawkes celebrations, and whatever ceremonies previous inhabitants of these lands may have had to mark the coming of winter and the season of darkness. Many thousands of people descend on Bridgwater each year to see the colourful procession, and the fireworks display. What it all means is anyone's business to say, but it nicely fills the social gap between summer and Christmas.

Chapter Six

SOMERSET: HIGHLANDS AND ISLANDS

The shapes of the mist, slowly moving along, exquisitely beautiful;
passing over the sheep they almost seemed to have more life than those
quiet creatures. The unseen birds singing in the mist.

Dorothy Wordsworth's Journal, in the Quantocks, 1 March 1797

THE BEST OF SOMERSET?

Somerset in early May is entering into its white period. Cow parsley
marches along the verges, still upright and vigorous—later it flops and
straggles and looks bedraggled—there is may blossom (hawthorn) in the
hedgerows, the first elderflowers with promise of sparkling wine and cor-
dials, the great candles of the horse chestnuts already heavy and listing
drunkenly with pollen and rain. May is Mary's month, and even on a grey,
wet morning the countryside shakes itself and shimmers with light and
renewal and the promise of sunshine to come.

Lytes Cary is not the sort of place you would stumble on by accident,
although the A303, a major trunk route to the West Country lies close by.

So too does Somerton, the ancient capital of the land of the summer people. But the lanes twist and turn and the very signposts seem intended to deter and confuse rather than encourage and enlighten the traveller. The National Trust guidebook describes it as a "comfortable jumble of gables" built of local blue lias stone—the sort of house that rises and then crumbles quietly back into the land from which it came. And that surely is what would have happened if it had not been for Sir Walter Jenner. When he found Lytes Cary in 1907, the great hall was being used as a cider store and the great parlour to store farm equipment. An enthusiast for William Morris and the Arts and Crafts movement, Jenner rebuilt and modernized while leaving the core of the late medieval house untouched. The Jenners were the vehicles by which this beautiful old house was transferred eventually to the safe hands of the National Trust, whose tenants Jeremy and Biddy Chittenden spent the second half of the twentieth century transforming the garden.

Our interest in Lytes Cary is only obliquely the garden, beautiful though it is. That oblique interest comes from an earlier garden here, that of the herbalist Henry Lyte. His son, Thomas, was a keen gardener too, taking special pride in his orchard of apples, pears, cherries, walnuts, grapes, plums and peaches. (The present orchard includes medlars and quinces, old fruits that grow well in Somerset, and are the subject of renewed interest in recent years.) Henry Lyte the father was a scholar, reputed to have retired to his study to avoid a cantankerous stepmother who no doubt dominated daily life in the panelled communal hall with its high raftered roof. In 1578 he published the *Niewe Herbal,* an English translation of a Flemish herbal illustrated with many fine woodcuts. A first edition, on loan from the British Museum, lies open at "spurges"—great and small. Lyte, a meticulous recorder, describes them thus: "The leaves be long and narrow, like the leaves of a withie or almonde tree, the stalke breaketh abroad at the top into many other little branches." Like many gardeners of his generation, Lyte was excited by the new and the exotic, by fruits such as the pineapple and the pomegranate. He preferred the violets bred for the garden with their "deepe blewe colour" to the woodland varieties "without flavour, and of a fainte blewe or pale colour", a view now so heretical we should be thankful that Lyte kept to plants and not religion as his subject of study.

Lyte did have wider interests, mainly the history of his own family and of the British in general. He developed complex genealogies which showed that the British were descended from the Trojans. It all seems very unlikely, though as we shall see in Chapter Seven, John Wood the Elder in Bath a century and a half later had similarly wild notions about national identity. Lyte wrote this up in *The Light of Britayne* (1588)—he shared the Elizabethan taste for puns too, here punning on his own name—and presented a copy to Queen Elizabeth on the day she attended "old" St. Paul's Cathedral. His son Thomas followed this up in the reign of James I, creating a genealogy that traced the new king's ancestry back to Brutus. No doubt the king, recently imported from Scotland, was insecure in his new role. Thomas' reward was a gold and diamond locket with a Hilliard miniature of the king himself inside. Sycophancy ran in the family. When John Lyte created the great chamber in the 1530s, he added into the plasterwork of the ceiling the royal coat of arms and Tudor roses to honour Henry VIII, as well as his own swans and his wife Edith Horsey's—well—horses.

But family histories are histories of sadness and failure as well as joy and success, of rupture as well as continuity. The Lytes continued to live at Lytes Cary until the mid-eighteenth century, but they were in financial trouble. The figures did not add up and the Lytes were forced to move away. One descendant, Henry Lyte, was a Victorian vicar of Brixham in Devon, where he wrote the much-loved hymn "Abide with me".

CLEVEDON AND THE BRISTOL CHANNEL

Clevedon is a modest little town of sturdy stone villas. The sea is brown and eager on a day of wind; on a calm day silver grey (it is seldom blue in the Bristol Channel), a mid-morning high tide overwhelming the tidal swimming pool and beating on the rocks around it. Clevedon has views, and so is a suitable place for that favourite English seaside habit of sitting on a bench or deckchair and staring out to sea. On a clear day there is mile after mile of coast down channel past Brean Down to the purple Quantocks and Exmoor, while over on the Welsh side, the Black Mountains and Brecon Beacons clamber up the horizon. Clevedon is Victorian and proud of it. John Betjeman admired Clevedon and made a film about it. And the glory of Victorian Clevedon is its pier. Steamers still call here, the restored *Balmoral* and the *Waverley* on their journeys up and down the channel and across to Wales and Lundy or even up to Bristol on a good tide. Fishermen and women still fish here (well supervised by the Cleve-don Sea Angling Club: "My best catch is thousands and thousands of friends," said one member), and day visitors and locals still tramp the boards.

The pier is simple, beautiful, functional. It opened on Easter Monday 29 March 1869. On Easter Sunday that year it snowed, perhaps antici-pating an uncertain future. Like the drawing offices in the old Great Western works at Swindon, its framework includes old broad gauge rails (designed by Brunel but referred to as Barlow rails) brought across from South Wales. Given the constant strain of the tidal flow in these waters, the thin legs are actually stronger than fat ones that would have set up more resistance. But with an average 46-foot tidal rise and fall, the second highest in the world, it was a tricky technical problem. The pier consists of eight main arches on slim pillars that give it an almost gravity-defying appearance, floating high above the brown waters of the Channel. For a time all was well. The Eltons at Clevedon Court were satisfied that their investment was paying dividends in attracting visitors, and since they owned most of Clevedon, what was good for Clevedon was good for the Eltons.

The opening of the Severn railway tunnel in 1880 took business away from the steamers, and in 1894 they opened a pavilion and dance-hall to attract more people onto the pier. Excursion trips developed: the *Waverley* first visited Clevedon in 1886. From 1921 the firm of Campbell domi-nated steamer traffic on the Channel with their White Funnel fleet. At the height of the trade, they had eleven paddle-steamers on the Channel, and a day's blow at sea remained popular right through into the 1950s and 1960s. Then in 1970 came disaster: two spans of the pier collapsed during tests. "It looked like the end of the world," said the resident tollhouse manager. From the beginning there were plans to restore the pier. The Elton family were very supportive of early efforts, although Sir Arthur Elton, a leader in the new field of industrial archaeology, died in 1973. There were petitions, letters to editors, demonstrations and fund-raising, but no real progress was made. In 1979 the District Council proposed demolition, and this proved the catalyst for renewed action, culminating in a public enquiry in 1980. The council's aesthetic, technical and eco-nomic arguments for demolition collapsed. Betjeman was ill but sent a recording (you can hear that gravelly, slightly complaining voice: "I think it is a gem among coastal towns in England... Without its pier, Clevedon would be a diamond with a flaw"). By 1984 when the council conceded a 99-year lease, it was clear that the pier would have to be largely rebuilt, and this took place at Portishead Docks. State money was important in addition to local fund-raising and included large grants from English Heritage and the National Heritage Memorial Fund. Now it is National Lottery money that helps to keep the pier afloat.

And then there are the donations. Money for the new boards has been contributed by thousands of sponsors and this has become a real feature of pier life. The pier is part of a culture of sentimentality, in the best sense of that word: heritage is not just about beautiful and important buildings, but also that sense of the importance of place in people's lives and wanting to hand that importance on. The name plaques of the many donors that line the wooden seats running the length of the pier bear witness. Simple messages such as "God bless Nan (Dolly Hill) 1908-2006"—and more dramatically, quoting six lines from the Beatles, "And I love her":

Elizabeth Merritt
Will you marry me?
Michael Provis
Christmas Day 2001

One hopes she said yes, and that they will live happily ever after. Family loyalty and romantic love are both clearly still alive in Clevedon.

At the business end of the pier, where the boats dock, are two shelters and a handsome little pavilion with a café above, ornate and intricate wrought iron and stained glass in contrast to the functionality of the main structure. The restless slip-slop of the waves on the iron rails reminds us that humankind is energetic, creative and mortal. Upstream from the end of the pier one can see the southern (second) of the two Severn bridges. This is a landscape that may be about to change dramatically. Already there are the two Severn bridges rising above the mud-flats, sand-banks and swirling brown waters, and the compact, box-like structure of Hinkley Nuclear Power Station, tucked away in the corner of Bridgwater Bay but visible from all directions. Now there is once again talk of a Severn barrage to use the power of the sea to generate electricity. What was declared economically unfeasible in the 1930s may well be possible in our high energy life-style. Feasible, possibly, but whether it is desirable is quite another matter. Across the channel lie Penarth and the gleaming white new buildings of Cardiff Bay—the shiny new Wales of devolved government and commercial vigour, while further east there is still the old industrial decay of heavy industry around Newport. Past and future, nature and industry: that is the Bristol Channel today. There is no chance of waking up from an afternoon nap and imagining yourself in the Mediterranean at Clevedon.

Downstream the Mendips flare out in the bulky headland of Brean Down (wild strawberries and rare flowers in summer), the dumpy, pudding-basin profile of Steep Holm, a profile even more pronounced at low tide, and discreet little Flat Holm with its lighthouse. Springs and wells and magic are never far away in the Mendips, and Steep Holm is no exception. Phil Quinn describes the Monk's Well, just above East Beach, which "certainly supplied the small Benedictine priory which existed here in the Middle Ages." But its roots may be more ancient than that, "for a carved human face found in woodland above has been declared a 'shouting head', a Celtic symbol of life. Indeed it is even suggested that the head could have been part of a Celtic or Romano-British shrine built above the well." These extraordinary intrusions of the past into the present are an everyday occurrence in Somerset, but all the stranger here for occurring on what is now an uninhabited rock in the middle of the sea. Both islands have served as retreats and sanctuary for monks, Vikings, Anglo-Saxons, smugglers and cholera victims. Some have gone in search of silver. Both islands were fortified during the Napoleonic Wars, and again in the Second World War.

Steep Holm is now a nature reserve, with a unique claim to fame. It is the home of the Steep Holm peony, a large, carmine pink flower. Most probably it was introduced by the monks, since the peony was a vital part of the medieval *materia medica*: John Gerard's 1597 *Herball* prescribed it for afflictions as varied as jaundice, nightmares, "torments of the belly" and "disease of the minde". Yet the peony was not "discovered" on Steep Holm until 1803, so it is possible that it had been introduced by some passing botanist. Even Gerard was known to have faked a peony at a site in Kent.

Flat Holm remains a working island, with its lighthouse and its residential education centre. On Flat Holm Marconi experimented with his wireless method of sending messages, and it worked—so Flat Holm can claim to have received the first ever radio message across water in 1897. Potential visitors need to know that Steep Holm is English and Flat Holm Welsh; Steep Holm may be visited from Weston-super-Mare, and Flat Holm from Barry. To visit both on the same day involves two return trips and transfer from Barry to Weston. Stern places, these islands.

Clevedon is almost synonymous with the name of Elton, and the family home, Clevedon Court, is now in the safe hands of the National Trust. The Eltons were creative eccentrics to match even the Aclands whom we shall meet first on Exmoor, and later in South Devon. The current eleventh baronet is a TV producer, while it was his industrial historian father who passed the Court to the Trust in 1960, while securing permission for the family to continue living there. At the end of the Victorian era, the eighth baronet, Sir Edmund, managed to combine being a studio potter (Elton ware) with chairman of the Urban District Council, and founder and captain of the fire brigade. His pieces on show include a beautiful three-handled loving cup to celebrate the peace in 1918 and an orange brown glaze with an incised sunflower (the pottery was established in 1881 as the Sunflower Pottery). His interest had grown from watching men in Nailsea brickyard making tiles. He neatly fits in with the mood of the Pre-Raphaelite Brotherhood and the Arts and Crafts movement in rejecting "modern" industrialized approaches and returning to more basic manual techniques.

The cult of the English country house has become so firmly embedded in the national psyche that the assumption is that every grand country house now in the hands of the National Trust once belonged to an ancient landed family. This is far from being the case. The Eltons were a family of Bristol merchants and entrepreneurs. The Court was purchased by the first baronet, Abraham, in 1709, using a fortune built up mainly on the Bristol brass industry. It was the fifth baronet (1755-1842) who was the first to live in Clevedon on a permanent basis and develop and improve the town.

The house has many artistic and literary connections, celebrated in the various items and pictures on display. Jane Octavia Elton was married to a clergyman called Brookfield who had been friends with the novelist Thackeray at Cambridge. Both were unhappily married, and at Clevedon Thackeray is supposed to have declared his love for Jane Octavia in 1848. But it was a love that could not thrive openly amid scandal, and it was quietly dropped. The friendship ceased in 1852, but Thackeray never forgot her. She lives on as the inspiration for the character of Amelia Smedley in *Vanity Fair*.

HANNAH MORE AND HER SISTERS

The first three Sir Abraham Eltons were all mayors of Bristol and had a fine house in Queen Square, though this was sold after the third baronet went bankrupt in 1745. They all belonged to the Society of Merchant Adventurers, trading in lead, tin, calamine, copper, coal and property, with interests in shipping (no doubt including the slave trade), glass-making and banking. The Reverend Sir Abraham, the fifth baronet, was a shareholder in the Clifton Suspension Bridge, and his second wife laid the foundation stone on the Clifton side of the gorge. Yet there were other aspects to Bristol and other aspects to the Elton family. Sir Charles Elton had been disinherited by his clergyman father when he married Sara Smith, daughter of a non-conformist Bristol merchant. He earned a living as a journalist and classical scholar. In the State Room at Clevedon Court is a large picture by the Bristol artist Edward Villiers Rippingille, called "The Travellers Breakfast"—a smaller copy is in the Coleridge Cottage at Nether Stowey. The picture imagines the coming together of a large circle of Bristol acquaintances—intellectuals, artists and businessmen, including various Elton family members, Charles Lamb, William Wordsworth, Coleridge and Robert Southey.

Bristol, then, was a lively place to be at the end of the eighteenth and beginning of the nineteenth century. One of the most interesting characters it produced was Hannah More, a contentious and controversial figure, who lived to the ripe old age of eighty-eight. Initially she and her sisters were founders of and teachers at a successful girls' school in Bristol. Later she tried literature and the theatre, taking a particular interest in David Garrick and having a play put on in Bath. Gradually her interests turned more to religion and slavery, and in the 1780s she met William Wilberforce. "God almighty has set before me two great objects," she wrote, "the suppression of the slave trade and the reformation of manners"—of morals, that is. Her pen turned from the fashionable Blue Stocking literature to religion and politics. There were twenty sugar refineries in Bristol, all operating on the produce of slave plantations, while houses in both Bath and Bristol were being built from the proceeds of slavery or the slave trade, or both. While the position of women in public life did not allow women to take part in mainstream politics, an issue such as the abolition of the slave trade was very much a women's sphere. Among More's friends was John Newton, the captain of a slave ship before seeing the light of religion and joining the church. He would become famous as the author of the hymn "Amazing Grace".

Hannah More's friendship with Wilberforce was to lead to further developments in her life. Hannah moved into Cowslip Green at Wrington, south of Bristol on the edge of the Mendips, in 1785. The following year, Wilberforce visited, and an excursion was arranged to visit the picturesque gorge and cave at Cheddar. But Wilberforce was scarcely a man to focus on the picturesque and blot out the foreground, which was dire poverty. He reported on his return: "The scenery is very fine but the poverty is dreadful. Miss Hannah, something must be done for Cheddar. If you will be at the trouble end, I will be at the expense." Hannah and her four sisters set about the task. They schemed and pleaded, made friends with local farmers and squires. A house was rented and equipped, money spent on teachers, uniforms, equipment, books and bibles. Soon 120 children were in attendance. Despite ridicule and opposition, Hannah More's "Sunday" Schools (so-called because most children worked, and initially it was not possible to teach them except on Sundays) expanded through the district: Shipham and Rowberrow in 1790, Congresbury, Yatton and Axbridge in 1791, Nailsea in 1792, Blagdon in 1795, Wedmore in 1798. Wilberforce, a serious man, returned to visit the schools—on his honeymoon.

Some questioned the teaching of these rural children and whether learning to read might not give them ideas above their social position— or worse; following the French Revolution the 1790s especially was a decade of fear. At Wedmore, and then Blagdon, the spectre of non-conformity was raised by the established church. Blagdon was a particular centre of controversy, with Hannah refusing to dismiss a teacher suspected of Methodism. In this paranoid and poisoned public space, the French regicides of the 1790s had quickly become identified with the English Puritan regicides of the 1640s. Accusations of heresy, letters and pamphlets were aired. It was a member of the Elton family, as the local magistrate, who absolved the teacher of the "crime". But accusations continued and eventually the school was closed and the teacher found work elsewhere. The French Revolution made everything more difficult for moderate reformers like Wilberforce and More. Indeed, the two issues of slavery and revolution became entwined. The revolutionary government in France abolished slavery in 1794. With war between Britain and France raging, slaves in many of the West Indian islands revolted. More in particular moved to separate herself from radicalism, most famously in the phrase: "From liberty, equality and the rights of man, good lord deliver us." Tom Paine's book *The Rights of Man* was banned and his effigy burned on Beechen Cliff above the city of Bath. In the coal-mining district of Kingswood north and west of Bristol, where John Wesley had sought to gentle the natives by setting up a school, there were food riots.

THE WORDSWORTHS AND COLERIDGE

All down the Bristol Channel coast, across the misty levels, the Quantocks are, as it were, in attendance. Some centuries ago little thought was given to these wild hills. John Leland (*Itineries*, 1535-43, spelling modernized) travelled "all by forest, barren and moorish ground, where is store and breeding of young cattle, but little or no corn or habitation." By the end of the eighteenth century new ways of looking at landscape dictated that the Quantocks were to be considered sublime, and where not sublime, then certainly picturesque. Collinson's *History of Somerset* (1791) described the "steep and lofty hills" between which were "deep vales and hollow glens". The sides of the valleys were "scarred with wild rocks". Just a matter of taste, one might say, but it was a new taste that was to attract to the Quantocks three of the best-known writers of that revolutionary decade of the 1790s.

Nether Stowey is not so much picturesque as ordinarily pretty in a rather West Country way. There are terraces of pretty stone cottages, rendered and colour-washed. There is a fast-flowing stream (a leat) running down Castle Street. But it is a quiet town, for all the busyness of the water, more Marie Celeste than Ancient Mariner—the name of the pub ("Sky Sports live here") opposite the Coleridge Cottage in Lime Street.

Samuel Taylor Coleridge, son of a Devon vicar, was part of that revolutionary Bristol ferment in the 1790s. He lectured there brilliantly—so brilliantly and so incisively that he received death threats for his pains. With his fellow-poet Robert Southey he devised a scheme called "pantisocracy", a sort of primitive communism to be lived out in small self-sufficient communities. Coleridge's ideas were deeply rooted in the land, in a reverence for the land, and for other creatures. As Richard Holmes, Coleridge's biographer, writes:

> It was nature herself who must be the great teacher, and the essential role of education—and by extension, poetry and philosophy itself—must be as an affectionate interpreter of man's place in the natural world.

It was on a walking tour of Somerset with Southey in 1794 that Coleridge met Tom Poole, autodidact, tanner, local businessman and friend to Romantic poets in need. As early as 1792 Poole belonged to a book club in Nether Stowey that was reading Mary Wollstonecraft, the radical supporter of the French Revolution and the rights of women. By 1797 Coleridge had the additional burdens of a wife and child, disillusion with the French Revolution, the end of his friendship with Southey, the failed scheme for pantisocracy and an incipient opium habit. Poole found him a safe retreat here, a two-up, two-down cottage in Lime Street. Coleridge (quoted by Holmes) wrote the original credo of the urban down-sizer:

> I am anxious that my children should be bred up from earliest infancy in the simplicity of peasants... their food, dress and habits completely rustic. I never shall, and I never will, have any fortune to leave them: I will leave them therefore hearts that desire little, heads that know how little is to be desired, and hands and arms accustomed to earn that little.

There are so many connections, and there is not space enough or time to mention all of them. Coleridge married in 1795 and spent his honeymoon in Clevedon. His first meeting with William Wordsworth was probably at the Bristol house of the Pinney family, when Wordsworth was on his way to the Pinney country house at Racedown in Dorset where he spent two years rent-free with his sister. The Pinneys were not radicals, but rather a wealthy West Indian slave-owning family. Coleridge's first collection of poems was published in 1796 by his Bristol patron Joseph Cottle. But it was the collaboration between William Wordsworth and Coleridge, aided and abetted by Dorothy Wordsworth, that was the most significant and the most controversial. Even if we excise the considerable contribution of Dorothy to *Lyrical Ballads* (1798), the controversy remains. Certainly there is more Wordsworth here than Coleridge, although the single best-known poem is undoubtedly Coleridge's "Ancient Mariner". Already in the 1930s Sylvia Townsend Warner had Dorothy's notebooks available, and was determined to write Dorothy back into the story of English Romanticism. She concluded that "Dorothy Wordsworth's Journal is still the truest guide to this landscape; a landscape, one might say, that matches her in sensibility; for its components of heath and sea and woodland sink into one's mind not so much for their natural beauty as for their aptitude to respond like an Aeolian harp to the minutest changes of sky and mood and weather." Coleridge had noted the same on first meeting Dorothy: "Her eye is watchful in the minutest observation of nature." Dorothy confided to her journal: "He is a wonderful man. His conversation teems with soul, mind and spirit." To all three, Coleridge, Dorothy Wordsworth and William Wordsworth, Nature, with a capital letter, remained the source of ultimate truth.

It was Tom Poole who found a large, comfortable house for the Wordsworths in the Quantocks, so that social relations and poetry might expand in friendly (if rather strenuous) country walks. All three might have felt that Nature had supplanted the French Revolution as their chief source of inspiration. But politics returned to haunt them. When the Wordsworths moved to Alfoxden Park in 1797 they threw a housewarming party. John Thelwall, a radical democrat who had served time in prison for his beliefs during the 1794 Treason Trials (he was acquitted), delivered a fervent address which reached the notice of the Home Secretary. It was not just Thelwall but the general behaviour of the trio which aroused suspicion. All that walking, all that watching, the nocturnal excursions, the obsessive interest in water... On 11 August 1797, Dr. Daniel Lysons of Bath wrote to a government minister:

> My Lord Duke,
> On the 8th inst. I took the liberty to acquaint your Grace with a very suspicious business concerning an emigrant family, who have contrived to get possession of a Mansion House at Alfoxton (sic), late belonging to the Revd. Mr St Albyn, under Quantock Hills—I am since informed, that the master of the House has no wife with him, but only a woman who passes for his Sister—The man has camp stools, which he and his visitors carry with them when they go about the country upon their nocturnal or diurnal expeditions, and have also a Portfolio in which they

enter their observations, which they have been heard to say were almost finished—they have been heard to say they should be rewarded for them, and were very attentive to the River near them—probably the river coming within a mile or two of Alfoxton from Bridgewater (sic)— these people may possibly be under Agents to some principal at Bristol…

No-one was ever arrested. By 1798 Coleridge and the Wordsworth were ready to move on; there is probably no particular significance to be attached to the non-renewal of the lease on Alfoxden, other than the doubts of the senior member of the Pinney family about his tenants. As Coleridge put it in a letter to his brother: "I have snapped my squeaking baby-trumpet of Sedition and the fragments lie scattered in the lumber-room of Penitence." Eventually he was to rewrite the whole episodes as one of the great jokes of English literature – the story of Spy Nozy, in fact the philosopher Spinoza, of whom the government agent had overheard them speaking. But in the deadly, paranoiac atmosphere of the 1790s, it had been far from a joke.

Nature, despite the best efforts of humankind, is still lovely in the Quantocks, and along the coast where the hills tumble towards the sea. Kilve at low tide, with its long tilted limestone pavements, as if laid by a team of skilled Somerset masons, is as lovely a shoreline as anywhere in England. There are fossils in the shale beds sandwiched between the limestone. The nuclear reactors at Hinkley Point are safely out of the way round the corner to the east, where the footpath passes an old wartime pill-box and a small lighthouse. To the west, Watchet and Minehead both show. There are warm rock pools busy with children seeking out marine life stranded there until the late evening high tide, the distant lapping of waves on sand and mud, and the sea-gulls settling to an afternoon nap on a rocky promontory. Out to sea, the misty coast of Wales, Steep Holm, standing high and proud above the tide, and little Flat Holm squashed onto the horizon by some giant footstep. As unlikely as the nuclear power station, oil was discovered at Kilve in 1916 and in 1924 Dr. Forbes-Leslie set up his Shaline Company to extract oil from shale. It proved too expensive, and now the oil retort house is already almost as romantic a ruin as the Chantry, established there in 1329 for five priests to pray for the soul of Simon Furneaux. Now cream teas can be taken among the crumbling stone walls.

Utopia and Dystopia on Exmoor
Beyond the Quantocks is Exmoor. On a clear day, it can be seen from the
Mendips or from Glastonbury Tor. On a murky day, there is still a smudge
on the western horizon, until rain obliterates it. West of Kilve is the pretty
little harbour of Watchet, once an important port with a light mineral
railway running down from the hills above. There is a statue of the Ancient
Mariner on the quayside, erected as part of the Millennium celebrations,
and several millennia older, a holy well next to the church of St. Decuman
high on the hillside above the town, lovingly restored and cared for and still
occasionally used for baptisms and services. St. Decuman is one of a
number of Irish and Welsh saints in this book, all with colourful and unlikely stories—in this case his arrival by sea with a cow on a raft of faggots,
his beheading by a madman, and the restoring of his head in the waters of
the holy well. The Watchet Boat Museum on the quayside celebrates the
"Watchet flattie", a particular kind of shallow draught vessel much used for
coastal traffic in the Bristol Channel until recent times. Sue Clifford and
Angela King, authors of Common Ground's *England in Particular*, have an
engaging description of Watchet lighthouse: "a small, red, hexagonal tower
with a slate pagoda roof, rather like a tall pillar-box." Equally engaging are
the local boys who while away the quiet hours by leaping into the harbour.
The cold water appears to do them no harm.

A little further west, Minehead is a respectable Victorian seaside resort
which has survived the arrival of the stately pleasure-domes of Butlin's
Holiday Camp and the revivalist efforts of the steam enthusiasts on the
West Somerset Railway to re-emerge as the starting-point of the South
West Coastal Path. There is a fine sculpture by Owen Cunningham to
mark this departure, beaten metal hands holding out a map that plots part
of the whole devious circuit from prim Minehead to the naturist beach at
Studland in Dorset. Six hundred and thirty miles is a lot of walking, and
the present author is not among those hardy types who have completed the
circuit, although he did once manage the hundred miles from Bude to St.
Ives in Cornwall in an especially benevolent March spring in the 1980s.
Through the sculpted fretwork the walker looks back at the brown waters
and flat coast-line of Bridgwater Bay. There are sterner landscapes to come.

Above Minehead lies North Hill: gardens and villas, dahlias and
chrysanthemums, azaleas and hydrangeas in season. But after that, travelling the coast by water, there is little to mark the work of men and women.

At Porlock Weir, grey-green sea and white breakers mark where the sea has broken the shingle bank that once protected a stretch of farm-land which is now fast reverting to salt-marsh. Beyond are green fields and wooded slopes, and above the bracken-and-heather-and gorse heights of Selworthy Beacon. The woods come right down to the sea, interrupted only by the occasional rock fall. There is Glenthorne House, sitting precariously in a steep combe above a low cliff, and further west waterfalls plunging straight into the sea. At Countisbury Point, already now in Devon, the tidal flows are swift and confused, and the neat little white Foreland lighthouse tucked into the side of the cliffs is a reassuring presence. Here too, buried beneath the waves, is experimental equipment busy generating electricity from the vigorous tidal flows.

Inland, Exmoor tells a rather different story. In winter the burnished gorse climbs steeply towards the grey heavens. The rain is implacable, now turning to drizzle, now to snow. When it stops, the mist can come down in minutes, enveloping gorse and bracken and animals and trees in a single white nothing. Wild it may be, untouched nature it is not. The wild ponies and red deer may run free across the moors but their health and numbers are carefully monitored. The grazing of sheep and cattle, as on Dartmoor, are controlled by ancient rights and customs, and the landscape is the

product of a careful balance between humans and nature. It is grazing that prevents the reversion of the countryside to woodland, although there are extensive tracts of woodland still. One family, the Aclands, owned much of the land from the coast across Selworthy Beacon and up to Dunkery Hill. Since the Aclands turned over their huge holdings in West Somerset to the National Trust, the Trust has sought to balance the interests of visitors, of nature and of agriculture, supported in turn by the Exmoor National Park. But problems erupt from time to time.

Hunting has been a major problem. The Aclands, especially before 1800, were great stag hunters. When the National Trust acquired the Holnicote (pronounced "Honeycot") land in 1944, the donation was accompanied by a "memorandum of wishes", which the Trust was required to respect. It is not legally binding, but states a clear wish that the estates should be run on the same principles and in the same manner as in the past. This includes progressive elements such as fair treatment for staff (some Acland pensioners continue to live rent-free) and protection of flora and fauna. But it also includes the continuation of shooting and fishing and hunting. Eventually this led to major row within the National Trust. Sir John Acland sided with the Trust majority, and against many of his landowning friends, over the banning of stag-hunting at Holnicote. There is acceptance now within the family and the Trust that social conditions and views change and that what was acceptable in 1944 may not be so in changed times. Yet the deer numbers still have to be controlled to preserve what we have come to expect as wild Exmoor.

As suggested, the interest of the Acland family post-1800 turned into rather different channels. Sir Thomas Dyke Acland was a friend of Hannah More and William Wilberforce and one of the strongest opponents in parliament of first the slave trade, and then of slavery itself (abolition of the trade in 1807 is only half the story). He preferred his gentle Killerton estate in Devon to wild Holnicote in Somerset, but was determined to "do something" for his West Somerset tenants as well. In 1828 he had a group of picturesque cottages built at Selworthy Green for estate pensioners, inspired by the "cottage orné" style of Blaise Hamlet in Bristol. As conditions deteriorated on the land, he recognized, like a few other landlords, the responsibilities as well as the ancient rights and privileges of the landed aristocracy. The cob and stone cottages, finished in the familiar Acland mustard yellow limewash, with their trade-mark semi-circular bread ovens and massive chimneys, can be seen in most of the villages between Selworthy, Porlock, Dunkery, Bossington, Luccombe, West Luccombe and Horner.

Of course, part of the attraction of prettifying the villages was to impress visitors, both the Aclands' friends and increasing number of tourists visiting the area in search of "wild" scenery. And as Gillian Darley notes, "At Selworthy Green the folk gathered under the walnut trees on the village green merited quite as much attention as the scenery." Selworthy was long considered to be of relatively recent construction, but the current view is that like the other 170 cottages and 14 farms on the estate, most date from the medieval period and were adapted to Romantic tastes in the early nineteenth century. Selworthy would certainly have benefited most from this process, because as a "retirement village", farm buildings and paddocks were removed to create the green around which the cottages squat. Like the Aclands, the National Trust has had to balance the desire to keep up external appearances with tenants' desires for rather more up-to-date interiors. Mains sewerage and inside toilets are both less than fifty years old in many of the houses. Visitors are well catered for with discreet car-parks and public toilets in each village. Cream teas are superb at Selworthy, but probably no better than at Kilve, or Horner, or one hundred tea-rooms in the western counties of England. At Horner there is an ancient packhorse bridge and even a caravan site, the caravans painted green and protected by one of those high beech hedges that keeps its red-brown leaves all winter long.

Not everything on Exmoor, though, is or has been sweetness and light. Samuel Palmer did some of his most magical paintings on Exmoor in the early years of the nineteenth century. One of them, painted in 1835 and now far away in the Victoria Art Gallery in Melbourne, is of the coastal hamlet of Culbone, near Porlock. The church of St. Beuno, dedicated to yet another Welsh saint, is often referred to as the smallest in England. Sylvia Townsend Warner has it "lying in its narrow combe as neatly as if it were a nut which a squirrel had put away for winter." Shirley Toulson and Judith Yarrow, modern painters who have tracked the course of Palmer through the West Country tell a sadder tale of this village. In the Middle Ages there was a leper colony, and a squint on the external wall of the church was probably designed to allow lepers to observe the priest blessing the sacrament without risk of infection to other parishioners. Culbone was a woodland community; there was charcoal-burning and the charcoal was sent across to South Wales to smelt iron, while there was also bark-stripping for tanning in the woods hereabouts. There are certainly the remains of old cottages to be seen near the church. Culbone is nearly, but not quite, a deserted village. It is still remote, accessible only to walkers on the Coastal Path, the old coastal road long ago eroded by cliff-falls; fog and thunderstorms and exhaustion can also deter the would-be visitor. But it is good to still have ambition.

It was precisely this wilder, more primitive version of Exmoor that appealed to the novelist R. D. Blackmore. A popular jingle recalls that:

Culbone, Oare and Stoke Pero
Parishes three, no parson'll go to
Culbone, Oare and Stoke Pero,
Three such places you'll seldom hear o'.

Well, Blackmore certainly knew about these parishes; his grandfather had been rector of Oare from 1809 to 1842, riding across the moors to conduct services there every second Sunday. Blackmore is remembered for one book, *Lorna Doone* (1869), a novel which continues to sustain tourism on Exmoor. It is long, it is often tedious, it is not to modern tastes, but it is also a cracking good yarn for fast readers—those who can happily skip-read long novels. The mystery is not why none of his other novels was successful, but why *Lorna Doone* became one of the best-selling books in the language. And what language, too! Blackmore took great interest in dialects, and there is much playing with the variations between Devon and West Somerset grammar and vocabulary (we must be frank that although Oare is in Somerset, the "Doone country", like Exmoor itself, is shared between the two counties). It is his use of dialect that places the novel so firmly, as does the use of local names: there are Ridds buried in the churchyard at Oare, where the fictional Jan Ridd and his Lorna were married.

Blackmore's interest in local peculiarities does not really extend to landscape or the natural world except in the scenes where he describes the impact of the great frost of 1684/85 on the wildlife and livestock on the moors. It lives in folk memory because normally winters are mild here; the snow comes and goes, but periods of deep frost are rare, and the cottage gardens in the villages have flowers all winter long. Blackmore is obsessed with the aristocracy and rank in general. The Ridds are of good yeoman stock, and Blackmore mentions several times that when Alfred was at Athelney, "he had a Ridd along with him." Most curious of all, the Doones are both aristocrats and Roman Catholics, which places them in a curious position in a part of the world where the distinction between Anglicanism and non-conformity was the most significant social divide. Confusingly, in the novel several Doones manage to fight on the side of Monmouth in 1685 against an openly Catholic king, a rare example of the use in fiction of this painful episode in Somerset history. Perhaps Lorna's Catholicism is an oblique tribute to the Catholicism of Blackmore's own wife.

CECIL SHARP IN SOMERSET

> I sowed the seeds of love
> And I sowed them in the Spring.
> I gathered them up in the morning so soon
> While the small birds do sweetly sing.

Traditional

The careful reader, map open on the floor, will have detected a circular movement in this chapter, and a consideration of Cecil Sharp's work in Somerset takes us back to somewhere near our starting-point at Lytes Cary, to the village of Hambridge, to be precise. The story begins in Adelaide, Australia, where Sharp met Charles Marson, a young English clergyman. Marson was appointed vicar of Hambridge in 1895, and immediately took a strong interest in the lives of his parishioners. His life and ministry had been touched by Christian Socialism, and he tried to put his beliefs into practice. Not only did he symbolically wash the feet of poor village boys on Maundy Thursday, but he also helped to found a branch of the Independent Labour Party in Langport in 1908, and argued for better housing for the village folk. It was at Hambridge in 1903 that Cecil Sharp recorded John England, Marson's gardener, singing "The Seeds of Love". Sharp's method was to write the words down, to notate the music, and to take photographs of the singers, and all this material is now stored at Cecil Sharp House in London, the headquarters of the English Folk Song and Country Dance Society.

Now "The Seeds of Love" was a common enough song, sufficiently well-known to be performed in music-halls, and hence part of an urban singing tradition too. But Sharp's visit to Hambridge is rightly celebrated as a pregnant moment in the revival of interest in English folk music that took place towards the end of the nineteenth century. It was Sharp's introduction to working "in the field". Maud Karpeles, Sharp's biographer, tells the story thus:

> Cecil Sharp was sitting in the vicarage garden talking to Charles Marson... when he heard John England quietly singing to himself as he mowed the vicarage lawn. Cecil Sharp whipped out his notebook and took down the tune; and then persuaded John to give him the words. He immediately harmonised the song; and that same evening it was sung at a choir supper by Mattie Kay, Cecil Sharp accompanying. The audience was delighted; as one said, it was the first time that the song had been put into evening dress.

Later it was to be arranged by Ralph Vaughan Williams, another avid collector of English folk songs. It is not surprising that this tremendous interest in English folk songs was occurring at precisely the point in history when a true folk culture was dying on its feet. We saw how in Dorset, Thomas Hardy was quite clear that the life and lives he was memorializing were already in the past. At the shearing supper in *Far from the Madding Crowd*, (1874) Bathsheba sings a ballad called "The Banks of Allan Water". It is one of the comic yokels, Joseph Poorgrass, rather the worse for drink, who murders "The Seeds of Love". But in the film version it is Julie Christie, playing the part of Bathsheba, who sings "The Seeds of Love", and again we can recognize a popular song taken up and "improved" by a character of higher social rank, just as Sharp himself had harmonized the tune, and Vaughan Williams had introduced it into the classical repertoire.

In an important chapter in *The Country and the City*, Raymond Williams takes particular issue with Cecil Sharp. His attack strikes a rather glancing blow, criticizing Sharp for dealing in the remnants of rural life. Yet of course that was why the work seemed so important to Sharp—to preserve something of a way of life, of a culture, that was fast disappearing. Williams stirs himself into a mighty lather, and draws to a defiant climax in which he rejects what he sees as the "betrayal" of real rural issues:

> The song of the land, the song of rural labour, the song of delight in the
> many forms of life with which we share our physical world, is too im-
> portant and too moving to be tamely given up, in an embittered be-
> trayal, to the confident enemies of all significant and actual
> independence and renewal.

It is certainly true that Sharp's work emphasized rural themes even
where there was evidence of other kinds of economic activity. The singers
he listened to on his regular visits to the King's Head in Coleford, a coal-
mining village in the Mendips, belonged to the agricultural rather than
the mining community. Later Coleford was to play a small but distinguished role in the 1926 General Strike, when the army was sent in to
subdue the strikers.

None of this is to minimize the importance of Sharp in Somerset, and
the volumes of *Folk Songs from Somerset* that he published between 1904
and 1909. He collected in Hambridge and Langport, in Bridgwater and
Harptree, in Minehead and on the Quantocks and Exmoor. He collected
from those in regular employment—gardeners, withy strippers, weavers,
blacksmiths, sailors and dress-makers—as well as from seasonal farm
labourers. Bearing in mind the criticism by Williams, it is interesting to
note that in urban Bridgwater he collected from brick-workers, and from
others who were in the workhouse. Jack Barnard, one of his best sources,
was unable to walk or read and write, but nevertheless had a repertoire of
150 songs. Workhouses were indeed a good source of songs but also the
eventual fate of a number of singers: George and Lydia Wyatt at West
Harptree were singers, George an agricultural labourer, but after his death,
Lydia ended her days at Clutton workhouse. Not all the singers had such
an unhappy end: Fred Crossman at Huish Episcopi had a successful
market garden; Louie Hooper at Hambridge became quite a celebrity, was
recorded by the BBC during the Second World War, and both she and
her sister Lucy White have entries in the *Oxford Dictionary of National Biography*.

As for folk culture, it is alive and well in Somerset, though not nec-
essarily in the hands of agricultural labourers. The old songs are sung, the
old tunes played. There are new harmonies and new arrangements, indeed

new songs. The number of apple orchards may have declined but wassailing ceremonies to secure the health of those apple-trees that survive have spread in recent years. Carnival is widely celebrated, mummers' plays are performed outside pubs and at village fairs, the ash faggot is burned at Dunster on Christmas Eve; the streets of Minehead echo to the sound of beating of drums on May Day, as the Hobby Horse, a character we shall meet again at Padstow in Cornwall, tours the town.

Roman Somerset

Charles Marson's Hambridge is not the only Hambridge in Somerset. A second village of that name lies a little further north. It is easy to find on the map, just to the west of the A37 striding confident and straight across the countryside from Shepton Mallet to Ilchester. The village of Lydford-on-Fosse lies on the A37 (most villages lie to one side or other of it) and gives the game away. This is a section of the ancient Roman Fosse Way, stretching from Exeter on the English Channel north to Bath, Cirencester, Lincoln and eventually the North Sea coast. For anyone who doubts this, it is enough to drive this particular road and watch the miles unfold in a remarkable straight line across the green fields of Somerset. Another route led east from the mining area around Charterhouse on the summit of the Mendip Hills, and was the route for transporting tin and silver towards the south coast. Lindsey Davis used this as the basis of the plot of the first of her Roman detective stories (*The Silver Pigs*, 1989); her detective Falco spends time at the mines enquiring into a conspiracy about the export of silver ingots. During his time there he endures hunger and privation, much of it due to the foul winter weather of the Mendips. Clearly the author had done her homework well. Local people still refer to this route as the "Roman Road", striding across the hilltops in total disregard of later settlements.

There is the heroic story of the Romans in Britain, full of reckless and warlike British (Celtic) leaders battling their lives away against the "foreign" invaders. There is a story of trade and empire. Then there is another story, which at least in Somerset is about relatively peaceful co-existence. It is probable that settled British tribes in this part of the world (best not to call it England yet) were trading with the Romans even before the invasion of the Roman armies. Many were quick to welcome the newcomers and adopt their lifestyle, including more sophisticated agricultural and building methods. Spelt, the tall, graceful bread-making grain now happily restored to the fields of Somerset, was probably brought in by the Romans. The list is almost endless. The Romans brought wine, and they brought vines too (again, vineyards have returned with some success to modern Somerset, particularly on the south-facing slopes of the Mendips). Almost certainly, apples as we know them today in Somerset were a Roman introduction, the sour "crab" apples of the natives being definitely not to Roman tastes. The walnut, a tree which for many is almost as much a symbol of Somerset as the apple, with its silver-grey bark, its plump green fruits that hide the brainy nuts inside and its liking for the vicinity of human habitation such as old farmhouses, is another Roman introduction. The list grows: cabbages, peas, celery, onions, parsnips, leeks, turnips, cucumbers, radishes, carrots and asparagus, plums, pears, cherries. It is impossible to imagine the average Farmers' Market or allotment without the Roman Empire.

The locals may scoff and ask "What did them Romans ever do for I?"—a question also asked of governments, local councils, the European Union and the United Nations—but, yes, the Romans did a lot for thee and I. On the farms and smallholdings around Ilchester, even the pattern of weeds is suggestive of Roman introductions mixed with more useful seeds—chamomile, corncockle, cornflower. It was the Romans who first realized the value of Ham Hill stone, and used it in the construction of the Fosse Way, the same glowing orange stone shipped across the levels to provide the decorative carvings of so many rural Somerset churches.

Given what we now know about cultural mix and fusion in Roman times, the site at Upper Row Farm in the parish of Hemington, ten miles south of Bath, is of special significance. It appears that the site was continually occupied through the Iron Age and Roman periods, and archaeological evidence has uncovered both typical Iron Age round houses and a Romano-British villa. The hyphen tells the story. The setting of the villa is especially splendid, on a gentle south-facing slope with superb views to Longleat Forest (the modern remnants of the medieval Selwood Forest) and the chalk scarp now dominated by Westbury White Horse and its attendant cement works factory. Gordon Hendy, the owner of Upper Row Farm until his death in 2008, was a farmer of the old school, yet happy to share his farm with the enthusiasts from the Bath and Camerton Archaeological Society (not to mention the BBC's Time Team in 2006) with their complex geophysical survey equipment, and happy to allow them the use of one of his barns (the old cheese barn) to serve tea and cakes on open days. He remembered his own parents making cider on the farm, and planted a new cider orchard which is just beginning to bear fruit. He also set aside a plot near the house as a demonstration Roman garden, where the fruit and vegetable and herbs that would have been familiar to the Romans in Somerset have been planted. For those whose interest in the Romans begins and ends at the Roman Baths in Bath, this is a delightful and rather different image of Roman Somerset.

Chapter Seven

BATH AND BRISTOL

Consult the genius of the place in all:
That tells the Waters or to rise, or fall,
Or helps th'ambitious Hill the heavens to scale,
Or scoops in circling theatres the Vale,
Calls in the Country, catches opening glades,
Joins willing woods, and varies shades from shades,
Now breaks, or now directs, th'intending Lines;
Paints as you plant, and, as you work, designs.
Alexander Pope, "Epistle to Lord Burlington", 1731

Let Bristol for commerce and dirt be renown'd,
At Salisbury pen-knives and scissors be ground;
The towns of Devizes, of Bradford and Frome,
May boast that they better can manage the loom;
I believe that they may;—but the world to refine,
In manners in dress, in politeness to shine,
O Bath!—let the art, let the glory be thine.
                    Christopher Anstey, *The New Bath Guide*, 1766

THEORIES OF ORIGIN

Roman villa life in rural Somerset was comfortable and homely, but Roman life in Bath was never less than grand. That much at least can be gleaned from even a brief visit to the enormous baths complex that extends beneath the modern city and has so slowly come to light again over the centuries. Bath was a city for relaxation and pleasure and trade. The therapeutic value of the waters had been recognized even before the Romans arrived; the story of the leper-king Bladud cured by immersion in the waters while herding pigs is just one way of representing this. By the time the Romans arrived in England in AD43, the "sacred spring" belonged to the Celtic god Sul, worshipped amid the muddy woods where the three hot springs emerged and drained out into the River Avon. The early decades of Roman rule were troubled times, and in Bath the Roman leaders took special care to pacify local feelings by attaching the Celtic god to their own veneration of Minerva, the goddess of wisdom and healing. But they went much further, building a very large complex of ritual baths where pilgrims could immerse themselves in the hot, sulphurous waters. No longer was Sul Minerva to be allowed to skulk among the trees. The Roman name for Bath, Aquae Sulis, the waters of Sul Minerva, confirmed the annexation of the older beliefs to Roman power and organization. Like all sacred springs, the place where the hot waters bubbled up to the surface was seen as a meeting point of the day-to-day world and the spirit world. The gods needed to be placated, most noticeably by the offering of coins. One particular feature of Bath that has come to light in recent excavations is the existence of messages written to the goddess on metal plaques, often asking for vengeance on enemies.

The temple precinct and the baths silted up in the post-Roman period, but it now seems that at no point was belief in the therapeutic value of the waters abandoned. In the Middle Ages several charitable hospitals clustered around the baths to provide accommodation for the poor. Bath continued to attract the sick and lame of all social classes, and whatever the contested nature of the actual healing value of the waters, many were to return home satisfied, as much by the break from routine, the fun and games of Bath, the good company.

Yet this emerging leisure industry was still only a side-issue for Bath. Although it is hard to imagine it today, Bath in 1700, before the great Georgian building boom, looked much like other prosperous Cotswold wool-towns. Chaucer's Wife of Bath, of course, was a first-class weaver, well able to compete, as Chaucer tells us, with the weavers of the Low Countries. Spinning, weaving and the sale of cloth continued to account for the majority of jobs in the city.

The transition from Cotswold Bath to Georgian Bath, accomplished by a determined and entrepreneurial city council undeterred by notions of preservation, is a story too well-known to occupy us greatly here. Perhaps the history of a single building will tell all that is needed. That building is the Cross Bath, still to be seen in all its Georgian splendour next to the gleaming new spa buildings of Thermae Bath Spa. It was the most fashionable bath, as it was the most private. Musicians accompanied the bathers who could drink chocolate while relaxing around the elaborate Melfort Cross, erected in 1688 to celebrate the birth of James II's son. His consort, Mary of Modena, whom we last met in Chapter Five complaining of her allocation of prisoners after the Monmouth rebellion, had come to the Cross Bath to take the waters in 1687. Fortunately for Bath, the future protestant Queen Anne was also a true believer in the value of Bath waters.

From 1783 the Cross Bath was rebuilt by Thomas Baldwin, who was both architect and town planner. His later scheme to create Bath, Beau, Hot Bath and Union Streets required the destruction of several existing medieval streets and houses, and much archaeological evidence. When he was sacked by the Corporation, John Palmer took over and ingeniously moved Baldwin's north-facing serpentine front to face east along the newly created Bath Street in the 1790s. Palmer was later to be the architect of Lansdown Crescent with its elegant wrought-iron railings, certainly the highest, possibly the finest, and probably the least visited (because of the climb involved to reach it) of all Bath's crescents. By the twentieth century, Bath was a more workaday, more ordinary city. Swimming, rather than bathing, was all the rage, and a public swimming pool at Beau Street was constructed in 1923, using the spa waters, suitably cooled. The elegant Cross Bath declined in status to become the "Tuppenny Hot". Then, in 1978 disaster struck. A young swimmer died from a rare strain of meningitis possibly contracted from the natural bacteria in the earth's strata through which the spa water passed, after she had taken part in a swimming gala at Beau Street. The spa waters were shut down.

Thanks to some brilliant scientific work, a way was found to circumvent the problem, and a project was devised to re-found Bath as a spa centre using National Lottery funding. The rest—project mismanagement, gross over-spending on the budget, rows between the council and the contractors—is, as they say, history, although rather raw and recent. The re-opening of the facilities in 2006 meant that those who could afford the prices could once again enjoy the delights of bathing in the warm waters. There are, admittedly, concessions for the long-suffering council tax payers of Bath, who had also enjoyed a free Three Tenors concert in front of the Royal Crescent to celebrate the opening in 2003 (a mere three years too early).

The Cross Bath remains quite separate from the main Nicholas Grimshaw building, and completely different in its feel. John Palmer's late eighteenth-century plan has been retained, the Victorian trappings and the ducks which colonized the place in the late twentieth century removed. Floating there in the hot water on a crisp winter day, with the surrounding Bath stone buildings etched against a blue sky, will always be a powerful experience of the force, the generosity and the mystery of nature. And mystery it is, for still no-one knows where the waters come from. The most probable location lies in a deep aquifer below the Mendips, posited but never seen: perhaps the waters represent the rainfall of a few hundreds years ago; others with equally fine scientific credentials have proposed up to 10,000 years ago. The poet Ted Hughes described water as "the ultimate life—the divine influx". These are the words carved around the rim of the water sculpture by William Pye through which the spring waters pass—the point at which the springs rise to the surface under natural artesian pressure. But what produces the pressure? Where do the waters come from? There is a vast secret here, hidden for ever from us in the geology of the Mendip hills. So to float in the Cross Bath is partly to be in tune with the spirit but also to be reminded how very little we know about the world we live in.

Across the road, John Wood's Hot Bath is the medical centre of the new complex, with its treatment rooms and its thermal pool looking very similar to the pictures of "taking the waters" in the exhibition at the visitor centre in Hetling Court. The new Grimshaw construction—the Royal Bath—is a remarkable building, offering so much diversity in such a small space. From the outside it can appear a boring bottle-green glass cube. Inside, though, is another cube, this time of Bath stone. And you realize that the glass itself is transparent from the inside so there is always that feeling of being part of the city, even before you reach the star attraction of the roof-top pool. The lower indoor pool, the Minerva, with its sensual, curving shape, occupies the exact spot of the Spartan municipal pool of yesteryear. From the floor rise four great mushrooms which support the whole of the stone cube above, including the weight of all that roof-top water. It is a place for whispers and for intimacy as bathers float in the sulphurous waters or lie and relax on chairs, as if mesmerized by the continual play of water reflections on the ceiling. The next two levels up are the simple changing area (some have called this Spartan...) and a floor of treatment rooms, elegant little individual curved pods within the cube. Up again is the steam floor, and here the interplay of circles and cubes is continued: there are four circular steam rooms, each with its own scent, and a central area of powerful overhead jets of water.

And so to the roof, which is a very special place indeed. It is probably not the best view in Bath—the city from the wooded heights of Beechen Cliff still claims that distinction—but it is a remarkable feeling to be within the heart of the old city, so close to the tower of Bath Abbey and the three ancient charity hospitals on three sides of the new spa. There is even the "carbuncle" on the backside of the 1960s Technical College building, made famous by John Betjeman, and behind which the wintry sun is setting. There is Prior Park, there is Sham Castle, the lovely Bath skyline from Combe Down to Bathampton Down, the last rays of the sun on Bath stones, the last few brown leaves of late autumn, the lights coming on up Widcombe and Bathwick Hills. Unlike the other spa areas, the rooftop pool is a place for chatter and laughter, between friends and family groups, but also between complete strangers, recalling some of the social past of the city. The sun goes down, the moon comes up. There is city and country, water and dry land, light and darkness, the square and the circle. It seems almost time to admit that the saga of the Bath Spa project may have a happy ending.

Let us return briefly to King Bladud, cured of his leprosy and restored to his throne. John Wood the Elder, visionary town-planner, architect and surveyor and undoubted father of Georgian Bath, had some interesting thoughts on Bladud. Bladud is the biographical crux on which rest Wood's implausible theories of an ancient British architecture based on the dimensions of Noah's Ark and the Temple of Solomon. Romans, Greeks and

Britons, he believed, had built on God-given Jewish principles. Wood's Circus and Royal Crescent (the latter mostly the work of his son, John Wood the Younger) in this reading are symbols of sun and moon, the same sun and moon worshipped by the ancients, the same sun and moon that now rise and fall above Bath's revived spa. The dimensions of the Circus approximate to both the stone circles at Stonehenge and the infinitely more appealing stones in the quiet village of Stanton Drew, just south of Bristol, where thoughtful folk still leave offerings of pebbles and flowers and nuts to celebrate the movement of the seasons. It is good to know that even the most unlikely theories of the New Age have Georgian precedents.

THE CITY AND THE COUNTRY

(Pope is walking in a very orderly English park and raises his hat to "Mr God")

"Dear Sir", he said, "I must confess
This is a chastely ordered land,
But one thing mars its loveliness,
The stars are rather out of hand"—

"If they would dance a minuet
Instead of roaming wild and free
Or stand in rows all trim and neat
How exquisite the sky would be."

William Golding, "Mr Pope"

The novelist Henry Fielding had a keen sense of what the world should look like. Born at Sharpham Park, near Glastonbury, and raised near Mere in Dorset, he saw the proper ordering of landscape, ideally as part of a gentleman's park, as having moral value. He wrote *Tom Jones* in Twerton, a fact that now seems implausible. Twerton is the other side of Bath, working-class, industrial, grimy. Yet in Fielding's day Brunel's grim Great Western Railway viaduct that strides straight through this part of Bath glancing neither to left nor right was still nearly a hundred years away. There were pleasant water-meadows, and fields stretching up to the high scarp of the Cotswolds at Lansdown. Go a little up into Twerton, to the football ground (the view from Bath City's Fair Trade tea-bar at Twerton Park is without parallel in English football) or the City Farm, and you will get the idea. And when he was not sitting in Twerton writing and mourning his wife Charlotte, immortalized as the sweet Sophia Western of the novel, he was living the good life up at Prior Park with his friends Ralph Allen and Alexander Pope, sometimes even his novelist sister Sarah Fielding, although it must have been hard at times to ignore her preference for the novels of the distinctly more respectable Samuel Richardson.

It has often been stated that Squire Allworthy is somehow modelled on Fielding's patron, Ralph Allen. Firstly and quite clearly, Henry Fielding wanted to please his open-handed benefactor. Many of Allworthy's good points might be seen to reflect well on Allen, especially his generosity. Fielding wrote in *Tom Jones*:

> Neither Mr Allworthy's house nor his heart were shut against any part
> of mankind, but they were both more particularly open to men of merit.
> To say the truth, this was the only house in the kingdom where you
> were sure to gain a good dinner by deserving it.

Yet such a simple equating of Allworthy and Allen does not quite seem to hold water. Allworthy is an innocent abroad in a heartless world, and not altogether an admirable figure. He does not have either the knowledge of the world or the common sense of Allen. Further, Allen was not a rural squire; Prior Park (unlike other landscaped gardens such as Stowe, Wilton and Stourhead) did not have a home farm and tenant farms to support it. Allen was an entrepreneur, not a local squire. He had made a fortune out of reforming the postal trade between Bath and London, and invested much of the money in acquiring the stone quarries on Combe Down, financing improvements in the river navigation between Bristol and Bath to reduce transport costs, and building a tramway down what is now Ralph Allen's Drive to carry stone to the riverside. Most noticeably, he commissioned Prior Park as an advertisement of the virtues and properties of Bath stone, which he wished to see adopted across the country, and in London in particular. It has to be said that these quarries are now a considerable problem for the city, creating subsidence on a large scale. Some of the caverns are being filled in with concrete, while others are being reinforced as they are the home to large numbers of rare bats.

While the house remains a private school, the landscape gardens are now in the careful hands of the National Trust. Large amounts of money have been spent restoring the upper area known as the Wilderness. Dating from the 1730s, this was the first part of the landscaped garden, but had become overgrown and virtually forgotten for many years. Pope is the inspiration behind this. Grottoes, urns, bridges, temples and cascades were the language of this landscape movement, aiming to "improve nature", a kind of intermediate stage between the obsessively formal gardens of earlier times and the Romantic notion of "wild nature". It has little of the fantasy, little of the beauty of Stourhead.

In the second stage of the park development, the Palladian bridge at the lower end of the gardens was built. But it was linked to the upper gardens and house by a central cascade with planting either side of it. In 1760 all this was swept away by Capability Brown, unifying the whole with a great sweep of parkland and strengthening the planting on either side. This planting has now reached maturity and has encroached rather onto the parkland area. From the bottom looking up, the Wilderness is quite invisible. But from the top the whole drama of Bath is exposed, the

Pulteney Bridge, Bath

old city with its abbey and gasworks nestling down in the valley, the Georgian city climbing up to the heights of St. Stephen's Church, Beckford's tower with its golden cap rising above Lansdown, the distant clump of trees on Kelston Knoll. This is Bath, the setting, the "genius of the place" as Pope would have it, but also a certain balance between built-up area and open spaces passed down from one generation to the next, despite the many follies of the City Fathers.

Ultimately, Palladian bridges are all more or less copies of the work of the Italian Andrea Palladio (1508-80). English examples include Wilton House (1737), Stowe (1739) and Prior Park (1755). The Russians built one at the Tsarkoe Selo palace at Pushkin, outside St. Petersburg, in 1771. They are statements of power and wealth, order in architecture as in society. Yet in England the Palladian bridge was more than just a sign of wealthy, enlightened garden design. To have a Palladian bridge was the signature of the Boy Patriots, a dissident Whig group opposed to the insipid rule of Robert Walpole, and supported for some time by Fielding, who before he settled to novel-writing and the law had been a highly successful (and controversial) political journalist and playwright. It has been suggested (by Tim Mawl) that the Palladian bridge at Prior Park was part of a complex play of interests between Ralph Allen and William Pitt, the future prime minister. If this is so, it seems to have been a successful ploy. The bridge was built in 1755, and Pitt became a Bath MP in 1757.

If there is sadness as well happiness in Henry Fielding's life, this is even truer of his sister Sarah, who lived in Widcombe at the foot of the Prior Park gardens. She felt trapped between her dissolute brother, her lack of a secure and independent income and her own strict moral views. The personal experience of bereavement comes into her novel *David Simple: Volume the Last* (1753), her three sisters all dying in a seven-month period in 1750-51. But she was also able to reflect some of her remarkably advanced social ideas—for example the idea of the foursome as a single economic unit in which resources could be shared. She quotes Pope:

Where Order in Variety we see
And where, tho' all things differ, all agree

not in respect of landscape gardening but the notion of a harmonious society based on mutual respect. Sarah was involved in plans with the well-known Bath Blue Stocking Elizabeth Montagu and her sister Sarah Scott to set up a community of women along the lines of Scott's 1762 novel *A Description of Millennium Hall.* Death intervened.

Women were important in eighteenth-century Bath, even if it is the men (Fielding the novelist, Allen the entrepreneur, Beau Nash the gambling Master of Ceremonies, John Wood, father and son, the architects) who got the plaudits. There was Selina, Countess of Huntingdon, friend of George Whitefield and the Wesleys, who established one of her Connexion's chapels here. It is now the Building of Bath Museum, built, in a supreme irony and at the height of the Georgian building mania, in a neo-Gothic style. It was another way to flag up her disapproval of the moral chaos of Bath, its dedication to conspicuous consumption and social climbing, even if tempered by a concern for charitable giving. But it was charity with an edge of self-interest: the General Hospital (later the Royal National Mineral Hospital and now the Royal National Hospital for Rheumatic Diseases, but still known affectionately in Bath as "The Min") provided for the poor as the three medieval hospitals near the springs had done, but also made sure that the most crippled, physically disabled "cases" were kept away from the public gaze. Later there was Hannah More, and at a similar period, either side of 1800, there was Jane Austen.

If Jane Austen has become a national industry for film and television producers, she is also a local industry. She has her own museum and her own guided tours (why no statue, then?). Jane Austen is too well known to detain us long. She did not like Bath, but was genteel and knowing enough to play this perverse taste down in the novels. The two novels substantially set in Bath, *Northanger Abbey* and *Persuasion*, are the first and last she wrote (although *Northanger Abbey* was not published during her lifetime). Thus while Catherine Morland is glad to be in Bath, full of plans for shopping, enjoyment and excursions, Anne Elliott is reluctantly driven there by family misfortune and represents a rather more jaundiced view of a once great city moving into nineteenth-century decline. Jane Austen was a great walker, walking to such unfashionable places as Charlcombe, the weaving village of Twerton, or Weston, where most of the city's laundry was done by a fierce and independent tribe of women. While such walks are referred to in her letters, they do not substantially enter into the novels, other than in the broad social satire of Catherine Morland's climb up Beechen Cliff, where Edward Tilney dismisses the still lovely view of the city as "unworthy to make part of a landscape". The most telling criticism of Austen comes, though, not through her limited interest in fashionable ideas about landscape, but in the limited social vision of her novels. Raymond Williams' critique still rings true:

> Yet while it is a community wholly known, within the essential terms of the novel, it is as an actual community very precisely selective. Neighbours in Jane Austen are not the people actually living nearby; they are the people living a little less nearby who, in social recognition, can be visited. What she sees across the land is a network of propertied houses and families, and through the holes of this tightly drawn mesh most actual people are simply not seen.

Such, it would seem to some of us, natives of this city, is still the case.

THE TWO CULTURES

It is sometimes difficult to keep up with eighteenth-century Bath. So many of the great and good seem to have passed through Bath, so few of the social movements and political agitations of the century are unrepresented there, that in a sense the history of Bath at that period can be written as almost national rather than local history. Bath produced, or rather lured to itself, one of the great mavericks of that turbulent turn of the century in 1800: William Beckford. Beckford was the richest man in Europe, though his money did not come from Europe, but from the slave plantations of Jamaica. Scratch the surface of late eighteenth-century wealth and slavery is so often there. Beckford's most visible monument in Bath—the gilded half-Italian, half-Greek tower on Lansdown known as Beckford's Tower—was refurbished with the money Beckford received as compensation for the abolition of slavery in the British Empire in 1833.

Beckford was formidably well read and equally well travelled. He studied Goethe in German; he wrote a novel in French, *Vathek*, which is considered to be a key work of French literature; he was an Orientalist, well versed in Arab and Persian culture and history; he knew the bizarre flights of architectural fantasy in Piranesi's designs; he was the greatest collector of his time. His official twenty-first birthday party was followed by a four-day unofficial orgy, designed by Philippe Jacques de Loutherbourg. Ostracized by society after a homosexual scandal, he spent much time travelling.

Then there were the buildings: the lovely Palladian Fonthill Splendens in Wiltshire built by his father replaced by the sublime Gothic (but jerry-built) fantasy of Fonthill Abbey; finally there was the Tower. In Bath Beckford lived as a recluse in Lansdown Crescent, with his own private landscaped garden route up to the Tower, which he visited daily. It was a way of turning his back on both the crumbling away of his own life and fortune, and on the hated neo-classicism of Bath. From his carefully restored reading room in the belvedere at the top of the Tower it is impossible to see any of the Georgian splendours of Bath. Beyond the hills south of Bath rise the Mendips, while the foreground is taken up by the sprawl of modern Weston and, across the river, Twerton. Perched 800 feet above sea level, and a few flights of stairs above that, it is a place to be visited in a winter gale—a secure port in any storm, and there were plenty of storms and few ports in Beckford's long life. Beckford's Tower is an odd sort of pilgrimage, but one worth making

The gulf between the two cultures of arts and science was scarcely acknowledged in the eighteenth century, as the life and work of the astronomer William Herschel demonstrate. He came to Bath in 1765 to work as organist at the newly opened Octagon private chapel in Milsom Street. He promoted concerts, in Bath and in Bristol. His sister Caroline came from Hanover to keep house for him, to sing in his concerts and to be his personal assistant. Herschel spent increasing time in the garden at night, studying the stars through his telescope. Caroline was required to sit with him and record his findings—not least the discovery of Uranus. In her memoirs she complained of being put upon and unloved, short of both friends and money. Eventually she came to be recognized as William's partner rather than his assistant. In contrast to Newton's view of a "clockwork universe", as Michael Hoskins points out, William Herschel believed in the principle of "Plenitude". This stated that rational beings were to be discovered everywhere in the universe, not just on earth. (He rather spoilt things by including the sun and the moon as unlikely locations for these rational beings.) What Caroline believed is less clear. When William died she viewed the future with trepidation as a "chamber of death" where she might reflect on her "isolated situation". She lived for 25 years more, received the gold medal of the Astronomical Society of London, and when her nephew John Herschel, Professor of Astronomy at Cambridge, visited her, he found her happy and contented. Undeterred, she rewrote her memoirs in her nineties, leaving all the pessimism in. For a woman who never grew beyond 4 feet 9 inches tall, probably as a result of smallpox in childhood, to live to the age of 98 years was a remarkable achievement.

If arts and science were considered quite compatible, then to move from science to its applications in technology was nothing. From the various learned societies that existed in the second half of the eighteenth century grew not just the Bath Royal Literary and Scientific Institution (now returned to its rightful home in Queen Square), but also the Bath and West Show, once peripatetic but now anchored to a site near Shepton Mallet. The Bath Philosophical Society (1779-85) had no fewer than eleven members who were or later became Fellows of the Royal Society. William Herschel was a member, as was Joseph Priestley. William Smith, the father of English geology, was hereabouts too. He came to do a useful job of work, surveying a line for the Somerset Coal Canal, which would enable coal to be transported more cheaply from the coalfields of North Somerset. It was a demanding job, but one that brought him into close contact with the scientific community in Bath. As he dug into the earth, he made the observations and deductions in the Jurassic limestone beds that would eventually lead him to draw the first map of the geology of England—in the rather overblown title of Simon Winchester's book, "the map that changed the world."

One is tempted to suspect that about 1800 everything began to go faster, including history and time. Hard on the heels of the canals came the railways, and hard on the heels of Smith and his canal came the over-named Isambard Kingdom Brunel and his Great Western Railway. Winchester's notion of a "map that changed the world" refers to the contribution that Smith's work made to an eventual dating of our world that made nonsense of the claims of religion that God had created the world in seven days. Brunel changed Bath in ways that Bath cannot have begun to suspect but which are still visible today. Brunel was in a hurry; the Board of the GWR pressed Brunel; Brunel pressed his foremen; the foremen pressed the navvies. They died in their numbers, especially during the construction of Box Tunnel, where Brunel chose to strike dramatically due west from Chippenham to Bath rather than taking the more circuitous route through the Avon Valley.

In Bath itself Brunel made the passage through Sydney Gardens, a pleasure ground where Jane Austen had enjoyed herself, with dramatic landscaping echoing the similar passage of the Kennett and Avon Canal a few years earlier. But then it was up and over, over the river on a high bridge, then a massive viaduct (including Bath Spa station) creating a new wall to the southern edge of the city, and then cuttings and the long viaduct through Twerton. Many houses were demolished, although in Twerton an unlucky few were offered as compensation a new life underneath the railway arches. A new world had arrived. And it was a dirty world too. Those who remember Bath before the end of the steam era will agree: forget the golden light; most of Bath was at best grey, at worst, black. Bath stone and industrial pollution simply do not mix.

All Ship-shape and Bristol Fashion

Generations of untidy West Country children were brought up on the injunction to keep their toys, books and bedrooms "all ship-shape and Bristol fashion". The origin of this expression is not so much the reputation of Bristol sailors as well-organized, tidy workers, but the chaos at Bristol harbour each time the tide went out and ships bottomed out on the thick Bristol mud, their masts and spars spread-eagled at crazy angles. The only way to avoid objects flying around both above and below decks was to have everything carefully stowed and secured before the tide ebbed. It must have been an amazing sight—hundreds of ships tied up among the medieval garrets and churches of England's second city (only Norwich ever rivalled it for that title). Now the harbour is dry land, and after a largely unsuccessful career as a traffic roundabout, it is now the post-Millennium Bristol Centre with its fountains and abstract sculptures.

Old Bristol begins at St. Mary Redcliffe, called by the first Queen Elizabeth "the goodliest, fairest and most famous parish church in England". The words were probably penned by a courtier, but great cities like flattery and the words are remembered. This is a church to rival the Augustinian abbey (now Bristol Cathedral) on the Gloucestershire side of the river. Yet Bristol is in neither Somerset nor Gloucestershire, for as early as 1373 the rich merchants, fed up with being subject to the courts of both counties, paid the Crown for a charter which declared Bristol to be the county of Bristol. The most noticeable feature of St. Mary is the vaulted, stepped hexagonal north porch. Here by tradition sailors and emigrants came to ask for blessing, for the spire of St. Mary would have been clearly visible from the quayside. There is city and state here—the

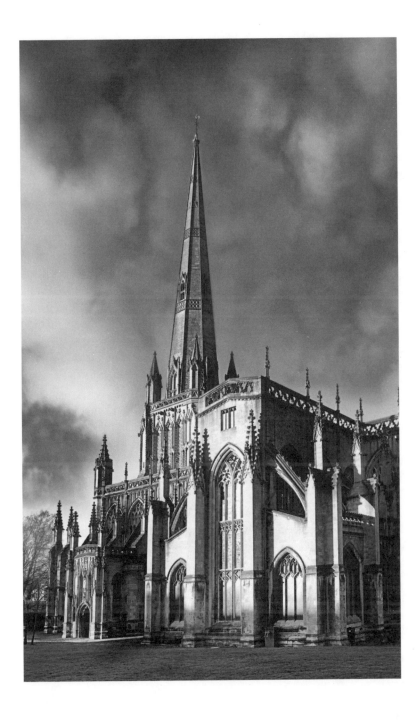

niches contained statues of the kings of England, while the corbels featured townsfolk. The dedication was to Mary, star of the sea. Those coming here no doubt included pilgrims bound for Santiago de Compostela, the Galician shrine. A modern icon shows St. Nicholas in his bishop's robes holding John Cabot's ship, the *Matthew*, while the whale bone brought home by Cabot from his 1497 journey to North America lies nearby.

One of the most famous sons of St. Mary Redcliffe was Thomas Chatterton (1752-70), poet and fraud, remembered by a life-size seated statue in Bristol's Millennium Square. His uncle the sexton allowed him access to the old manuscripts stored in the room above the north porch. At the tender age of fifteen, he produced a set of poems, claiming that they were in the main the work of the invented Thomas Rowley, secretary to the real William Canynges (see below). Eventually his work was discredited and Chatterton himself shunned. He committed suicide by taking arsenic in London, but his work was taken up and admired by the Romantics, initially Southey and Coleridge, both of whom were married in St. Mary. Keats wrote an ode to him, the French writer Alfred de Vigny a play and the Italian Leoncavallo an opera. Poor Chatterton, not least of the many historical footnotes that still draw visitors to St. Mary Redcliffe.

William Canynges was four times mayor and three times member of parliament for Bristol in the fifteenth century. He employed 800 men. Probably most of the money for rebuilding St. Mary in that century came from him, though other merchants probably made contributions too. Their merchant marks can be seen carved in stone around the church, and thus is Bristol's mercantile history written into the fabric of the city. In the south transept is one monument to Canynges and his wife, lying side by side, but after her death he was ordained into the priesthood, which earned him a second memorial—on his own, in priest's robes, in white alabaster. Much of the trade of the city was in cloth and wine and fish, but from the earliest days there was also a darker human trade. In Anglo-Saxon times many were sold into slavery in Ireland and this trade was organized mainly through the port of Bristol. We know this, because the medieval historian William of Malmesbury explained how St. Wulstan of Worcester paid many visits to Bristol in the early Norman period in an attempt to eradicate the trade:

For many people, brought from all over England, were dragged off to Ireland in hope of greater profit; they offered for sale slave girls, both virgins and those already with child… young people of both sexes, with the beauty of free men and unspoiled by age, who are daily exposed publicly for sale.

There are many links between Bristol and America. Cabot, whose presence imbues the north porch at St. Mary Redcliffe, reached Newfoundland in 1497, the first of a series of expeditions that sought a northwest passage to the Pacific. There is a seagoing replica of the *Matthew* at the Floating Harbour (the wet dock which eventually solved the problem of the tides and the mud). Its skipper, when it sets sail, is the same enterprising young man who runs the modern blue and yellow passenger ferry services that buzz busily around the city. Cabot is revered in Bristol—his tower sits high on the south edge of Clifton, with splendid views down to the cathedral, the Floating Harbour, Brunel's Great Britain, and across to the Mendip outlier of Dundry Hill, which limits Bristol's expansion to the south. Another fine sailor, Admiral Penn, is buried in St. Mary, while just across the road is the site of Bristol's Quaker graveyard, an oasis of peace at a busy traffic intersection. Penn was Cromwell's commander but also served under Charles II. He captured Jamaica from the Spanish and, according to the St. Mary guidebook writer, as its first governor "stripped it of its wealth causing terrible hardship to its people." He loaned money to the king, and when he died, his Quaker son called in the loan, and received land in America instead. Such is the story of the founding of the state of Pennsylvania by William Penn.

REMEMBERING SLAVERY

But talk of America, the sea, the Atlantic trade always ends in talk of slavery. As we have seen, medieval Bristol was involved in the white slave trade, but the trade for which it is most remembered, and most often reviled, was the seventeenth- and eighteenth-century trade in black Africans. There was some direct trading with the colonies, but the most typical pattern was the triangular trade, taking cloth and metal objects and trinkets out to Africa, the "middle passage" of slaves from Africa to the Caribbean and America, and then cotton and sugar and tobacco back to Bristol for refining and manufacturing. Slavery is the dark secret that lies behind so much of the wealth of Bath and Bristol, the other side of the conspicuous consumption of Georgian Bath and Regency Bristol. And not just Bath and Bristol: in Porlock they caught and salted herrings to sell in Bristol as food for the unwilling human cargo of slaves. In the years leading up to the abolition of the trade (1807) and of slavery itself in the British Empire (1833) it was much spoken about. A long silence followed. Only in recent years, with the presence of a large black population (mostly of Afro-Caribbean origin) has it been again spoken of in Bristol. Bristol rioted in 1980. Although the immediate cause was a police raid on a black café in St. Paul's, growing poverty and unemployment and disillusion with the city too hastily rebuilt after war-time bombing had much to do with it. Black youths were singled out by the heavy-handed tactics of the police, but as a perceptive website reports: "Contrary to popular belief, the riots in St. Paul's were not strictly race riots. They were part of a long Bristol tradition of riotous action by the city's poor against perceived injustice which dates back to the early 1700s at least." Most spectacularly, Bristol had burned in 1831 when the mob, infuriated by the rejection of the first Reform Act, took to the streets and burned and looted the Mansion House. Around 250 of the rioters were killed or seriously injured. The young Charles Kingsley described it as "Dante's Inferno" and noted the distant tower of Dundry church reflecting the red glow of the flames.

It is deeply ironical that the man most associated with the Bristol slave trade was also the man who endowed many of the city's good causes: Colston School, Colston's Almshouses, Colston Hall, Colston's Charities. Edward Colston owned sugar plantations in Jamaica and in 1698 took full advantage of the ending of London's monopoly on trade with Africa. From then until the later years of the eighteenth century when it was overhauled by Liverpool, Bristol was the capital of English slavery. Some owners treated their slaves better than others. For example, John Pinney organized the inoculation of the slaves on his plantation against smallpox, while at the same time advising his overseers against calling out the doctor to them. This is the same Pinney at whose house Coleridge and Wordsworth first met, and who provided rent-free accommodation for the Wordsworths in Dorset. Ultimately, to talk of a "good" slave-owner is a nonsense, and the only surprise is that the trade and the ownership of slaves continued as long as they did. Some black slaves ended their days as servants in Bristol, and some escaped, but it is fanciful to think of the rioters of 1980 as at the end of anything other than a highly convoluted historical chain of displacement and exploitation

Bristol has been at the heart of discussions in recent years, culminating in 2007, the two hundredth anniversary of abolition of the slave trade, about the collective guilt of the English. But at this distance it is a difficult argument to sustain. White English people have had their own struggles, some of which are reflected in this book. Landlords, factory owners, those who have led us into wars for which there was little popular support, the list would not only be endless but contested at each twist of the way. Perhaps better to celebrate the moral strength and courage of those who fought the evil of slavery from without, and those black people who resisted from within in the numerous revolts which pepper the history of the slave trade and the slave plantations of the Caribbean. Better too maybe, as suggested in the previous chapter, to think further about the links between different sorts of oppression and the growing evidence that causes such as political liberty, the emancipation of women and the rights of black people may have common roots and common ideals.

BRUNEL'S BRISTOL
Brunel and Bristol belong together. In 1833 Brunel was appointed as engineer for the Great Western Railway main line from London Paddington to Bristol. The original entrance to the station lies on Temple Way and is often missed by those arriving at or leaving the modern Temple Meads station. This station building is, at the time of writing, occupied by the Commonwealth Museum, the pivotal role of which in articulating Bristol's recent debate about slavery must be acknowledged. Now it may move to London, which once again throws into doubt the use of this historic site. Behind the museum, and running parallel to the road leading up to the modern entrance, is Brunel's splendid train shed, with its vast hammerhead roof still intact, now sadly used as a car-park and as a pedestrian exit by those wishing to take the ferry into central Bristol. Across the road is the rather Dutch-style headquarters of the Bristol and Exeter railway, and the modern curved station reflects the need to link together these two lines and thus provide through working to the south-west. The main frontage to the street is pure fancy, a church-like structure with a solid central tower and decorative pinnacles, its crenellations reflecting those on the Temple Way frontage of Brunel's first station. It is as imposing a setting as any station

in England, the modern and practical dressed up to play the fanciful and the historical.

A similar combination of the practical and flamboyant is found in Brunel's Clifton Suspension Bridge, which spans the Avon gorge at its narrowest but highest point, hundreds of feet above the brown waters and mud of the Avon. There is little relationship between the economic importance of Brunel's bridges and the care and attention he lavished on them. Clifton was "my first child, my darling", yet its practical importance is far, far less than the Royal Albert Bridge across the Tamar west of Plymouth, which for the first time created an all-weather link between Cornwall and England. The Clifton Bridge links two largely recreational areas, Clifton Downs and Leigh Woods. Perhaps for this reason, the bridge was in continual financial difficulties and not completed until after Brunel's death. Peter Aughton, in his fine book about Bristol, waxes lyrical about the bridge, and indeed its graceful span is as much an artistic achievement as a technological one. It belongs, it occupies a space, it symbolizes a city.

One cannot say more of any human artefact than that. It is a preferred focus for leisure visitors to the city, but also over the years has been the preferred point of exit for the many suicides lured to Clifton by Brunel's bridge.

Back at the Floating Harbour, Brunel's steamship, the *Great Britain*, lies finally at rest. Like so much else that Brunel achieved, it was a splendid failure. Brunel thought big, and thought in diagrams. To him, a steamship line to New York would be a natural extension of the main line of the Great Western Railway. Steam was the coming thing, and to carry sufficient coal for the crossing involved building big. Yet it is also obvious that Bristol with its narrow tidal river was at the limit of its use as a sea-going port. The *Great Britain* never did make a commercial trip from Bristol, and it was Liverpool—the same Liverpool which had taken over the slave trade from Bristol at the end of the eighteenth century—which now became the *Great Britain*'s home port. Only five years after her maiden voyage to New York in 1845, she was sold and put to use on the Australia route, providing luxury for the few like the first England cricket team who could travel first class, and hardship for the many who travelled in steerage. A quarter of a century later, she was bizarrely converted to sail, and by the First World War was being used as a coal store. In 1937 she was scuttled off the Falkland Islands, or Islas Malvinas. Few remembered her glorious past, fewer still thought she might have a future.

Yet in 1970, surrounded by as much emotion as witnessed her first launch by Prince Albert in 1843, the *Great Britain* was back in the Floating Harbour. Vast crowds saw her homecoming, passing under Brunel's Suspension Bridge for the one and only time in her life, a rotting, rusting present for the people of Bristol. Such a restoration project takes time, and as so often in modern England it was the National Lottery that came to the rescue, financing a dry dock which would lift her delicate timbers clear of the water, while preserving the illusion of a ship at a quayside. On a winter's day with the riverside sky full of cloud and sleet and hail, the warmth and comfort of the ship come as blessed relief. The saloon has mirrors, marble columns and Corinthian capitals, although later on deck, in the wintry sunshine again, one of the five resident engineers explains that these are simply the iron frame of the boat, round metal columns that can be seen at their best in the cargo hold, then covered with plaster to look like marble. It is the sort of illusion the Victorians excelled at. The visiting schoolchildren, some from an expensive private school and others not, love the domestic cosiness of it all and the mannequins dotted around the lounge. No doubt in Victorian times, one set of children would have been happily catered for in First Class, while the others roughed it in Steerage. The ship is laid out as it might have been in about 1860 when it was busy carrying migrants to Australia. And there is still that white line on the deck, separating Steerage from First Class, which might not be crossed, a line smudged but still present everywhere in contemporary England.

Chapter Eight

SOUTH DEVON

Either the great resources of a country can be owned by private individuals, or they can be owned by all individuals in common. It is most important that anyone who vaguely hopes for any third alternative should sit down and write out in black and white what the alternative can be. Otherwise he should accept my contention that there are only these two alternatives.

Sir Richard Acland, 1941

THE ACLANDS AT KILLERTON

The Killerton estate lies immediately north of Exeter and, unlike the Acland family properties in Somerset, is very accessible indeed. From Dolbury Hill Fort, an Iron Age settlement on a volcanic outcrop with extensive views over countryside, there are the sights and sounds of the M5 to the south and trains on the main line from London Paddington to Exeter to the north. It is a busy countryside, quarried in more recent times. There is a splendid grove of mature beech trees rising above and blackberries in profusion below. These trees were part of the landscaping of the "Clump" by John Veitch for the Acland family in the eighteenth century.

So who were these Aclands, whose influence was so widespread in Somerset and Devon? Anne Acland, wife of Richard Acland who donated Killerton to the National Trust in 1944, describes them engagingly in the National Trust guide to Killerton as a family who had risen from very modest beginnings by "sheer genetic luck". Each generation produced at least one male heir, and the Acland men had an uncanny knack of marrying rich and fertile women. By the time of Elizabeth, John Acland was a sheriff, justice of the peace, member of parliament and benefactor of the poor. A trend had been set. The Civil War was a set-back, the family declaring for the king in a county that by-and-large, especially in nearby Exeter, was staunchly for parliament. In the eighteenth century family fortunes were restored again by marriage, most notably that of Sir Thomas Acland to Elizabeth Dyke, who brought with her both her name (all future baronets were "Dyke Acland") and rich landholdings in Somerset, including Holnicote. This particular Thomas was delighted with Holnicote, became an enthusiastic Master of Staghounds and seldom visited Killerton at all. It was only after 1770 that he addressed himself more directly to the arts of peace, and to Killerton, and determined to build a house and park in the fashionable eighteenth-century style.

Thomas Acland was also a good talent-spotter, and the talent he spotted was John Veitch. John was a young man of less than twenty years, a Scotsman who had walked from Edinburgh to earn his fortune and was working for a London nurseryman. Acland employed this young man to "make a park." The design that Veitch came up with enhanced the qualities of the landscape, and in particular the contrast between the rolling farmland below the house and the great upthrust of Dolbury Hill above it. John Veitch remained at Killerton for a long time, including twenty-three years during which he managed the estates single-handed as well as setting himself up as an independent nurseryman nearby. Acland was less fortunate with his architect. James Wyatt came up with a grand classical design to be placed further up the hill in a dominant position. There were difficulties, and the plan never materialized. Instead, there was a hasty rebuild on the more sheltered site where the house is still today. The result is that the house is completely overshadowed by its garden and park and setting. From the flowered terrace there is a gentle view across the sloping countryside towards Exeter airport, electricity pylons, the estate villages, the site of the new Cranbrook extension of Exeter and the distant hills of

East Devon that shut off the view to the sea There is gently sloping parkland with mature trees fading imperceptibly into the tenant farms beyond. But further up the gardens towards Dolbury are magnificent views of rolling farmland and distant Dartmoor, all laid out in an on-off shimmer of late afternoon sunshine cascading between the clouds. Landscape at Killerton is in three clear sets: the garden and park, the farmland, the wild moors. But it is never a quiet place, with the permanent hum of traffic on the M5 to add to the busy bees, the squabbling birds and the wind sighing in the trees—first luscious acers and tree-sized rhododendrons, then giant redwoods, Spanish chestnuts, the remains of a cedar of Lebanon the crown of which has been taken down, and then the beech clump on Dolbury.

In 1808 another Sir Thomas Dyke Acland assumed the title. Where the eighteenth century had been about stag-hunting and pleasure, the nineteenth century was about social responsibility and good causes. This was the Sir Thomas whom we saw being a good landlord in the villages on the Holnicote Estate in Somerset, and the same improved mustard yellow cottages in villages such as Broadclyst bear evidence to the same determination to do the right thing by his tenants. His wife Lydia was from the same wealthy banking Hoare family who had taken on Stourhead in the previous century, and as a young woman had had much contact with the evangelical movement, with Wilberforce and the abolitionists. It was to be, by any standards, a remarkably successful marriage partnership. Under Lydia's instruction, John Veitch fenced off part of the deer park and laid out the flower borders and shrubberies which are the immediate ancestors of the present ones. Sir Thomas, or Great Sir Thomas as he came to be known, supported all the major causes of the century, including abolition of the slave trade, Catholic emancipation, parliamentary reform, the abolition of slavery itself and the repeal of the Corn Laws. As a Tory MP he managed to make few friends among his landowning neighbours in Devon, Somerset and Cornwall, to which the Acland empire now extended.

But Killerton is more than a house and garden and 130,000 visitors a year, as John Channon, the property manager at the Killerton and East Devon Estate office, explained. The estate was an inalienable gift to the National Trust in 1944, so the Trust must keep the freehold. There are 6,500 acres of which 1,300 acres are woodland, mainly in Ashclyst Forest, 21 tenanted farms and 250 houses and cottages. The Trust has resisted the move to large agribusiness farms in recent years, and the average size of 200 acres is small by modern standards. There has also been a move away from dairy, with the estate now including arable and mixed arable-stock farms. The Aclands have gradually disengaged from the management of the estate, and Dominic, son of Sir John Acland, is himself a tenant farmer at Sprydon. The estate is at the forefront of the new role of farmers as custodians of landscape and environment as well as producers of food. Initially the Trust saw the estate simply as a way of financing the house and garden. Then with the success and popularity of Operation Neptune and the acquisition of coastline in the 1960s, it became more interested in nature conservation. Now every time a farm is re-let the Trust looks for radical solutions. Part-time farming is now on the agenda, as it allows some marginal land to revert to woodland, pasture and fen. Farmers are encouraged to raise traditional breeds—Devon Red and Dexter cattle and Dartmoor ponies—and to encourage butterflies and flowers. For both farm and cottage tenancies, the Trust gives preference to local people wherever possible, thus keeping communities together in ways that are difficult if market forces alone are at play.

It was Sir Charles Thomas Dyke Acland, described by Anne Acland as "the last Edwardian", who initiated the process by which the Acland lands passed into the hands of the National Trust. In 1916 he gave the Trust a 500-year lease on 800 acres of Exmoor, part of the Holnicote Estate, thereby doubling at a stroke the holdings of the fledgling organization. However, the process by which the remainder of the Acland holdings passed to the Trust is quite complex, and extremely interesting. As we have seen, both social responsibility and political involvement ran in the family. By this time the family politics were firmly Liberal (with a capital "L"); in 1926 David Lloyd George chose a rally of 19,000 people at Killerton to launch the Liberal Party's new land policy. Yet almost everywhere except in the West Country the Liberal Party was in retreat. This was an age of extremes. In 1935 Richard Acland became Liberal MP for North Devon, but in the spirit of the 1930s his heart was never entirely in the Liberal Party cause. He became convinced that the only solution to the crisis facing Europe, the rise of fascism on the one hand and authoritarian communism on the other, was a moral crusade for public ownership. To distinguish this from the socialism of the Labour and Communist parties, he revived the seventeenth-century idea of "common wealth", though it was not until 1942 that the Common Wealth Party took shape. That same year the Beveridge Report had been published with its ideal of a welfare state in which the three evils of poverty, unemployment and sickness would be eradicated by fixing a safety net to catch the victims of social and economic change. More broadly, both Beveridge and Acland were responding to a general sense that the future could and should be different from and better than the past. At its peak, spurred on by Acland's "revivalist fervour", the new party had 15,000 members. Daringly, it defied the wartime gentlemen's agreement that where by-elections occurred seats would be uncontested. Common Wealth won three more seats in Parliament.

Perhaps the world had changed more than even Richard Acland believed possible. The 1945 election was a landslide victory for the Labour Party, and Common Wealth disappeared beneath it. Acland himself resurfaced in 1947 as Labour member for Gravesend, a seat he held until 1955 when he resigned because of his opposition to nuclear weapons. The career of this exceptional man then took a further twist. He entered teaching, and eventually became a lecturer at St. Luke's Training College in Exeter. By an extraordinary turn of fate he ended his career as warden of the St. Luke's hall of residence—at Killerton House. How had this come about? As his son tells the story in the Killerton National Trust guide, Richard Acland had conceived the plan in 1942 of selling off all the family estates in order to finance his new political party. John was only three years old in 1942 and even if he had been listening could not possibly have remembered the reply from Richard's wife Anne: "the estates are not just property; they are communities of people for whom I feel responsible." It was a reply fully in keeping with the history of the family into which she had married.

Eventually 1,500 acres were sold, and the remainder passed to the National Trust in 1944. The Aclands and Killerton survived the war, but not the furniture which had been put into store in Exeter. This was destroyed in the Exeter blitz. It is the war-ravaged townscape of Exeter and Plymouth, and other bellicose matters, to which we shall now turn in this chapter.

WARSCAPES: EXETER AND PLYMOUTH
Some of the most tragic episodes of the Second World War were the air-raids inspired not by the desire to destroy military targets but simply to

inflict damage on the cultural legacy of great cities. In 1942 Hitler launched the so-called Baedeker raids against selected English cities, including Bath and Exeter, in retaliation for massive RAF attacks on the historic Baltic port cities of Lübeck and Rostock. If we did not make reference to this in Bath, it is because, as Barry Cunliffe remarks, "given the scale for large-scale devastation the escape of so much of Georgian Bath was remarkable." Much of the damage was done in the thickly populated suburbs west and south of the city centre such as Oldfield Park. A total of 417 people died in two nights of bombing, yet only the Assembly Rooms, completely refurbished as recently as 1938, were left to be completely rebuilt again after the war.

A week later it was the turn of Exeter. The death-toll on 4 May 1942 was 156, much lower than Bath, yet the raid transformed completely the centre of Exeter. Famous old buildings such as St. Lawrence and the College of the Vicars Choral disappeared from the map. Much of the shopping centre was flattened. What we see today is almost two cities. There is the Cathedral Close, its buildings dwarfed by the massive honey-coloured stone of the cathedral with its twin Norman towers. Then there is the rather poor quality and hasty post-war rebuilding, and we all know and sympathize with the why of this, and the new wave of late twentieth- and early twenty-first-century re-rebuilding. It is less easy to sympathize with the latter. So within the town centre area there are a few (mainly religious) medieval buildings in red sandstone, the orange-red brick of post-war rebuilding and the glass and steel constructions of the new age. Even in the Cathedral Close the cranes that are driving the new Exeter skywards tower above the remnants of an earlier culture.

A little later in this chapter we shall examine some of the connections between Devon and America, which go beyond the rather accidental fact that the *Mayflower* was forced to pause the trip of the Pilgrim Fathers and put into Plymouth for repairs. But first that other nation which shares North America—Canada. Among the many interesting memorials in Exeter Cathedral is the one to John Graves Simcoe, first governor of Upper Canada and founder of Toronto, "in whose life and character the virtues of the hero, the patriot and the Christian, were so eminently conspicuous, that it may justly be said he served his king and his country with a zeal exceeded only by his piety towards his God." In general, we have made little of monumental inscriptions in this book, not because they lack interest but because they deserve a whole book to themselves. We make exception for Simcoe. The memorial itself is flanked by the figure of Simcoe and an equal-sized Canadian Indian, naked apart from his cloak and carrying a tomahawk. Simcoe carries a musket. Walford Chapel, near Honiton, once part of the Simcoe Estate, "is maintained in perpetuity by the Ontario Heritage Foundation as a place of pilgrimage." The Canadian Second World War Memorial is at Broadclyst, one of the Killerton villages. Sadly, and in defiance of the convention that death the great leveller demands that the dead should be listed in alphabetical order, the memorial in the church of St. John the Baptist has separate lists for officers, non-commissioned officers, and men.

If Exeter might be considered an unfair target for bombing, then the same would presumably not apply to Plymouth. Plymouth has always been a military town, or rather a naval town. It is difficult to imagine a story (we shall treat it as such and not enquire too much further) as quintessentially English as Drake playing bowls on Plymouth Hoe while waiting for the arrival of the dreaded Spanish Armada. The Hoe is still a lovely place, open to the sea and the south and the salt, turning its back upon the city, its massively ugly shopping centre, the dockyards at Devonport, the pubs and restaurants and marinas of Sutton Harbour and the Barbican. From the Hoe there is so much green that it is hard to imagine that you are in the heart of the only large city south-west of Bristol. To the west, across the water, are the green heights of Mount Edgcumbe Park, now nearly into Cornwall. Immediately ahead lies Drake's Island, the first line of protection for the city and its docks and harbours. To the east the rolling green hills of the South Hams, and another small piece of the large history of the United States of America.

AN AMERICAN MYSTERY IN DEVON

The South Hams in late April is a patriotic place to be, with the red, white and blue of the banked hedgerows all the way down the lanes from Totnes to the sea: ragged robin, milkmaids (stitchwort) and bluebells. At Slapton Sands, despite an irritating, warmish rain and Start Point glowering northwards in gloomy silhouette, the great shingle bank is flower-decked for spring with pink and white valerian, bladder campion, sea-pinks. There is no sea view from the road, which lies below the level of the shingle bank. But it does allow the prospect of the fresh-water lake of Slapton Leys with its village and Field Studies Centre behind. Now the lake is a nature reserve with reed-beds, gorse, scrub and crab-apple. "And only man is vile"—the words of that old hymn creep into consciousness from a long-forgotten past—bleak, silent passengers sitting in their cars, but always facing the gloomy sea, the rain tapping, then hammering more insistently on the car-roofs. But then the rain eases, and it is time to set out and discover the American mystery of Slapton Sands.

The conservation scheme for the area, as at Studland, leaves some scope for "natural" evolution—a little more shingle here, a little less there, the colonization of plants on the upper levels of shingle, the balance of open water, reed beds and wet woodland on the other side of the road. But the village of Torcross itself takes no chances, sheltering behind its high defensive sea-wall. The first thing you come to going southwards towards Torcross from the Strete end of the beach is a small obelisk on the sea side of the road that begins to tell the story of Slapton Sands. The first mention, then, of the United States of America, the 3,000 local people who evacuated the area at such short notice in the final weeks of 1943, and the appreciation of the American Army authorities. It is dedicated to "the people of the South Hams who generously left their homes and their lands to provide a practice battle area for the successful assault in Normandy in June 1944." The villages are listed—a litany of ordinary lives disrupted and transformed by world affairs and a world war (remembering that war is always a failure of diplomacy, or of politics)—Blackawton, Chillington, East Allington, Sherford, Slapton, Stokenham, Strete and Torcross. Lives arraigned in strictest alphabetical order. Generous it may have been but people had little choice, given exactly six weeks to move themselves, their furniture and their stock out of the area. Some had never been away from their home village, some never returned, many were put up by friends and relations outside the immediate battle-zone.

The memorial talks of the "saving of many hundreds of lives", presumably through rigorous training, but the real story here is about lives lost, some would say unnecessarily in ill-planned and ill-conducted exercises. The story unfolds around the Sherman tank at the entrance to the village of Torcross and adjacent to the car-park. In all, 746 men (army and navy) died when Exercise Tiger was intercepted by fast German torpedo boats operating out of Cherbourg on 28 April 1944. Two landing craft were sunk and another crippled, as a line of these craft

moved towards Slapton. Here Ken Small, almost single-handedly responsible for the recovery of the Sherman tank from the sea in 1984, and the subsequent uncovering of much of this tragic story, used to sit in his car and wait for visitors, talk to them about Exercise Tiger and sell them copies of his book *The Forgotten Dead*. It has sold 140,000 copies and is still on sale in the little post office. People want to know, and the truth will usually out—eventually. The shop assistant's father was from Torcross, was in the army during that same war, and knew nothing about the disaster till years later.

Now we now know that the 746 who died in the cold, unforgiving sea that April night were not the sum total of deaths in the West Country as the Allied troops prepared to invade France. Altogether, 946 men were lost during training exercises. The West Country's contribution to the Normandy landings was very great, with 485 craft setting out from Dartmouth (one-eighth of the total) and a further 66 from Salcombe. The official US Navy memorial of 1984 asserts that valuable lessons were learned but one wonders. More personal is a note taped in a plastic cover to the Sherman tank, gradually acquiring a more and more sculptural quality under its many layers of protective black paint, in memory of "Ike" Osteen of the US Army Postal Unit who was here at Slapton from February to May 1944. He died on 20 February 2007 in Colorado. The message is a simple one: "Rest in peace, old pal."

Whatever one feels about war, about military secretiveness and incompetence, there is no doubt that this memorial at Torcross has helped many families come to terms with loss and grief. There is something indefinable and sad about Torcross—the tank and memorial with their red wreaths and poppies against the grey waters of Slapton Leys and the green hills of Devon, and in the other direction the grumbling, restless shingle of the beach. Sad, too, the continual sighing and sucking of the undertow as each wave breaks and runs out of energy. The flags (the Stars and Stripes and the Union Jack) are at half-mast—we are only two days on from the commemoration of 28 April, two days on from new wreaths and messages which will continue to haunt the summer visitors.

But there is still a place called Hope. Indeed, there are two places in the South Hams of Devon called Hope—Inner Hope and Outer Hope. It was at the Democratic National Convention in Madison Square Garden, New York, in July 1992 that Senator Bill Clinton spoke that unforgettable line "I still believe in a place called Hope," which would have been unforgivably corny if he had not happened to come from a long line of Clintons in a small Arkansas town called Hope. But what of Hope in Devon, Inner and Outer? The little sandy coves with their holiday homes, pub and shop nestle in neighbourly fashion between fierce red-brown cliffs and offshore rocks, with a tiny church and a church cat and a belfry, a favourite haunt of the local seagulls, standing above and between the coves. In the past, serious-minded Inner Hope with its recently restored Fishermen's Reading Room of 1908 and Methodist chapel had little to do with church- and pub-going Outer Hope. There is still rivalry, but at least they are now on speaking terms. Beyond Hope, the National Trust land stretches out to the headland of Bolt Tail with marvellous views of the rock-strewn seas across to the village of Thurlestone and the gentler coast stretching down towards Plymouth. The rain clears towards evening, the children come down to the beach with their buckets and spades and shouts and laughter. It is hard not to feel hopeful at Hope.

ON DARTMOOR

We fired our guns and the British kept a 'comin'
There wasn't nigh as many as there was a while ago
We fired once more and they began to runnin'
On down the Mississippi to the Gulf of Mexico.

Jimmy Driftwood

Between 1812 and 1814, England was at war with the United States of America. The Battle of New Orleans took place in 1815, after the conclusion of a peace treaty in faraway Europe, but is remembered as the one great American triumph of that war. In 1936 a high school teacher, Jimmy Driftwood, wrote a song about it in order to interest his history students in the subject. It was to become very popular on both sides of the Atlantic. So clearly relations between England and the United States of America have not always been as cordial as memories of the Pilgrim Fathers and Slapton Sands might suggest. Not far away, on Dartmoor, American prisoners from the war of 1812 were kept in this newest and harshest of England prisons. Indeed, Dartmoor Prison, just outside Princetown at the very heart of this high moorland country, was built to house prisoners of war, and the first inmates were 2,500 French prisoners in 1809. It only became a convict prison in the 1850s, when transportation of convicted criminals to the colonies became less viable as the increasingly respectable communities of Australia voiced their opposition to having yet more of Britain's undesirables dumped on their doorstep. Now it houses 600 inmates, of whom seventy work on the prison farm. Princetown church also owes its existence to convict labour. Its granite was quarried by the French, while some American prisoners worked on its interior.

Dartmoor Prison is both on the moor and of the moor, its grey granite profile as much a part of the landscape as the tors (shattered granite outcrops) which rise in strange forms above the surrounding heather. Yet as the prison farm suggests, this is not a wilderness landscape. The man who first imagined the prison, Sir Thomas Tyrwhitt was also the man who founded Princetown. He envisaged it as the centre of a project to reclaim Dartmoor as farmland, one of the more ambitious and wilder schemes of eighteenth-century agricultural improvement. Unlike John Knight's successful nineteenth-century scheme to clear and enclose much of Exmoor

Forest for farming, the Dartmoor project failed. Yet like Exmoor, it is wrong to see Dartmoor as wilderness. There is a good deal of farming still on Dartmoor, with farms and fields between grey stone walls across the lower slopes and in the sheltered valleys. Even on the higher slopes, apparently the home of the wind and the wild birds, the signs of human activity are never far way. The sheep, the cattle and the ponies are part of a complex system of grazing which prevents the moor reverting to woodland and scrub.

Dartmoor Prison also features in one of the best known stories of Sir Arthur Conan Doyle, *The Hound of the Baskervilles* (1902). Conan Doyle did not invent the myth of dark Dartmoor, neither are the risks entirely imaginary. Yet he is surely responsible for the persistence of this particular way of looking at one wild corner of a country where, in general, the landscape is groomed and tidied almost to the point of boredom. Conan Doyle did go to Dartmoor to do his field-work, but as Christopher Frayling points out, he was not a stickler for accuracy:

> …wild orchids do not flower on Dartmoor or anywhere else in mid-October, any more than bitterns, even then almost extinct, mate in the autumn; the bogs on the moor were nothing like the quaking slime of Grimpen Mire; Dr Watson's and Stapleton's descriptions… could fit almost any Gothic wasteland.

Conan Doyle stayed in comfort at the Duchy Hotel in Princetown, now the splendid and entirely to be recommended High Moors Visitor Centre. On his way back to London, the great man played cricket for the Incogniti at select Sherborne on 3-4 June, at the beautiful Lansdown Cricket Club ground in Bath on 5-6 June, and at posh Cheltenham on 7-8 June. They are rather different West Country landscapes to the one he conjured up in *The Hound of the Baskervilles*.

A key source for Conan Doyle lay twelve miles away from Princetown in Lewtrenchard in the form of an Anglican priest, the Rev. Sabine Baring-Gould. In 1900 Baring-Gould published *A Book of Dartmoor*. This gentleman seems to have been considerably under-employed on his parochial duties. In addition to writing the hymn "Onward Christian Soldiers", he wrote useful books about the topography of the West Country and about folklore. For a dozen years he collected folk songs through the length and breadth of Devon and Cornwall, published as *Folk Songs and Ballads of the West* (four volumes, 1889-91). He began to work with Cecil Sharp, who was a regular visitor to Lewtrenchard. For the revised 1905 edition of *Songs of the West*, Cecil Sharp took over as musical editor. The two men also collaborated on *English Folk Songs for Schools* in 1907.

Yet Baring-Gould's speciality was very tall and very unlikely stories. He brought the traditional "Widecombe Fair" into print, according to Frayling "the song which the Devon regiment sang as it marched against the Boers." For this we respect him; less so for his accounts of werewolves and other monstrous apparitions supposed to inhabit lonely places. There is a duality in Baring-Gould. For Frayling:

> *A Book of Dartmoor* was a plea for a certain kind of conservation, and a polemic in support of the efforts of the new Dartmoor Preservation Society to control "wanton trippers", over-zealous restorers, enclosing farmers, tin-miners and the military authorities who were turning the place into a shooting-range.

Yet Dartmoor became, for Conan Doyle and a large part of the English public, a symbol of physical and moral wilderness and chaos. Less than half a century later, T. S. Eliot in "East Coker" (*Four Quartets*, 1944) could appropriate the word "grimpen" (an imaginary name used by Conan Doyle) as meaning a bog or mire, but with all the overtones of horror, of "fear and frenzy" which it had acquired by then. He wrote:

> In the middle, not only in the middle of the way
> But all the way, in a dark wood, in a bramble,
> On the edge of a grimpen, where there is no secure foothold,
> And menaced by monsters, fancy lights,
> Risking enchantment.

It is a relief to turn to the words of Satish Kumar, whose 2008 film *Earth Pilgrim* set a new standard for what is possible in the much abused medium of television:

> I see the bees buzzing, collecting a little nectar here and a little nectar there. Never too much. Never a flower has complained that a bee has

taken too much nectar away. Nature in balance. But this balance is tipping. Human beings go to nature and take, take, take, until all natural resources are depleted. Honey bees never do that. If I can learn that lesson of frugality and simplicity, I will be learning the art of living.

Like the Wordsworths he is a great walker, a great observer, an ex-Jain monk who has exchanged walking round the deserts of Rajasthan in India for the green expanses of Dartmoor. Unlike Eliot's dark spiritualism, haunted by nightmare visions of violence and chaos, Kumar's view of Dartmoor in all its seasons is full of beauty, of potential, of the need to make peace *with* the earth in order that we can then have peace *on* the earth. It is a dream in the great tradition of Blake, of Gandhi, of Martin Luther King.

Let us, then, look again at Dartmoor. This is an ancient landscape, marking several thousand years of human activity. Ten thousand years ago, it was a densely wooded area, the haunt of hunter-gatherers, and there are still great stands of oak, as lovely in winter as in summer, as Kumar notes, with the yellow lichen and green moss coating their skeleton outlines. But in later Stone-Age times people made clearings in the woods for farming, built stone circles and avenues for ceremonial purposes and developed the simple clapper bridges which for many centuries enabled people to move around the moors and keep in touch with neighbouring communities. They also mined and traded tin, and from well before the Roman period traders came from the Mediterranean to both Cornwall and Devon to buy tin. In the first millennium AD Dartmoor became depopulated, but in the second millennium was repopulated. Much of the moor is common land, with a complex system of rights that sustains a certain way of life, a specific landscape—rights to cut and burn turf as fuel, to cut bracken for animal bedding, to graze ponies, sheep and cattle on the moor, all overseen by a manorial reeve. The National Park is thus the guardian of not just a great wilderness, but also as complex an economic and social system as one would find anywhere in Europe.

Dartmoor is also one of the world's great archaeological sites. Of course, many of the sites are only to be visited by those who are able and willing to walk quite long distances over moorland to reach them. Still others are within the military zone, which we shall return to in a moment. But one of the best sites, Merrivale, is a mere ten minutes' walk from a car-park on the B3357 Tavistock-Two Bridges road, with a regular bus service from Tavistock passing close by. There is a stone circle, a single standing stone (a longstone or *menhir*), cairns and an avenue of standing stones, the remains of burial mounds and signs of round houses (there are 5,000 of these on the moor), everything to suggest in fact a complex and well developed settlement. Add in the rather unusual spring combination of bright summer sunshine, a sky of purest, palest speedwell blue, a north-easterly winter gale, seven Dutch tourists determined to linger and twenty hikers who marched straight through the settlement looking neither to left nor to right, and you will get the impression of a special place on a special spring day. There was also the gorse, which flowers all winter and comes to a climax in spring—the gorse that the Swedish botanist Linnaeus first saw on Putney Heath in London and declared to be one of the greatest sights in nature. He would have loved the moors of the West Country. The ceremonial elements of this landscape would appear to be 4,000 years old, the round house remains only 3,500 years old; by that time, about 1500 BC, the site was already clearly recognized as a sacred one and the houses were carefully placed so as not to interfere with it. No-one knows, though everyone can have their own theory, what sacred rites may have taken place here, but the quiet Dutch tourists clearly felt that special aura of the place, even if the loud English walkers did not. The present author felt himself more inclined to the former than the latter, even stopping to count and photograph seven stony tors that can be seen protruding from the surrounding moorland.

Later periods are represented too at Merrivale. There are several abandoned quarries visible in the immediate vicinity. The track of the Princetown railway, the main traffic of which was granite and prisoners, can be seen marching across the hillside, following the contours. Alluvial tin was extracted from local streams. The nineteenth-century water leat still flows orange-red between the two pre-historic stone rows, and remarkably still provides a supply of pure water to the cottages at the bottom of Longash Hill. An upright stone continues the tradition of using granite slabs as markers; it is carved on one side with A for Ashburton, on the other T for Tavistock to mark a route between the two towns. One rather sad aspect of the history of Merrivale is its use in 1625 as a Plague or Potato Market. Bubonic plague was rampant in nearby Tavistock and supplies of food for the town were left here for the surviving inhabitants to collect. According to tradition, coins for payment were left in vinegar-filled jars, the vinegar acting as an antiseptic.

And so, by a circuitous route, we have returned to matters military. One third of the open moorland on Dartmoor, over 30,000 acres, is retained as military ranges by the Ministry of Defence, and not usually open to the public. Military use of the moor began during the Napoleonic and Crimean wars. From the 1890s there was a permanent camp and artillery range at Okehampton. During the Second World War, nearly all the open moorland was used for training purposes: draw a rough triangle between Okehampton, Lydford and Princetown, and the size of the present three sets of ranges becomes apparent. Under the 1985 Dartmoor Commons Act, most of this land is common land, but there is only public access when the ranges are not being used; since additionally, walkers and riders have to be on constant lookout for the possibility of unexploded ordnance, and tolerate the visual intrusion of military markers and the occasional low-flying aircraft, it sounds less than an attractive proposition.

As in South Dorset, the army works hard at its public relations, maintaining a website, explaining the military rationale behind its activities and the (dubious) environmental advantages of its occupation of the moor. The aim of the National Park Authority is to free Dartmoor from live firing, but even this limited aim is not universally supported. A public consultation revealed a majority of only 52 per cent against the practice of live firing on the moor. Passions run high. One particular part of the military's public relations deserves further comment: the Ten Tors Challenge, promoted by the army for groups of young people looking for a challenge. This involves hiking between 35 and 55 miles across rough moorland in two days, navigating via ten tors on the way. Each year several thousand teenagers are involved. In 1996 a total of 2,100 of the 2,400 competitors had to be evacuated from the moor after a blizzard. In 2007 a young woman was killed during a training hike, swept away in a stream swollen by heavy rain. Perhaps, after all, that dark, depressing image of Dartmoor promoted by Sabine Baring-Gould, Conan Doyle, the prison and the army may still contain an element of truth.

THE ENGLISH RIVIERA AND DARTINGTON

It is time for further mention of the Great Western Railway. West of Exeter, Dartmoor presses southwards and there is no obvious lowland route towards Plymouth and Cornwall. Brunel, always the showman, decided to make a virtue out of necessity. The Great Western strikes first due south from Exeter, down the west bank of the Exe, past the pretty little ferry village of Starcross. There are water-meadows and cows protected by a stout sea-wall. There are mud-flats at low tide and this estuary is an important wintering site for birds. Herons wait patiently for tide and fish, while Exmouth sparkles across grey waters. From Dawlish Warren right down to Teignmouth, the railway carves out a line along the sea-wall itself, occasionally flashing into short tunnels in the crumbly red cliffs. It was a bold gesture, and is one of the most photographed stretches of railway in the world, but one that looks increasingly perilous. Every few years the winter storms cut the line and every few years it is patched up. But with climate change, rising sea levels and increasingly severe winter storms, this cannot go on. Even in my lifetime, the red cliff stacks off Dawlish have diminished. Perhaps the next cutting of the line will be the final *coup de grace*, and the railway will have to seek a new inland route. Meanwhile, it struggles on.

And so to Totnes on that lovely river, the Dart. It is tempting to write "that loveliest of English rivers", but everyone has their favourite and such judgements are rhetorical rather than truthful. The Dart introduces us to the sunken river valleys which litter the coastline all the way down into Cornwall—the Dart, the Avon, the Erme, the Yealm, the mighty Tamar that for much of its length separates Cornwall from the rest of England, and then in Cornwall the Looe River, the Fowey, the Fal and the Helford River. Each estuary is tidal, each is loved by birds (herons, kingfishers, egrets) and boat people. Much of the time the woods come steeply down to the waters. They are rivers best seen from the water, for often the river hides behind a curtain of trees and treacherous steep banks. But for the moment we shall turn our backs on these tidal waters and look upstream. Totnes is a fine, busy town, full of shops, proper shops. You can shop down the whole great length of its main street and visit a castle and a church as you do so. The houses here battle with the weather: tile-hanging, colour-washed rendering, painted weatherboard—anything to keep the weather out. There are real butchers, whole foods, clothes, fruit and vegetables, New Age paraphernalia and books. It feels like a town, and is deservedly busy.

There is no doubt that Totnes has benefited not just from the visitors attracted by its shops and its restored steam railway (the Dart Valley) but from the presence a few miles upstream of Dartington Hall and its various educational and cultural activities. The story of Dartington begins in 1925 with its purchase by Leonard Elmhirst and his American heiress wife Dorothy. They took over an estate sharing the general poverty of rural England between the wars. They wanted Dartington to be an exemplar of rural regeneration as preached by the Indian writer Rabindranath Tagore, but there was no unified business plan: weaving, forestry, sawmills, the-atrical and musical productions were piecemeal moves towards a broadly conceived end. Leonard Elmhirst's views on agricultural modernization, which aimed to make rural lives more sustainable, would scarcely feature in a textbook on sustainable agriculture today: he introduced the battery methods of rearing hens, he pressed mechanization, he tore out hedges to increase field-sizes. On the other hand, his forestry would be regarded as a model of sustainability: timber grown on the estate, processed at a timber-mill on the site, and then used as a building material by a build-ing firm set up on the estate.

The arts were important from the beginning at Dartington—there was dance (Dorothy Elmhirst herself danced), there was music, there was Bernard Leach and pottery. All these different activities were (and are) held together by the Dartington Hall Trust. But above all there was the school. The school began with Dorothy's three children who came over from the United States after her marriage to Leonard. They were joined by children of workers on the estate, and of artistic *émigrés* from Central and Eastern Europe driven into exile in the 1930s. Sean O'Casey, the Irish dramatist, moved to South Devon so that his children could attend Dartington, two sons as boarders and then a daughter as a weekly boarder. Dartington Hall rapidly acquired an international reputation as a progressive school, its philosophy reflecting that of the estate—respecting and developing needs and talents of individuals within a supportive community. The children contributed to the domestic work of the school, engagingly described as "useful work", and took their studies seriously, which did not happen in all progressive schools of the period. The education may have been child-centred, but there was an expectation that children would take advantage of the high-quality opportunities available to them, and be concerned with the common good. Nothing was too good for the school. William Lescaze, a Swiss-American architect working in the International Modern style, was employed to design High Cross House for the headteacher, Bill Curry. He also designed boarding accommodation for the students, and pigsties on an estate farm. Furniture for the single study-bedrooms was purchased at Heal's. At the other end of the design spectrum, the medieval Great Hall was lovingly restored, using timber from the estate. Of course, the war changed a great deal at Dartington; the disappearance of the lavish provision of domestic staff was the seedbed for "useful work" which proved not only practical but also educational, teaching practical skills and respect for property and the environment, and so became a permanent feature of the school.

From the 1920s through to the 1960s Dartington Hall School was a kind of utopia in a decidedly sub-utopian world. It is described as such by former pupils and teachers. In the 1970s and 1980s the memories change. Some of these later pupils had already been in trouble at expensive private schools and were sent to Dartington Hall as a school-of-last-resort. Freedom became taken for granted, rather than a privilege which in turn demanded (at least expected) in return commitment and a sense of responsibility. It proved difficult to find leaders of the calibre of Bill Curry, or of Hu and Lois Child who had succeeded him as joint heads in 1957. Relations with local people deteriorated over issues such as nude bathing and adolescent sexuality. Finally in 1987 the school closed. But Dartington itself was far from finished. One of its most distinguished old boys, Michael Young, for fifty years a trustee of the Dartington Hall Trust, wrote of the lasting influence of the school:

> I have been working for most of my life from the branch office of Dartington that I set up in Bethnal Green in East London [the Institute for Contemporary Studies, founded 1952] from which with Dartington support have originated the Consumers' Association and the magazine *Which?*…, the Advisory Centre for Education…, the National Extension College and the Open University… and the College of Health.

It is a formidable achievement for a restless young man taken under the wing of the Elmhirsts in the 1930s.

Dartington lives on, not just in the fine buildings to be seen on the estate, but in its Arts Centre, its College of the Arts, its International Music and Literature festivals, its shops in the old Cider Press building, its summer schools, and its ability to change and to generate controversy. In Totnes it has an interest in Totnes Books. In far away North Devon there is the well-known Dartington Glass factory in Great Torrington. Less well-known outside the West Country is the work of the Beaford Arts. There is a residential centre at Beaford, near Torrington, but drama and musical events are organized each year in villages from Lynton on the Somerset border to Holsworthy on the Cornish frontier. The work at Beaford included the seventeen-year project of James Ravilious in the 1970s and 1980s to document in black-and-white photography the lives and work of North Devon people. Both Dartington Glass and Beaford were a response to post-Second World War social and economic conditions in North Devon that mirrored the decay the Elmhirsts had found in South Devon in the 1920s.

Satish Kumar is a frequent lecturer at the Schumacher College at Dartington, which is addressing the old issue of rural regeneration but in ways which recognize that the earth's resources are finite and must be cared for. Robin Tanner was a friend of the Elmhirsts and taught many weekend and longer ten-day courses at Dartington on the place of the arts and crafts in education, thus neatly linking two of Dartington's main interests down the years. In his autobiography Robin Tanner describes his first visit to Dartington in the early 1950s as "a deep and lasting influence upon me and ultimately on Heather and Dietrich too." Dietrich Hanff was their adopted German Jewish son who became a primary school teacher. Over the years Tanner taught many courses there, linking practising teachers with practising craftspeople such as Phyllis Barron the block-printer, or Lucie Rie and Bernard Leach, the potters. He remembers especially Sunday evenings in the Great Hall, when Heather Tanner would give talks, illustrated by readings by Robin extracted from the commonplace books both kept for many years. "Dartington," he wrote, "which had so much to give, also somehow exacted the highest standards from us all." It is exactly what those early students of Dartington Hall School felt about it too. Dartington courses lived long in the memories of those fortunate enough to experience them.

Chapter Nine

NORTH DEVON

This afternoon as I swam there, alone, a family of kingfishers flew through the arches of the bridge, seven young ones and two parent birds. It was as though the sun-bow was broken up, enlarged, made animate. The young ones were not so brightly coloured as their parents, whose backs were a copper-flame sapphire green. They cried out when they saw me, a keen hard whistle, and sped away immediately, followed, after hesitated flying around the pool, by the seven young ones.

Henry Williamson, *Goodbye West Country*, 1938

BOUNDARIES

North Devon includes the fringes of both Exmoor and Dartmoor and a great swathe of country based on three great rivers all beginning with the letter "T". Of these, two are wholly in Devon, which comes as somewhat of a relief. The Torridge flows north through Great Torrington to the sea at Bideford. A little further to the east, the Taw drains the western slopes of Dartmoor, reaching the sea at Barnstaple, and then joining with the Torridge to create a large estuary banked by mud-flats and sand-dunes.

The third great river is the Tamar, which for most of its course from near the cliffs of North Cornwall to the sea at Plymouth, forms the boundary between Cornwall and Devon. We might also mention its junior partner, the Tavy, draining the south-western flanks of Dartmoor. The whole area of the Taw/Torridge basin has been colonized by Henry Williamson—or, to be fair to that author, by his literary creation, Tarka the Otter. Williamson's home was at Georgeham, north of Braunton on the north bank of the Taw estuary. Tarka, on the other hand, roams the area at will, and thus justifies the appropriation of this whole area as "Tarka country". The railway line between Exeter and Barnstaple has become the Tarka Line, while the Tarka Trail, itself incorporating some of the closed lines in the area, covers 180 miles in a giant figure of 8 centred on the market town of Barnstaple.

How far this identification of the whole area with Williamson's watery world is justified is up the reader and the visitor to judge. Certainly in these pages we shall be mentioning others who have passed this way and deserve a note in our cultural history. We shall examine in a little more detail whether the strengths of Williamson as a writer are or are not diminished by his weaknesses as a man. This would not be an issue if we were intruding into a private life. But some of the events in which Williamson was involved were very public events, as we saw in Chapter Four over the death of T. E. Lawrence. Further, Williamson wrote about them and placed at least a partial version of them in the public domain. Thus we shall be concerned with his deserved reputation as a writer of imaginative fiction, as an inspiration to many to become involved with natural history and the protection of wildlife. But we shall also be concerned with how his public stances bear on his reputation as a writer.

A wide view of what we might mean by "North Devon" comes from a journey along the thirty-nine miles of the Exeter-Barnstaple line, which links North Devon to the London to Plymouth and Penzance main line. Indeed, this is so far from London that it is possible to arrive in Barnstaple in time for breakfast by catching the overnight sleeper train from Paddington. This countryside, especially in early spring, contains so much of the quintessence of Devon—a quiet, undramatic landscape, well populated by animals, birds, flowers and villages. The only town of any size comes early—Crediton, once the seat of the Bishops of Devon. But that was a long time ago, over a thousand years in fact, and Crediton is happy to be a quiet little market and commuter town, with a prize-winning café in the railway station buildings that serves not just rail travellers but locals too in search of tea and home-made cakes and sociable chat with their friends. It is only February, and some of the water-meadows are still flooded from the winter rains (which is, after all, what water-meadows are for, rather than for building houses). But the snowdrops and primroses are blooming along the hedgerows, the first lambs with their absurdly long and fluffy tails are finding their feet in the fields. There are plenty of field-trees, skeletal and grey against a blue sky. It could be summer but most of these careful trees will wait another two or even three months to burst into leaf.

The train jolts and rocks and grumbles up to the summit at Copple-stone—this is not luxury travel by any means—and then gathers speed for the long descent down the valley of the Taw. This is one of Tarka's rivers, a lively, rushing river tumbling over stones and gravels, gradually slowing to a mature slate-blue stream winding its way through water-meadows to reach the muddy waters of the estuary at Barnstaple. The country is opening out, startled sheep run foolishly away from our noisy advance

Pannier Market, Barnstaple

which is now unstoppable until we hit the Barnstaple buffers. The catkins dangle enticingly from the hazel bushes, there are white-washed farm-houses with slate roofs, stone bridges and always the grey-green of the woods. Occasionally flashes of something brighter too, not just primroses, but gorse bushes on the rougher ground, a pink camellia in a cottage garden, a pheasant on a field of winter wheat.

Barnstaple is a famous town. And not the least of Barnstaple is its enormous covered Pannier Market. There are similar structures in most North Devon towns, but this is the biggest and the best. The general markets on Thursday, Friday and Saturday are the liveliest, mixing local produce with plants and flowers, shoes and books, crafts and bric-a-brac. Friday has always been the most popular day, a market the roots of which can be traced back 800 years. The stately current building, like the row of shops opposite called Butcher's Row, dates from 1855. It is a quin-tessential building of the Victorian railway age, a long hall with a central nave of iron columns and girders supporting clerestory windows that infuse the bustling scenes below with a sympathetic natural light. With the building of the new market, the High Street where previously the stalls had been set out each market day, was improved with fine Victo-rian façades, often hiding much earlier interiors. Barnstaple's other Vic-torian iron relic—the curving line of the railway viaduct that led the railway across the sometimes turbulent, sometimes flaccid tidal waters of the Taw and onwards to Ilfracombe—was blown up in 1976. No longer is it possible to experience the frightening trip across the Taw in flood. With the closure of the Ilfracombe line, the bridge had become ex-pendable, and the railway now terminates in an industrial estate south of the river. Such was the twentieth-century notion of progress. Fortu-nately the old Barnstaple Town station on the north bank has survived, together with its signal-box, splendidly renovated as a special school. The removal of the railway bridge has left the view clear for the town bridge, ancient stone, much rebuilt, such that every arch is supposed to be different.

The fame of Barnstaple is best seen in its museum and heritage centre. Indeed, North Devon is a land of good museums. Regretfully, we shall not have space to describe them in detail, but Bideford, South Moulton, Braunton and Fremington Quay are all worth a second look, no doubt to be joined by Great Torrington when it re-opens as a heritage centre. What comes over in all these towns is the status of North Devon as a trading depot. Wool and cloth-making was based partly on local production, but wool was also imported from Ireland, and finished cloth exported to Europe. Likewise, the pottery made from estuarial clays was traded to Wales, Ireland, Northern Europe and eventually to North America. Barnstaple was a law unto itself. It did not receive a charter until 1556 but behaved as if it did have one, claiming the charter had been lost, despite threats and visitations from London. Privateering, which most visitors would call piracy, was a popular activity; the town still prefers the term "privateering" as suggesting an element of state sponsorship rather than mere law-breaking. Fishing was important too, the boats working as far away as Newfoundland. Much of the catch was salted, not for home consumption but for export to France and Spain, where the Catholic Church insisted that Friday fish was a central tenet of the faith. As the estuary silted up, trading and fishing moved downstream to Bideford, Appledore and Clovelly, but even in winter, with few if any tourists in evidence, Barnstaple remains a lively and effervescent little town.

Barnstaple may be remote, but like so many fine old West Country towns it is central to our national history. In the seventeenth century, the merchants, the leading citizens, were staunch Protestants and parliamentarians, unlike South Moulton and Torrington which were both royalist strongholds. Barnstaple was occupied twice by royalists, the first time expelled by a popular rebellion of the townsfolk, the second time by the arrival of General Fairfax's invincible army. In 1685 French Huguenot refugees flocked to Barnstaple from La Rochelle, for centuries one of its main trading partners. And then came John Gay, born in 1685 and a pupil at the Grammar School. A bright boy, Gay became secretary to the Duchess of Monmouth. This good woman, betrayed more by her husband's infidelities than his politics, had her estate seized by the revengeful James II but restored by William and Mary. Gay knew Alexander Pope, and was always in search of rich patrons, although increasingly acquainted with the seamier side of London life. He wrote copiously, but is remembered for one great work, *The Beggar's Opera*. It was first performed in 1728, and Hogarth painted scenes from it. Lavinia Fenton, who played Polly, was much admired by the Duke of Bolton. (And yes, dear reader, she married him.) Gay wrote 69 songs, using tunes from popular songs and dances, which obviously contributed to its success. Within four years he was dead, and Pope, ever the loyal friend, was a pall-bearer and wrote a few lines of epitaph:

> Of manners gentle, of affection mild
> In wit, a man, simplicity, a child

If only all our complicated, messy lives could be summed up so eloquently!

CHARLES KINGSLEY COUNTRY

Just north-west of Bideford, facing due west out to the Atlantic swell, lies Westward Ho! This is a good bathing beach, and a less good surfing beach, more popular with local surfers than with those who come from London and Birmingham in search of perfect waves. There are some beach-huts, shops and accommodation. To tell the truth, it is a nondescript place, but why is it here and why the curious name and the even more curious exclamation mark? Westward Ho! is the only town or village in England with such curious punctuation, and is probably the only town or village named after a book. The author was Charles Kingsley, novelist, Christian and Westcountryman.

Kingsley was born at Holne, a lovely village on the southern, sunny fringes of Dartmoor, with views one way of the tors of the high moor, and the other way distant glimpses of the English Channel. His father was the vicar there. But it was perhaps his father's time as vicar of Clovelly (1830-36) that influenced the then teenage Kingsley the most. Clovelly now is the chocolate-box image of the seaside village, a village that you have to pay to get into at all, with a single steep street plunging down to a tiny harbour. But harbour it is, the only safe haven between the Taw estuary and Boscastle in Cornwall. It was here that Kingsley learned to love the sea and the life of boats and sailors that were the true inspiration for *Westward Ho!* A full account of Kingsley's life is impossible here, but we should note in passing the influence on the young clergyman's life of the Evangelical movement within the Church of England, of the Christian Socialism of F. D. Maurice, of Muscular Christianity (he preferred to call it Christian manliness) and of Thomas Carlyle. As a boy, Kingsley had experienced at first hand the power of the mob in the 1831 Bristol riots, and his was the path of reform rather than of revolution, very much in the tradition of Hannah More. His best-known work, *The Water Babies*, was a plea for an end to the employment of young children in the chimney-sweeping trade.

So what of the 1855 novel *Westward Ho!*, a tale of Elizabethan seago-ing? It is rather more readable than *Lorna Doone*, though no more to the modern taste in story-telling. Its opening paragraph evokes Bideford, the salmon and the two rivers. There was already a tradition for Williamson to draw on when he started to write about this area. This is the novel, above all, of the civilizing mission of colonialism and empire, in which Kingsley had a strong interest since his own mother had been born in Bar-bados, the daughter of a slave-owning sugar planter. So our hero Amyas gazes westwards towards Lundy:

> And as he stands there with beating heart and kindling eye, the cool breeze whistling through his long fair curls, he is a symbol, though he knows it not, of brave young England longing to wing its way out of its island prison, to discover and to traffic, to colonise and to civilise, until no wind can sweet the earth which does not bear the echoes of an English voice.

For empire read free trade, free movement of people, the spread of the Protestant faith.

A central interest of the book for the modern reader is Kingsley's treat-ment of the indigenous peoples of the Americas, where much of the action of the novel is set. Blacks and Indians are inferior but slavery itself is wrong, and the participation of English colonialists in slavery is seen as wrong. Captain John Hawkins is taken to be the originator of Britain's involve-ment in slavery, and there is a sad scene, obviously influenced by the long march of the abolitionist movement, in which the novelist imagines his mother's death: "Lady Hawkins bowed her weary head and died, the groan of those stolen negroes ringing in her ears, having lived long enough to see her husband's *youthful sin* become a national institution, and a *national curse* for generations yet unborn" (author's emphasis). Kingsley also at-tempts to contrast the "free" English with the slave-owning Spanish. When the English come across a line of chained slaves in the jungle ("naked, ema-ciated, scarred with whips and fetters"):

> ...a low murmur of indignation rose from the ambushed Englishmen, worthy of the free and righteous hearts of those days, when Raleigh

could appeal to man and God, on the ground of a common humanity, on behalf of the outraged heathens of the New World; when Englishmen still knew that man was God, and that the instinct of freedom was the righteous voice of God; ere the hapless seventeenth century had brutalised them also, by bestowing on them, amid a hundred other bad legacies, the fatal gift of negro-slaves.

Yet it is exactly the notion of a hierarchy of races, which was used to justify slavery, that pervades the novel. When Amyas first meets the naked Indian girl Ayacanora, his eventual wife, he identifies her as clearly paler than the "hundreds of those delicate-dark-skinned daughters of the forest". Kingsley goes on: "All the strange and dim legends of white Indians, and of nations of a higher race than Carib, or Arrowak, or Solimo, which Amyas had ever heard, rose up in his memory. She must be the daughter of some great cacique, perhaps of the lost Incas themselves—why not?" In an unlikely ending, this "Indian" heroine turns out to be English, or at least to have English blood, which presumably justified her marriage to our hero Amyas Leigh, sanctioned by his mother. Yet the fear of miscegenation is still there too; significantly, by the time they get together at the end of the novel, Amyas is blind, with its symbolic suggestion of impotence.

So what has this to do with the humdrum little tourist resort we see today? Precious little. It was the speculative builders who first thought of putting up villas here who considered that the name might be a good way to cash in on the success of the novel. Rudyard Kipling, another writer who tangled with the hard issues of race and empire, had the misfortune to spend four years of his boyhood here, as he recounts in *Stalky and Co.* (1899). He described it as "twelve bleak houses by the shore". It has improved, and the sands are still wonderful.

Henry Williamson at Home

From whatever point of view, the landscape of North Devon is among the richest in England. From the moors of Exmoor and Dartmoor a broad stretch of well-watered, fertile farmland stretches towards the sea. Only Yorkshire of English counties has more miles of roads than Devon, the vast majority of them traditional Devon lanes with high banked hedges and wonderful displays of flowers from spring through to autumn. Henry Williamson has a number of quite different ways of describing nature (landscape, plants and wildlife). In *Goodbye West Country*, a book we shall turn to in a moment, he restricts himself in general to a rather cool objectivity. In *Tarka the Otter* there is something more. This is a difficult book, which makes its enormous popularity even more surprising. The first edition was a private publication of only 100 copies in 1927. It was much reprinted in 1927-31, an illustrated edition was put out in 1932, and further editions have followed over the years. Disney tried to film it, but Williamson said no, and meant no. In 1979 the naturalist Gerald Durrell wrote a screenplay for a film narrated by Peter Ustinov. The viewpoint is always that of the wildlife. In the first sentence we are introduced to the heron Old Nog. Other named creatures occur in the book: Tarka himself, the rapacious otter hound, Deadlock, who killed Tarka's mother. There is Halcyon the kingfisher, quite different from the more naturalistic description of kingfishers that heads this chapter:

> It may have been that the Quill Spirit had painted the bird with colours stolen from rock and leaf and sky and fern, and enriched them by its fervour, for the bird's feet were pinker than the rock veins in the cleaves of Dartmoor, his wings were greener than opening buds of hawthorn, his neck and head were bluer than the autumn noonday sun, his breast was browner than bracken.

Yet the background is the life, and more often than not the death, of many thousands of unnamed creatures. And this killing is not just for food, since Williamson makes it clear that otters can kill for sport, for fun, just as men kill otters for similar reasons. Williamson is unflinching in his intention to present the realities of nature. He shows animals at play, at rest, at work, travelling, mating, rearing young. It is surprising that such an unrelenting portrayal of nature red in tooth and claw became such a favourite among children, though no doubt edited (expurgated, to be more frank) versions by publishers such as Puffin must have helped. Here surely is the secret of Williamson's success—the ability to present nature in human terms, while at the same time emphasizing that nature has its own social rules that are very different from those of human beings.

Goodbye West Country is in many ways the more interesting of the two books for the adult reader. It centres on the events of the 1930s, during the period of Williamson's intense interest in Hitler, and before his departure for Norfolk where he had a relatively unsuccessful career as a farmer. Williamson presents here his views on Hitler as the "Leader" who is going to prevent a repetition of the disaster of the First World War—he writes movingly of the Christmas truce on the Western Front in 1914 (a talk rejected by the BBC). He also includes in the book criticism put to him about his views: "I am all for you when it comes to salmon and otter but violently opposed to your ideas of the great Mr Hitler" (an editor) or: "The spectacle of one of our more sentimental writers enjoying a sort of vicarious toughness by becoming (at a safe distance) the evangelist of the rubber truncheon is among the more interesting manifestations of current literature" (an article in *The Bookseller*). Williamson can also be very funny. He writes of *Lorna Doone*: "There are three things read more or less regularly in the large outlying district of the moor—*Holy Bible*, *The News of the World*, and *Lorna Doone*. The Bible supplies the spiritual needs, the newspaper supplies the human interest, and *Lorna Doone* supplies the summer flow of visitors."

But what of Williamson's own "human interest"? Opposite page 216 of *Goodbye West Country* is a photo of two women on the sands at Woolacombe, still one of the loveliest of the North Devon beaches. They are identified as Ann and Loetitia. We know that Loetitia was his wife and the mother of his children. But who is this Ann? He writes that "Loetitia and Ann are here, with all the children…" What he does not explain is that Ann is in fact Mfanwy, daughter of Edward Thomas. Mfanwy had sought out Williamson, feeling that his experiences of senseless slaughter in the First World War mirrored those of the father she had lost, had scarcely known. Williamson took her on as his secretary, and soon his lover. Both Mfanwy Thomas and her mother Helen Thomas wrote Williamson out of their respective memoirs. But Mfanwy left a published account of her first meeting with Williamson, imagining that her own father must have been like him: "so alive, with such a sense of fun, so interested in everything, and yet, in moments of silence, changing so rapidly, as though the world of 1914-18 were coming back…" The relationship dragged on, as did the marriage; finally in 1948 Williamson divorced Loetitia and took as his second wife a teacher from Bideford. It must have been very distressing. The only person who has come close to being frank about these matters is Williamson's daughter-in-law, Anne Williamson. From her we learn that in September 1933 two children were born to Williamson, one to each of the two women within a week of one another. Williamson was away renewing an acquaintance with a sixteen-year-old girl in Torcross.

For a family biographer, Anne Williamson is extremely frank. Her very title, referring to Williamson as the "last Romantic", reveals this. She sees him as incapable of reconciling his fantasies with the reality of the people around him, both in his relationships with women and with "great men". She points to the influence on Williamson of the mystical Romanticism of Wagner, Francis Thompson, Shelley and Richard Jefferies. She writes: "Henry Williamson uses all the symbols connected with the Romantics over and over again: death, darkness, wild scenery, the search for idyllic love, a surreal presence of the other world." When he appeared on the radio programme *Desert Islands Discs* in 1969, his final record was the *Liebestod* from Wagner's "Tristan and Isolde" and his book was Jefferies' *Story of My Heart*.

Of course, Williamson was not alone in his admiration of Hitler in the 1930s. Lord Rothermere wrote in the *Daily Mail* on 4 June 1935:

> The most prominent figure in the world today is Adolph Hitler. His master-mind magnetises the whole field of foreign politics… I am profoundly convinced that the better he is known to the mass of the British nation the higher its appreciation of him will be and the closer will become the relations between the two nations.

Williamson was heavily influenced by the aristocratic Etonian Nazi sympathizer John Heygate. Heygate had written as early as 1931 in an article about "pride of race", which is seen as uniting individuals and state, that "there are innumerable young men like me who are waiting for a great leader." It was Heygate who paid for the two men to attend the Nuremberg rally in 1935. But whereas Heygate changed his mind about Hitler and fascism, Williamson never publicly recanted his view of the *Führer* though he did come to see him as a "Fallen Angel". At this point in her book, Anne Williamson struggles with her own honesty. On the one hand she claims that Henry Williamson was not a fascist, but a naïve man who did not really understand politics. On the other hand, she admits that Williamson was a member of the British Union of Fascists, and that he published eight articles in the BUF journal *Action* during 1938-39. In June

1940 he was arrested and held for several days (Oswald Mosley was already in prison). His children suffered taunts at the village school they attended in Norfolk.

Yet it is also clear that Williamson, still traumatized by his experiences of the First World War, sincerely wanted Anglo-German *rapprochement* and peace. He wrote in *Goodbye West Country* that "Most people are the same as in 1914-1918", i.e. in favour of war, anti-German, "corroded by mental fear". But in backing Hitler, Mosley and the BUF he had simply backed the wrong horses. Perhaps it is kinder to remember another Williamson, the countryman, the naturalist, the writer who inspired so many adults and children to love the countryside that surrounded them. In 1973 it was Williamson who gave the address at the funeral of another great English naturalist, Kenneth Allsop, at Powerstock church in Dorset. It was money raised by the Kenneth Allsop Memorial Fund that supported the purchase of Steep Holm in the Bristol Channel as a bird sanctuary and permanent memorial to Allsop. Allsop's daughter Mandy returned the compliment by reading extracts from Williamson's own writings at a memorial service in London after his death in 1977. The address was given by the poet Ted Hughes. Williamson is buried in Georgeham churchyard, amid the serene quiet of the North Devon countryside that he taught generations of English people to love.

LANDSCAPE, ECOLOGY AND LOVE

During the 1930s Laurence Whistler, who was beginning to emerge from the shadow of his flamboyant elder brother Rex, met a young actress named Jill Furse. Like Whistler, she wrote poetry, a craft in which she had been encouraged by her grandfather Sir Henry Newbolt. What followed was one of the most poignant love stories of the twentieth century, which Whistler set down thirty years later as *The Initials in the Heart: A Celebration of Love*. The telling of the story was only made possible by Jill's early death from a blood infection just after the birth of their second child in 1944, towards the end of the Second World War. Their marriage more or less coincides with the war, and for most of the time they lived apart, so there were plenty of letters from which to reconstruct this emotional journey. In addition, both partners set down their feelings in verse.

Rex Whistler was best man at their quiet wedding at Salisbury Cathedral in the summer of 1939, with war imminent. By now the Whistler brothers' parents were settled at the Walton Canonry in the Close. Guests included Siegfried and Hester Sassoon, and Jill's grandmother Margaret Newbolt. Love finally allowed Laurence to, as it were, untangle himself from his brother. When he joined the army, he chose not to be commissioned into the same regiment as Rex. He wrote: "I had built with someone else a world quite different from his." The couple settled not in Wiltshire but near Jill's own family home in North Devon, in an isolated cottage near a hamlet called Halsdon. The nearest village was Dolton, on a tributary of the Torridge, where her parents lived. This, then, was the scene of brief interludes of happy togetherness. Laurence remembered it as an idyll, strongly contrasting with the frustrations and tedium of army life, and the emotional roller-coaster of Jill's continuing attempts to reconcile a serious, if undiagnosed, illness with a career on the London stage:

> So here, while the sun was still rising, we may have idled on the top of our world; but soon we dropped down through slender oaks, light-flashing with cobwebs, down by zig-zag bends, and out on to the open floor of a valley so solitary that I have often swum and run, worked and picnicked, naked all day. It is a valley of the salmon and the otter—Tarka passed through it on his travels—and of the buzzard, lazily pivoting high above, with stretched wings that are marbled when they catch the sun and all but transparent when it shines through them.

It is a scene of fable, a scene, perhaps, from Samuel Palmer: "Palmer spoke for our gratified twilights; the lineaments of our valley, like the shape of our living, would have won his approval, I think." The couple lived simply and happily, in a relationship that that was the obverse of the scenes enacted by the Williamsons' *ménage* in North Devon a few years previously. Quotations from Jill's letter, of her life in the cottage alone with her first baby, have an almost George Herbert quality about them in the intense pleasure she takes in "the daily round, the common task". And at the end of it all, at the end of so much tragedy, is that sense that Laurence Whistler shared with T. S. Eliot, that in some obscure way that is beyond human understanding, "all shall be well."

War and separation made the beauty more acute, the relationship that much more intense:

> Simplicity of living, happiness, beauty of season and place, came to-
> gether in extraordinary contrast with the anguish of the western world…
> It seemed as though the west had been suffocated by bad habits, an ap-
> palling accumulation of greeds and illusions, and thus driven mad—
> that it would disintegrate if it would not undergo a spring-cleaning to
> rediscover the shape and purpose of life.

The diagnosis is not unlike that of Williamson, but the political conclusions Whistler drew are quite distinct. He hated the snobbery and traditions of the officers' mess: "It woke a response in my natural radicalism; for
I was long-since impatient with the whole structure of the old class-ridden
England." He looked forward to change, to the 1945 General Election, in
a way that reflects the thinking of Richard Acland at the time, "a profound
revaluation". He was involved in the wonderful adult educational movement of the Army Bureau for Current Affairs, and included the Beveridge
Report (despite instructions to the contrary) in the discussions in his radio
unit: "For the first time in history young working-class men, with wonder
and cynicism, were being positively invited by 'the authorities' to weigh
and solve problems for themselves." Looking back twenty years later, he re-
gretted little of the pre-war world, "except a comparatively unspoilt countryside". "Modern Britain," he concluded, "is fairer." It is curious to find
such explicit politics buried within a love story, yet it clearly mattered to
Whistler.

GORGEOUS LYDFORD

> I oft have heard of Lydford Law
> How in the morn they hang and draw
> And sit in judgement after.
> At first I wondered at it much,
> But soon I found the matter such
> As it deserves no laughter.
>
> William Browne, "Lydford Journey", 1644

If much of North Devon is best accessed along the road and railway link
from Exeter, it may be preferable to head north from Plymouth through
Tavistock by bus or car to reach some of the western fringes. The main

road, the A386, skirts the fringes of Dartmoor, and some but not all of its length lies within the Dartmoor National Park. So does Lydford, although Lydford has little in common with the high moors which we described in the previous chapter—the setting for *The Hound of the Baskervilles*, Dartmoor Prison and the extensive remains of prehistoric people. At Lydford we breathe the first airs of Cornwall. The parish church, like many in Devon and Cornwall, is dedicated to a Celtic saint—St. Petroc. Twenty-seven churches in Devon and Cornwall are dedicated to him, as are one in Somerset and two in South Wales. He is also much venerated in Brittany. He may or may not have been a Welsh prince, but he certainly founded monasteries in sixth-century Cornwall, lived as a hermit near Bodmin and died in about 564. St. Petroc's is a fine church. But by the middle of the nineteenth century it was substantially in ruins, like so much else about Lydford. And then there was the West Gallery band and choir. It is the same old story that we told in Dorset (we omitted to mention that it happened at Moreton too)—a new vicar, the purchase of the organ, the ousting of the old music. Except that here the members decamped all together to the Bible Christian chapel. By 1872 the gallery in which they had worshipped God in their own musical idiom was tumbling down and removed completely.

Lydford is a town—well, a village now—that attracts all those who love to feel the rise and fall of history, of places once great cast down, of places cast down and then uplifted again. In pre-conquest times it was a strong place of the Saxons, a defence again the Danes in the east and the Celts in Cornwall, protected on two of its three sides by the gorge, of which more later. Its importance can be measured by the fact that it was one of four Devonian towns permitted to mint coins, using local silver, from 927 until it was sacked by the Danes in 997. The Danes went home content with their booty, and many Lydford coins are now on display in Scandinavian museums (Stockholm, especially) for this very reason. The Normans recognized immediately the defensive qualities of the site. By the end of the twelfth century, Lydford was an important town. The substantial remains of the keep can still be seen to the west of the church, except that its main function was always as a prison rather than a castle.

A major industry in Devon was tin-mining. The four stannary towns (Ashburton, Chagford, Plympton and Tavistock) controlled this trade. Transgressors against stannary law were shut away in this forbidding grey building at Lydford. Its reputation was terrible, as William Browne's poem suggests, and presumably this reputation was an important factor in enforcing the regulation of the trade. Those who suffered at Lydford were not just petty thieves or trespassers. In 1508 Richard Strode, MP for Plympton, spent three weeks in the dungeons at Lydford. He had complained that Dartmoor rivers were becoming polluted by the activities of the tin-streamers. The stannary towns objected, and their courts fined him £40 each and had him put in prison. The outcome is a curious and important one in the annals of English democracy; on his release, Strode successfully moved a bill in Parliament to ensure that in future MPs could speak their mind without threat of prosecution. In modern jargon, he had established the principle of parliamentary immunity.

Despite this long and proud history, what arrested the apparently terminal decline of Lydford in the nineteenth century was the railway. And with the railway came tourists. What the tourists came to see was not the town, or its church, or its prison, or its marker stones, but the gorge. Both the South Devon Railway (later Great Western Railway) and the London and South Western reached Lydford in the middle of the nineteenth century. At first the railways had very practical concerns, the transport of granite and metal ores to the docks at Calstock and Plymouth and of agricultural goods to markets in Plymouth and beyond. There were complications too, not least the adherence of the Great Western to Brunel's seven-foot broad gauge, the remains of which can still be seen used as fencing along the track of the long-defunct railway. Lydford acquired two stations, one for each company, next door to one another, and by 1890 Lydford Gorge was open for business, with the luxurious Manor Hotel catering for visitors from London keen to experience the wilds of Dartmoor and the picturesque charms of the gorge. All this history can still be appreciated at the "business" end of Lydford, a mile from the village centre. The centrepiece of the gorge, the Whitelady waterfall, was owned by the miller. He would collect sixpence from each visitor, allow sufficient time for them to descend into the gorge some 190 steps below, and then open the sluice gates to enhance the effect of tumbling water.

The hundred-foot waterfall falls into the gorge rather than through it. For those who like to draw out their pleasures or find steps difficult, there is a long, winding path down to the foot of the fall. This also means that the other sounds of the gorge—the breeze in the tree-tops, the sighing of

the young beeches reaching a climax and then fading, can be enjoyed, with the insistent plummeting of the fall kept for a while in the background. The Whitelady is a narrow, twisted white ribbon on a green background, for the rocks here are almost completely covered in ferns and lichens and flowers and small bushes. In spring, summer and autumn, the waterfall hides among the leaves of the trees that grow everywhere and in splendid disarray. From the fall, a path leads the mile through the gorge in the direction of the church and castle, to what in these days of National Trust ownership has become the main entrance, with tea-room and shop. If the River Lyd, flowing through the gorge, often appears brown in wet weather, this is because of the staining of peat from its source high on Dartmoor. At quieter times of year the water is crystal clear, the home of insects and dippers, those charming little brown-and-white birds which hop along the bank and then disappear under water to feed on insect larvae on the stream bed. There are herons and kingfishers too, in search of larger prey. Butter-flies flit through air, the trees are full of busy, noisy forest birds, it is almost as if someone had created a copy of paradise for human beings to enjoy.

At the Devil's Cauldron the water is squeezed between gloomy water-stained rocks on either side, polished into rounded, black forms by the constant action of the water. For those who venture along the often treacherous path clinging to the side of the rock-face, there is a reward. Ticker's Pool is a delightful, calm afterthought, light filtered from high above through the leaves of beech trees which begin bright and vividly green in spring and age to nut-brown by autumn. The water takes on shades of gold and turquoise, reflecting the light back onto the trees above, the composition structured by the black shadows from the tree-trunks falling across the pool. It is a place of grey wagtails, those most entertaining and companiable of wild birds, bobbing along the shingle bank, a place of peace and recollection and sensual enjoyment. It is the sort of place that makes you believe in the National Trust as guardian of our natural heritage.

LUNDY: ON THE EDGE OF THE WORLD

> It was a glorious sight upon a glorious day. To the northward the glens [combes] rushed down towards the cliff, crowned with grey crags, and carpeted with purple heather and green fern; and from their feet stretched away to the westward the sapphire rollers of the Atlantic, crowned with a thousand crests of flying foam. On their left hand, some ten miles to the south, stood out against the sky the purple wall of Hartland cliffs, sinking lower and lower as they treaded away to the southward along the lonely ironbound shores of Cornwall, until they faded, dim and blue, into the blue horizon forty miles away.
>
> Charles Kingsley, *Westward Ho!*

Such is Lundy. For Amyas and his crew of North Devon men from Clovelly, from Bideford, from Appledore and from Northam, Lundy is home, after their bizarre adventures in the Americas. Here are familiar rocks and familiar perils, familiar nature. But for the modern landlubber setting out from Ilfracombe or Bideford, Lundy feels like the unknown. For a start, it is distant. True, it is only eleven miles north of Hartland Point, but from Bideford or Ilfracombe it is 24 miles, a longer distance than the English Channel at its narrowest. Lundy is, at best, a smudge on the horizon, quite distinct from the ever-present form of Steep Holm in its brown estuarial waters. Yet Lundy is, by comparison, a relatively large

island, three miles long and half-a-mile wide, and as the cliffs and beaches of North Devon fade into the grey-green horizon, so the Dartmoor-grey, granite bulk of Lundy becomes a reassuring presence out to the north-west. For centuries Lundy served as a base for smugglers and pirates, a lawless fastness secured by the ocean and the weather from prying mainland eyes.

Things should have improved, when Thomas Benson, MP for Barnstaple, leased the island in 1750. But this was the unreformed parliament of ill repute, and Benson turned out to be as bad as any pirate. Smuggling continued, especially of tobacco from Virginia, as it had always done. Benson contracted to ship convicts to the Virginian colony, and many of these convicts only got as far as Lundy, where they were set to work on the inhospitable land. By 1793 there were seven houses and 23 inhabitants. Things did improve a little with the purchase of the island in 1834 by the Heaven family. Yet Lundy was still distant. The bishop brought over to consecrate the church in 1897 is credited with the awful pun "how difficult it is to reach the Kingdom of Heaven." He also claimed that his belief in purgatory had been reinforced by a particularly rough sea crossing. By this time quarrying was established on the sheltered east side of the island—on the west the birds still reigned supreme—but production ceased in 1868. The stone left around in the quarry, plus that used to build the quarry houses, was re-used in the 1890s for the church and the new lighthouse.

Eventually in 1969 the island passed to the National Trust who immediately leased it to the Landmark Trust. This interesting organization, which specializes in restoring rather unlikely historical monuments and financing them by letting to visitors, has made a remarkable success of Lundy. From March until October there are regular ferry services to the mainland, while in winter a helicopter service whisks passengers in just seven minutes from Hartland to Lundy. The various buildings at the southern end of the island—cottages, the old lighthouse and school—have been adapted as holiday lets. Apart from the lighthouse keepers, the main function of Lundy's small population is to service visitors. The heart of the community is the Marisco Tavern, providing not only food and drink, but also advice, information, a library, and good company. It is named after the De Marisco family who were lords of Lundy for several centuries after the Norman conquest.

Visitors come to Lundy for many reasons: for the isolation, for the scenery, or simply because it is there—but overwhelmingly for the wildlife. Stuck out in the Atlantic as it is, Lundy has a unique micro-climate that encourages the growth of many species that are rare elsewhere. Indeed, the strange-looking Lundy Cabbage is unique to the island. In summer the heathland that covers most of the island is bright with gorse and several shades of purple heather, and the trilling of skylarks can be heard above the shrill wind and the distant boom of breakers on the rocks. Some of the old quarries along the eastern side of the island have filled with water, their granite rock faces alive with honeysuckle, golden hair lichen and bracken. Where there is grass, it is jewelled with a thousand wild flowers. The balance is kept by wild goats, deer and ponies, and the half-wild Soay sheep, all introduced to Lundy in the twentieth century. On the wilder west and north sides of the island are the birds, and it is the birds that attract most visitors—the summer breeding sites on the cliffs of guillemots, razorbills, kittiwakes, storm petrels, Manx shearwaters, and the rather commoner herring gulls. Sadly, the puffins that are the most distinctive and emblematic of Lundy's inhabitants, and may well have given their name to the island, are at the extreme edge of their range and in decline. Besides its importance as a summer breeding-ground for seabirds, Lundy is also an important stop-over point for exhausted, migrant birds, boosting the Lundy bird-list to nearly 300 species.

Lundy's other environmental importance is maritime. In 1986 Lundy and the surrounding waters were declared Britain's first statutory marine nature reserve. In 2004 the eastern side of the island was designated a no-take zone in order to preserve and enhance stocks of marine life, such as lobster, crab and other shellfish. Diving has developed quickly as one of Lundy's major tourist activities. It is the only place around the coasts where all five British corals are found. Basking sharks are often seen around Lundy in summer. Grey seals breed in caves around the island and are often spotted both on the rocks and at sea. Like their Cornish cousins, they are inquisitive creatures who seem quite at home with human beings, and often nose down to see what the divers are up to. Lundy, finally, is a great place to watch the weather. From the Old Light, there is an unimpeded view of the Atlantic opening out with Wales on one side and Cornwall on the other. With a front approaching, there is grey upon grey upon grey of intermingled sky and ocean. It is time for Cornwall.

Chapter Ten

CORNWALL: PAINTING A PICTURE

Cuntelleugh an brewyon us gesys na vo kellys travyth (Gather up the fragments that are left that nothing be lost).

The Federation of Old Cornwall Societies

Cornwall starts very well indeed. Brunel's Royal Albert bridge across the Tamar is as splendid as anything he built, poetry in tubular steel, two great spans high above the waters of the river Tamar, the boats and houses like toys in a children's nursery far below and the miniature Tamar Valley line heading north on the Devon bank. Constructed in 1859, this single track bridge was the first connection between Plymouth and Cornwall that did not involve taking to the water. There is plenty of time to admire the bridge from the train. At the Plymouth end, the track does an almost right-angle bend, with a 15mph speed limit, and Brunel's signature states unequivocally: "I K Brunel. Engineer, 1859." (The year of his death.) A couple of miles south, hard by the enormous and flourishing Royal Naval dockyards, the Torpoint ferry still does a busy trade. But it is Brunel's neighbour, the new road bridge, completed in 1961, that has at last created a viable road link between Plymouth and Cornwall—an alternative to the tedious A30 route via Okehampton in Devon to the old Cornish capital of Launceston. By comparison with Brunel's bridge, the new suspension road bridge looks very ordinary indeed.

If Cornwall has started well by train, it does not last. Everything goes more slowly west of Plymouth. From London Plymouth can be reached in four hours, but it takes another two to reach Penzance. Cornwall is steep and hilly and awkward, and the line has been allowed to deteriorate over the years; repairs and maintenance patch up the damage but still it deteriorates. Ironically, one of the reasons for the slowness of Cornish trains is that Cornwall has managed to retain at least some of its branch lines. So the train must stop at Liskeard for the Looe branch, where the train screeches to a halt in a field and the driver must change to the other end of the train to slide down towards the kingfishers and the twin towns of East and West Looe that span the estuary. At Par a line strikes up and over the lunar white landscape of the china clay workings to Newquay, Cornwall's surfing capital and preferred holiday destination of the newly affluent young. At Truro there is the little branch line down to Falmouth and its docks, before the main line takes a new twist and heads towards the tin-mining country of Camborne and Redruth, the moors scarred with the chimneys of old pumping engines, and the north coast. At St. Erth it is still possible to change for St. Ives, a survival that has contributed much to St. Ives in recent years, as a park-and-ride facility here serves to keep many cars out of the cramped but ambitious fishing village. Only then does the line turn back towards the south coast, the familiar outline of St. Michael's Mount and the wheeling gulls of the terminus at Penzance.

Clay and tin and fishing: twentieth-century Cornwall was about decline. Agriculture and ship-building also suffered. Only tourism remained relatively buoyant, but tourism provides mainly part-time and seasonal jobs and little full-time work. Although unemployment has fallen in recent years, in line with other parts of the south-west, earnings remain low, men in particular earning only about three-quarters of the national average wage. With large numbers of people, especially retirement pensioners, moving into Cornwall from "up country" in recent years, house prices have risen and housing for local people has become a pressing issue. Against this backdrop Cornwall's status as a priority area for European Union funding is of great significance, and this is one of the few parts of

England where the European Union flag will be seen flying on a regular basis.

Conversely, the other flag that will be seen is the white-cross-on-a-black-background flag of St. Piran. St. Piran is seriously old: his stone Celtic cross standing among the sand-dunes at Perranporth was old enough to be mentioned as a landmark in a charter issued by King Edgar in 960. Not so his flag, only adopted as the Cornish flag by nineteenth-century Romantic revivalists. It may (or may not) be related to the Breton Kroaz Du, which has the colours reversed—black on white—and does have lineage. The invention of the Cornish flag is thus contemporaneous with the Revd. Robert Hawker writing the Cornish anthem ("And shall Trelawny live?/And shall Trelawny die?/Here's twenty thousand Cornish men/Will know the reason why!") in 1825 and submitting it anonymously to a Plymouth newspaper, masquerading successfully as a seventeenth-century popular song.

BOOM AND BUST

Cornwall, then, is an old country with a problematic present and a dubious future. By the middle of the nineteenth century, it was very prosperous indeed, its mines producing tin, copper and a variety of other minerals, some of them very rare. Cornish engineers led the way in the development of beam engines to pump water out of the mines. What Cornwall lacked was coal. The ore was taken from Cornwall and smelted and worked elsewhere, so Cornwall never developed the range of production industries familiar in other parts of industrial England. But in 1866 there was a collapse in the world price of copper, as new mines were developed in other parts of the world such as Australia, Canada and South America. Tin overtook copper as the chief mineral extracted in Cornwall, with smaller quantities of arsenic, but by the 1870s Cornish mining was everywhere in retreat. It is another irony that the world-famous Camborne School of Mines dates from 1888, by which time the industry was in slump.

Along with industrial slump went population decline. As ever, it was the young and ambitious who went first. In 1851 John Deason of Tresco in the Isles of Scilly, married Margaret Davey in Penzance. By 1854 they had reached the other side of the world, and the gold-fields of the state of Victoria, in Australia. If life was hard for the miners, it was worse for their women and children. Four children were born to this marriage, and by 1858, when their mother died, all four were dead. Undeterred, John Deason married Catherine McAndrew, a Scot from Fife, in Bendigo in the same year. Both lived into the twentieth century as did ten of their eleven children, the last dying in 1956. John Deason became famous in 1869 when he uncovered the monster Welcome Stranger gold nugget, at that time the largest ever discovered. The majority of these pioneer miners in Bendigo were Cornish, and Bendigo, a handsome town in upstate Victoria, renowned for its fine public buildings, has not forgotten its Cornish connections. The Cornish Association of Bendigo was the moving force behind the erection of a fine brass monument dedicated to the Cornish Miner. It depicts the man at work, hewing a great slab of rock. The rock is polished on one side and reflects the clear blue Australian sky. It makes one wonder why so few such monuments exist in Cornwall itself.

The engine houses that litter the Cornish countryside are silent relics of a past age. Daphne du Maurier described engine houses such as Wheal Cotes (or Coates) on National Trust land at St. Agnes Head as "memorials to daring and to courage, to the spirit of the miner himself, undefeated in adversity and loss, braving the centuries past, the centuries to come, symbols of a Cornish heritage." The last mine, South Crofty, closed in 1998. Yet there are still those who think that, given the right world price for tin, Cornish mining might still have a future.

The Federation of Old Cornwall Societies is the guardian of the past in Cornwall. Its website strikes a more cheerful note than the rather gloomy account above: in order to enter the site, it is necessary to listen to fiddler Mike O'Connor playing the Duke of Cornwall's Reel. The first Old Cornwall Society was founded in St. Ives in 1920. Its successors have spread widely through the towns and villages of Cornwall, and serve as a link to the Cornish diaspora, especially in Australia and the western United States of America. Charles Causley found signs of them in the Mojave desert and wrote in his poem "Calico":

And the Cornish were here, their names like granite
Scoured by a century of sun,
The vanished voices hymning to Zion,
Hollowed out by the accents of home.

In more recent years, in addition to much worthy antiquarian research, the OCS has encouraged the revival of many old folk traditions in Cornwall, including the Midsummer Bonfires and the events in Helston, Padstow and Penzance that we shall come to later in this chapter. It has also encouraged the revival of a language that was considered dead, a Celtic language closely related to Welsh and Breton. And as in Wales and Brittany, there is a Cornish politics too. In recent years a nationalist party, Mebyon Kernow, has returned a number of councillors in local elections in Cornwall. Indeed, in local elections in 2007, it returned more district councillors in Cornwall (seven) than either the Labour Party (four) or the United Kingdom Independence Party (one). No Cornish politician of any party can ignore that sense of a special Cornish identity, of a Cornish dimension to every issue, that plays so strongly on the Cornish consciousness. Once Cornish and Breton fishermen could understand one another in their native tongues; now many Cornish towns and villages are twinned with communities in Brittany, expressing an ongoing Celtic solidarity.

Cornwall has entered the twenty-first century full of optimism. On the north coast, at Delabole, which claims a thousand-year history of slate mining, the company is back in local hands again after a management buy-out. There are wind turbines in the fields and a buzz of excitement in the air. But as Daphne du Maurier wrote over forty years ago in the last lines of *Vanishing Cornwall* (1967): "The challenge is to the young." Du Maurier was an outsider who settled in Cornwall, who made Cornwall her own, and contributed much to the culture, as we shall see in some detail in the next chapter. Such incomers are welcome in Cornwall, not least as an antidote to the stereotype of the outsider who takes everything and gives nothing back. Also back in the twentieth century, Charles Causley was writing about a Cornish school roofed with Delabole slates:

And I recall another voice. A teacher
Long years ago, saying, "I think I know
Where all the children come from, but the puzzle
To me is, as they grow up, where they go."
Love, wonder, marvellous hope. All these can wither
With crawling years like flowers on a stalk;
Or, to some piper's tune, vanish for ever
As creatures murdered on a morning walk.

So often it is the brightest and best who have left for careers "up country". The hope remains that some at least will stay, their love, wonder and hope intact. To work, perhaps, at some of the more exciting ventures that recent years have introduced into Cornwall: the Eden project with its geodesic domes bringing new life to the clay districts, the Maritime Museum by the docks in Falmouth, the Tate's outpost at St. Ives—all new additions to the magical Cornish landscape as a landscape of both work and leisure, of inward and outward flow, of national pride.

PAINTING CORNWALL: NEWLYN AND ST. IVES

> Nostalgia comes each spring in London, for the rain, for the mist, for the mud and dung, for thick shoes and a mackintosh, for the glory that is Cornwall, the mystic Cornwall that goes to people's heads and makes them a little queer. It has not the grandeur of many parts, much is not what is called "old world" or "picturesque". Much is sordid—ruins of tin-mines and shafts and corrugated iron roofs, but it seems actually haunted; ghosts have a habit of stalking abroad and calling on even the least imaginative of us.
>
> Laura Knight, *Oil Paint and Grease Paint*, 1936

Cornwall is full of painters and paintings. Yet that happy state of affairs only dates back a couple of hundred years. Previously painting had been the prerogative of the London-based aristocracy, only spreading out into "the provinces" in the context of country seats. All that began to change towards the end of the eighteenth century, the artistic equivalents of Wordsworth and Coleridge discovering the joys of life on the Quantocks. Painters began to travel, to seek out new subjects: nature, picturesque or sublime, the remains of earlier cultures and civilizations, the everyday life of country people. The West Country shared in this outward movement of artistic activity, and distant, little known, "foreign" Cornwall achieved pre-eminence in this field. Turner's watercolours are an especially rich source for this Romantic view of landscapes, worked up in the studio from notes and sketches that in some cases date back to the 1790s. He painted Launceston, looking like an Alpine hilltop town, exaggerating the rise and fall of the land. He worked up the naval dockyard at Devonport (without, of course, the bridges) as an allegory of peace, the sailors being paid off, the storm clouds clearing to reveal a golden evening light over the Tamar. The drama of marine life is reflected in "Entrance to Fowey Harbour, Cornwall", which depicts a ferocious storm and a shipwreck from which people are struggling to escape in small boats. "Longships Lighthouse, Lands End" shows the lighthouse glimmering in the distance, while the storm rages and the sea claims more victims. His painting of St. Michael's Mount juxtaposes the rocky ruins with local people breaking up and selling timber from a wrecked ship on the beach.

Samuel Palmer was also fascinated by the wild and desolate coastal landscape of Cornwall on visits in the 1840s and 1850s. He went to the Lizard and painted at Kynance Cove. But above all he went to North Cornwall where the north-south tilt of Cornwall produces some of the wildest, steepest cliffs in Western Europe. Like Turner, he painted storm and wreck, but he also painted the calm of the sheltered little harbour at Boscastle and the magical scenes of Tintagel, with its vivid association with Arthurian legend. Nothing that the tourist industry has been able to throw at Tintagel can alter the magic of this rocky fortress, part Celtic monastery, mostly Norman castle, and the secrets that it may harbour of the life and times of the "once and future King".

In 1859, when Brunel's Royal Albert Bridge was opened, Cornwall was still remote, yet more accessible than it had ever been. In France painters had begun to gather in rural colonies to paint landscape and scenes of peasant life in the open air. They gathered especially in Brittany, at Concarneau, Pont-Aven and Quimperlé. They were joined by artists of other nationalities too, including the English. These artists espoused naturalism, everyday realism. Eventually and inevitably, this movement reached England. In 1884 Stanhope Forbes settled at Newlyn, a fishing port just down the coast from Penzance. And there he stayed. Artists came and artists went, but Stanhope Forbes stayed for the rest of his long life, dying in 1947. Forbes painted above all the life of the shore, the fishermen, the women who did many of the tasks ashore, the children playing on the beach or around the boats. Forbes' paintings are busy pictures, full of activity and the light of what he called "this shining, mirror-like shore". Nor were his paintings restricted to Newlyn. The Penlee Gallery in Penzance also features pictures of Penzance, of St. Michael's Mount and of inland settings. Forbes was also conscious that all this activity, picturesque as it might have been, had an underlying economic importance. "Fish Sale on

a Cornish Beach", painted in 1885, gives a precise account of people's livelihoods, as well as being a "signature painting" for the twenty or so artists who came to constitute the Newlyn school. Painting at Newlyn was a very public activity, no doubt to the amusement and at times consternation of the locals. The Penlee collection includes a photo of Walter Langley painting on the quay with an audience of three men and two children. Langley was responsible for one of the most beautiful of all the Newlyn pictures, "The Sunny South". A gardener rests on his long-handled Celtic spade, the fruit trees are in flower, the cabbage-patch thickly populated, the village lies below, with the sea and the sky beyond. Forbes kept faith with naturalism. He painted scenes that reflect contemporary musical life, including "The Violinist", a portrait of Walter Barnes, founder of the Penzance Orchestral Society, and its conductor from 1907 to 1942. He painted women at work, sewing flags in "Against Regatta Day" and doing war-work in "The Munitions Girls" (1917), now in the Science Museum collection.

A gallery was opened in 1895, financed by the Cornish entrepreneur and philanthropist John Passmore Edwards, but by 1899 Newlyn needed fresh impetus. In that year Stanhope Forbes and his wife opened the Newlyn School of Painting. He had long taken a role in encouraging younger painting; now this was formalized and students taken on. A number of the students came and stayed, Ernest Proctor and his future wife Doris (Dod) Shaw among them. Forbes proved an excellent teacher, encouraging students who wanted to turn to other styles of painting in addition to promoting his own naturalism. The colony was not a closed affair; Samuel John (Lamorna) Birch, whose name became so synonymous with the small settlement at Lamorna Cove, a few miles further south, that he later included it in his name, was a valued member of the artistic community at Newlyn. Established artists such as Harold and Laura Knight, who had been present at the artists' colony at Staithes in North Yorkshire, spent some time at Newlyn en route for Lamorna.

We are fortunate in having a very complete view of Laura Knight's career, as she proved an accomplished writer as well as artist. Her 1936 volume *Oil Paint and Grease Paint* was followed thirty years later by her autobiographical *The Magic of a Line*. Laura Knight took painting into new areas of activity. Initially she worked like other Newlyn and Lamorna painters, doing scenes of local life or posing figures among the coastal landscapes of Penwith. Later she was attracted by the circus and the theatre, painting clowns and ballet dancers, and during the war was a distinguished war artist and also drew at the trials of the leading Nazis in Nuremberg.

But it is her Cornish years that interest us here. From the beginning it was the light that fascinated her, and the way light both defined forms and transformed them. Soon after her arrival in Cornwall, she painted a large canvas of children playing on the seashore in the sunshine ("The Beach"). "A Summer's Day by the Rock Pool", which is on the cover of Laura Newton's *Painting at the Edge*, is typical of this period—adults and children playing happily among the rock-pools, while a female artist (perhaps Knight herself) paints the scene. This was an idyllic period in Laura's life. Colonel Paynter, the local landowner at Lamorna Cove, rented Laura and Harold Knight a house, built studios for both to work in and provided Laura with a painting hut at Carn Barges on the rocky coast. She invited friends and models from London to share her joy, and remembered half a century later how "In a private spot my young friends and models swam and dived in the deep pools at low tide or lay in repose on the rocks. How holy is the human body when bare of other than the sun." This work culminated in a large canvas finished at a studio in Newlyn but based on studies made in the open air. The locals, used by now to the artists painting fishing boats, landscape or even children playing on the beach, were by turns intrigued and shocked, but informed that with Colonel Paynter's approval, Knight could work in any way she chose. She presented the finished version of "Daughters of the Sun" at the 1911 Royal Academy and described in the 1936 book the reaction: "On its account I had there a *succès d'estime*, but not financially; I received an offer of three hundred pounds for it—to accept so great a reduction on the original price [£600] would have been an indignity." She then explains how the picture went the round of provincial galleries during the First World War, became damaged by water, and eventually she cut it up "in a ruthless mood". She concluded: "I felt a murderer."

It is not entirely clear from her own writing or from biographical accounts exactly what happened to Knight's work from this period. She wrote in her autobiography that a large collection of sketch books were damaged beyond repair when her studio was on loan to anther artist, adding the comment: "Among the work crowding my studio today there is no record of that intensive study covering many years—that of the nude figure in its natural surroundings." It is possible to put together a rather different version of events based on the experience of the Knights during those terrible war years. Laura was painting at St. Ives in 1915 when "the first restrictions against painting any part of the coast-line came into force… The restrictions became more and more severe; everyone was suspected as a spy; we were forbidden to work out of doors at all…" She also records that it became more and more difficult to get food, and that she had time out with a broken ankle.

For Harold Knight the war years were even more difficult. He registered as a conscientious objector, and was directed to farm work, despite the fact that he could probably have been excused service on medical grounds. He suffered from depression, a sense of isolation and rejection. Lamorna came to stand for lost youth, lost innocence. It remains a matter of conjecture whether, when the Knights left Cornwall for London at the end of the war, the "awful business" of clearing out the studios included the deliberate destruction of much of Laura's work from this period, including her sketch-books and the damaged "Daughters of the Sun". Her work became stronger and more varied, she became a respected public figure, but she never returned to the idyllic subject-matter of her Cornish work.

Even at Lamorna there were artists working in new and different ways, such as the surrealist painter, writer and occultist Ithell Colquhoun. Her "Scylla" (1938) in the Tate Gallery manages to be both a self-portrait in the bath and a scene of rocks and boat on the Cornish coast. While much of the early work at St. Ives is comparable in style and subject-matter to what was being produced at Falmouth, Newlyn and Lamorna, St. Ives was set to become an important focus of abstract art. Denys Val Baker, in his fascinating study of the arts and crafts in Cornwall (*The Timeless Land*), has an interesting quotation from Charles Marriott, an influential art critic of the first half of the twentieth century:

> Seen from a height such as Trencrom or Carn Galve the landscape runs to a decorative pattern; a sort of cloisonné effect of little green fields inset in a network of gorse-clad hedges. I have a notion that even in their abstractions painters such as Ben Nicholson get nearer to the peculiar magic of West Cornwall than did the painters of my day.

It is again that extra something that afflicts the English visitor to Cornwall. Ben Nicholson, who settled in St. Ives in 1939 and spent the next ten years there, described drawing a line as "like walking through the country from St. Ives to Zennor" (at last we have mentioned an ending-point of this book to match its starting-point in Avebury), and Val Baker comments that "Abstract painting comes from looking at the sea, the land, the sky; it is a visual experience." Piet Mondrian himself had evolved from painting beach scenes to the rigid abstraction of his later canvases. Terry Jackson, another St. Ives abstract painter, described how a painting "emerged" from observing the boats in the harbour at evening: "What I painted was an arrangement of form and colour which evokes for me a similar feeling."

Nicholson had visited Cornwall before 1939. In particular, he and his first wife Winifred had stayed with Kit Wood at Feock on the Fal Estuary in the summer of 1928. He painted two pictures ("Pill Creek" and "Pill Creek Moonlight") based on this visit. While still representational, all the emphasis is on the surface of the paint, and a limited colour palate. On this same trip, Wood and Nicholson visited St. Ives on a day-trip, met the primitive painter Alfred Wallis and bought some of his pictures. Nicholson later remarked: "He used very few colours, and one associates with him some lively dark browns, shiny blacks, fierce greys, strange whites and a particularly pungent Cornish green." By 1939, when Nicholson returned to St Ives with his second wife Barbara Hepworth and their three children (triplets), he had worked through cubism, through Calder, Miró and Arp, to his own particular brand of abstract, geometric relief paintings. If Cornwall had begun as an imitation of France, Nicholson renewed and refreshed the links with mainland Europe. During the 1930s he had visited Mondrian's studio twice, joined (with Hepworth) the theoretical group Association Abstraction-Création, and collaborated with the Russian constructivist sculptor Naum Gabo in the 1937 publication *Circle*. Gabo, fleeing the war, was to join Nicholson and Hepworth at St. Ives from 1939 to 1946.

The marriage did not survive but Hepworth stayed on at her studio at Trewyn in St. Ives, a distinguished leader of an artistic *milieu* that now transcended local, national and international divisions. Her sculpture "Single Form" outside the United Nations building in New York is a memorial to Dag Hammarskjöld, the Secretary-General so tragically killed in a plane-crash in Africa. Closer to home, she was a trustee of the Tate

Gallery from1965 to 1972. Bernard Leach the potter was her friend, and the two were awarded the freedom of St. Ives in 1968. After her tragic death in a fire at her studio in 1975, the studio and its garden were opened to the public, from 1980 under the control of the Tate Gallery. There her great abstract sculptures can be seen at their best, under winter rain and summer sun, amid the lush foliage of a sub-tropical garden. They include wire-sculptures, in which different planes are joined as if by the strings of a musical instrument, and at the heart of the garden is a giant sculpture that the visitor can walk through as well as around. It is abstract, and yet continually reminds the viewer of the great boulders that litter the Cornish landscape, the circles of standing stones and *menhirs* left by pre-historic people, the strange and magical stones with holes in them that so fascinated Daphne du Maurier. If nature abhors the straight line, which Nicholson's abstraction emphasized, then Hepworth's work, like that of her contemporary Henry Moore, remains firmly rooted in the natural, sensual world.

Hepworth is well represented too in the Tate St. Ives, a modest building dating from 1993 above Porthmeor beach, the heart of the old fishermen's quarter and incongruously the site of St. Ives' old gas-works. "Sea Form Porthmeor" is her response to the beach outside, while her "Menhirs" (in slate) and "Landscape Sculpture" (bronze) pay homage to the pre-historic landscape of West Cornwall. Here too is her friend Bernard Leach, Alfred Wallis' little paintings of the town, including one of those that Nicholson bought on that first visit in 1928, and a stained glass window by Patrick Heron. Much to see, then, if it is winter or the visitor is driven indoors by warm, summer rain.

ANOTHER KIND OF CULTURE

Unite and unite and let us all unite,
    For summer is acome unto day
And whither we are going we will all unite,
    In the merry morning of May.
                    Chorus of the Padstow Day and Night Songs

There is the material culture of Cornwall, how people have earned their living, the marks these economic activities have left in the landscape, the way that people's economic activities define them and their possibilities as human beings. Then there are painting, the visual arts, literature, dance, the sort of culture that is supported by the Arts Council, which goes on in theatres and concert halls and arts festivals. And then there is an altogether different sort of culture, what the English are inclined to dismiss as "folklore", what the Catalans and the Spanish value as "popular culture", a term devalued by its use in pop music or television soaps or novels sold in airport bookshops. Yet it is a term that might be reclaimed. Unlike the commercial forms of "pop" culture, it is not just marketed to people but comes from them, their history, their enthusiasm, their sense of fun and sharing. Once it was called Merrie England, the many festivals celebrated by the church, almost all of them drawing on earlier pagan traditions which celebrated the seasons, the harvest, the movement of the earth, the moon, the stars. The reformed church was supposed to have suppressed it, but it went underground; it happened but it did not exist officially—until the modern world rediscovered it, attempted to seal it in aspic, re-branded it as "folklore", a new way of killing the old ways. But then the people once more began to reclaim their birthright.

Cornwall is full of popular culture, some of it closely linked to the agricultural or solar year, some to fishing and the sea, some linked to the special male world of the miners—wrestling and the old Celtic sport of hurling especially. In this chapter we shall refer to just three towns: Padstow, Helston and Penzance, taking us through the months of May and June, from spring to high summer.

It begins at Padstow on May Day. Padstow is the home of the hobby horse ("'obby 'oss", or simply "'oss" in dialect), a fame it shares with Minehead in Somerset, where the 'oss co-exists quite happily with the Butlin's holiday camp. May Day in Padstow, especially if the sun shines, is an unforgettable experience. The hawthorn (May) blossom is out, the cars have been sent packing and the town has been decorated with greenery brought in from the surrounding woods (memories of Grovely here). The first surprise is the very high ratio of participants to visitors and onlookers; this is culture on a grand scale. Once there was one 'oss, the red or original creature. Now there are two, the red one having been joined by a blue 'oss. Most of the townsfolk are wearing the favours of one or another, but whatever the source of this breach, relations seem cordial. The bands may be limited in instruments (accordions and drums) but are large in numbers. Some families seem happily divided over which 'oss they support. Babies and dogs carry favours too. The main difference is that the party that supports the red 'oss is exclusively male while the blue 'oss party includes a significant proportion of young women. Could this be Cornish feminism at work? The basic dress is white for both women and men, with red or blue neck or head-scarves and sashes. Many have cowslips, bluebells or lily-of-the-valley pinned to their hats or dresses. The song is insistent, the tune simple; it is hard not to be drawn into the chorus—"unite and unite" (did they not unite at Grovely too?) to the accompaniment of the accordion.

Those who have only come out in the morning are told that it was "very wild" last night—there are processions with bands and choirs beginning at midnight and lasting until the early morning. Then there follows a break while people "go a-maying", gathering greenery and flowers from the woods. It is not clear whether the pubs have opened early, or simply failed to shut the night before. Control of the event lies with the two 'oss committees, and even the police do not know the exact route the processions are going to take. It is a day when people do not exactly defy authority, but turn their backs on it.

The tightly packed main square at Padstow is dominated by an enormous Maypole rising high above the modest little houses, decorated in greenery in its lower part and higher up by myriad flags and coloured streamers standing out against a china blue sky. The black silhouette of an 'oss surmounts the pole. The red 'oss has a home, in the Golden Lion pub, and must be enticed out by much singing and shouting in the street outside. Eventually he emerges, a body bearing a great black hood and symbolic head, as much bird as horse, twirling hysterically to the music. They have a hard time, these 'osses, tormented by their "teasers", pushed back when they attempt to rush at the crowd or inquisitively poke into an open doorway, and obliged to die every five minutes or so, to be then symbolically resurrected by the invocation of St. George and the sympathy and singing of their party, as in the traditional West Country mummers' plays. For Daphne du Maurier, the 'oss is both the scapegoat and the image of winter which is being driven out as surely as spring is being welcomed in. The hobby horse is a complex and ambivalent figure, and it is perhaps better to emphasize what May Day means today in Padstow: participation, fun, the renewal of the natural world after winter, the reclaiming by the people of the public space, and song and dance and laughter. Such things can make a town worth living in.

There is more to Padstow than May Day and the ritual chanting of "'oss, wee 'oss". The Camel River is a wide estuary here, and at both high and low tide there is a regular ferry service across to Rock. From here, it is a short walk to the chapel of St. Enodoc, lost among the sand dunes and the golf course. Over the centuries the sands crept in and for a time the vicar gained entry through a trap door in the roof. Or so they say. But in 1863 the little church was restored, and is now a popular tourist site. Sabine Baring-Gould—he of Dartmoor, folk song and scary stories—started it all off with a novel *In the Roar of the Sea*, popular in its day. John Betjeman, whom we have lost sight of since Clevedon and Bath, stayed in the area often, and chose to be buried here. His elaborate slate headstone can be seen in the churchyard, with Gothic lettering (perhaps acknowledging his German ancestry) and a profusion of decorative scrolls and flowers. There is a Celtic cross in the porch, found in an old boundary wall, and a beautiful Norman font.

St. Enodoc introduces a new subject, that of shipwrecks, and this will recur in these two final chapters. The bell at St. Enodoc was purchased from the wreck of an Italian ship, the *Immaculata*, which foundered on the appropriately named Doom Bar, a sand bar that lies across the estuary entrance. As recently as 1995 the sailing brig *Maria Assumpta* was wrecked near Pentire Point on the Rumps, a curiously shaped double headland with a narrow neck, which was once an Iron Age fortress. There is a memorial in the south transept of St. Enodoc to the three victims.

A week after May Day at Padstow comes Helston and the Furry Dance, perhaps better known as the Helston Flora Dance. This is still a spring, a May Day, celebration, but its date—8 May—is the feast of St. Michael the Archangel, Helston's patron, a good example of the Christian church taking over an earlier, certainly pagan, fertility celebration. Helston has probably seen better days—it was one of the Cornish stannary towns—hence the name of its main thoroughfare, Coinagehall Street, and a port until the river silted up in the Middle Ages. But it comes alive for the annual spring celebrations. As at Padstow, this is a day for the locals, emphasized by the very early start, 7.30 a.m., of the first dance, although it is also a focal point for Helston people who have gone away to make a living but still remember the town, and perhaps dancing through its streets as children.

There is an air of formality about Flora Day in Helston that is largely absent from Padstow. There are even police to control the crowds—it is important that there is sufficient space for the bands and dancers to process round the town. There is an official guide with a timetable and a map, very helpful for visitors who do not know the form. Dress is formal: even for the morning dance the men wear white shirts and ties, the women smart frocks; for the lunchtime and evening dances it is men in top hats and tails, their partners in long dresses, hats and gloves. The bands are uniformed, brass marching bands, making a sound very different from the lively accordions and drums of Padstow. The dance itself is of a stately processional type with occasional twirls, insignificant in itself except for one feature—its frequent departures down side alleys, through gardens and even through houses. This seems to be a distant relic of the idea of frightening off bad spirits (wassailing achieves the same end for apple trees), a view supported by the fact that houses in Helston used to be spring-cleaned in the week leading up to the Furry Dance. It is difficult to look too far for meaning at Helston, and even the name is contested. "Flora" seems to be an eighteenth-century classical revival term; "furry" from the Latin feria simply indicates a feast-day dance; "faddy" has also been suggested from an old English dance known as "The Fading". Floral Dance is simply the name of the tune.

These dances are marathon efforts, with large numbers participating, taking the dancers on a long circuit through the town beginning and ending at the Guildhall. The town is hilly and the dance requires stamina, especially on the long final drag up Coinagehall Street. Occasionally it all dissolves into giggling laughter as couples scuttle forward to try and make up a gap that has appeared in the procession. The midday dance is performed by local children dressed in white, the girls glowing with gloves on their hands and flowers in their hair, the boys looking rather solemn and self-conscious in their unaccustomed collars and ties. As at Padstow, the streets are lavishly decked in greenery, and lily-of-the-valley is worn by many of the participants.

From 8.30 in the morning, a rather remarkable ceremony, the Hal-an-Tow, takes place in seven spots around the town, at first sight a rather wilder event than the Furry Dance but with an interesting history. It seems to have been popular until Victorian times when, like so many other features of English life, it fell foul of Victorian disapproval of public rowdiness and drunkenness. It was revived by the Old Cornish Society in 1930, and is now firmly part of the celebrations, a different but now acceptable way of greeting spring. It has also taken on an increasingly nationalist sense, with the procession from one point to the next led by the Cornish flag, much whistling and chanting of "Oggy, Oggy, Oggy" and shouts of support every time St. Piran is mentioned. There is some wearing of the kilt in a handsome Cornish tartan that has become quite popular in recent years. At each point the handbell-ringer calls (relative) order and a declaration is read out in Cornish. There is also a song, the chorus of which is a simple incantation of the arrival of spring, but the verses of which manage to bring in such English luminaries as Robin Hood, Little John, St. George and Aunt Mary Moses. And the boastful Spaniards too, which may be a reference to the Spanish Armada, but equally may refer to their burning of Elizabethan Penzance. It is sung with great gusto to the waving of green boughs and an accompaniment of fiddles and tambourines. The welcoming speech, fortunately in English, makes a special mention of the Cornish diaspora and the arrival of "Cornish people from all over the world". Another warm welcome is found at the Blue Anchor pub near the foot of Coinagehall Street. For 600 years, this stone and thatch pub has both brewed and sold ales, and its strong Spingo beers are increasingly sought out by fans of real ale. The pub has been open all night, but still the beer flows in and out of the streets and houses, the dances and the Hal-an-Tow, just as it has for centuries past.

THE LIZARD AND PENZANCE
Before leaving Helston, it is worth making the short detour to the Lizard peninsula, England's most southerly outpost, where the spring begins in winter and in summer the cliffs are shrouded in exotic purple cloaks of naturalized Hottentot figs from South Africa, set off against the milky white of sea campion. The attractions of the cliffs and coves are obvious, and we shall not dwell on them, but there are other things happening on the Lizard. The Royal Naval Air Station at Culdrose regularly receives good publicity for its air-sea rescue work, as well as its important role in saving villagers from the floods at Boscastle in North Cornwall. It also has serious military work to perform, and the large golf-balls at the base may have something to do with this. (The smaller golf-balls flying around the Lizard are more of a hazard to the average visitor.) Next door, the Goonhilly satel-

lite tracking station with its trade-mark golf-balls and dish is an important international communications link. It received the first television pictures from the Telstar satellite in 1962.

St. Keverne is a neat and busy little inland village, very close to the home of Roskilly Cornish ice-cream, but also close to the Manacles, rocks that have claimed the lives of many sailors down the years. Before the days of lighthouses the spire of St. Keverne was a navigational aid, but only in good weather. In 1898 the nearly new passenger ship *Mohegan* ran aground on the Manacles en route for America. What happened next belies the black legend of Cornish wreckers, which we shall look at again in the next chapter. In all, 107 died, but 44 were rescued by the courageous men of the Porthoustock lifeboat. The village opened its church for the laying out of the dead, and its doors to family and friends of those who had died. The owners of the *Mohegan* paid for a beautiful stained glass window in the chancel which serves as a memorial to those who died. Outside in the churchyard, with its views across peaceful farmland to the sea, a memorial marks the mass grave of those who died (some bodies were embalmed and sent back to the US).

Penzance is the place to be for the midsummer festivities. Down by the harbour, as the *Scillonian*, the passenger ferry from Scilly, edges across the calm, mottled waters of Mount's Bay, is the fair, the complex iconography of swings, roundabouts, sideshows and shooting galleries. Next door is the Jubilee Pool. Perched above the sea, its smooth, white lines are a supreme achievement of that confident modernism of the 1930s, the lido to beat all lidos, the beguiling simplicity of the decade when everyone knew what they believed in, and the truth seemed so simple. Simple it was not, of course, but it took a world war and half a century of Cold War to demonstrate that fact. Everything is shades of blue and white here: the azure pool water, the blue pool wall, the white wall of the sunbathing terraces, the indigo sea, the Wedgwood sky. Meanwhile the silky banners waving above the pool introduce a wider palette and tell another tale.

Golowan, the Penzance midsummer festival, has developed in recent years into a week-long arts festival. Just as Helston's Furry Dance falls under the patronage of St. Michael, so Penzance falls under the spell of St. John, in whose name midsummer festivals continue to be celebrated in many European countries. Golowan is simply St. John's Feast in Cornish. The railway brought prosperity to Penzance, but it also brought a desire for respectability. Ancient rites such as midsummer bonfires and the rolling of blazing tar barrels were frowned on. From 1990 Penzance sought to restore something of this rich heritage, at once intensely local but also sharing in a much wider European celebration. Golowan today encompasses concerts, plays, talks, workshops, cabaret, comedy shows, fireworks, parades, poetry, ghost-walks and wrestling too. But the central events are packed into its second weekend when the town takes to the streets to the delight of locals and visitors. Darkness falls on the blue waters of the Jubilee Pool, the Mock Mayor is being chosen in a noisy, chaotic ceremony in a marquee nearby, the white pool terraces gleam luminously. Shortly before midnight the fireworks begin, red and blue and golden showers of light and noise reflected in the waters of the pool and the sea beyond.

There is little warning of what is about to happen. The Golowan band—accordions, drums, fiddles and woodwind—forms up and proceeds down the hill, led by a strange-looking character in white trousers and bow-tie, tail-coat, bowler hat and dark glasses, who bears a decorated staff. With his staff he beats loudly and insistently on the doors of what appears to be a lock-up garage. Suddenly the doors open and a snarling, black figure emerges, its wild head swaying above the heads of the mob (mob is the only word for what is happening here). This is Penglaz, the Penzance 'oss, resurrected from the distant past and a long sleep to terrorize and amuse the young of the town. Eventually the band reforms in the opposite uphill direction, and the dancers begin their strange and intricate Serpent Dance, a chain dance performed hand-in-hand in which strands of dancers weave intricate and confusing patterns through the crowd, the very symbol of modern community. "An eye, an eye, an eye," they cry, and no-one asks why as no-one knows the answer. They wind and twirl off into the darkness, leaving the very old and the very young to retire to their beds.

Saturday, Mazey Day, is about the children of Penzance and district. For weeks, months, they have been working with artists, designers and performers to put on a good display on this one great day. The result is a riot of colour and good humour. Many of the school and community groups have provided their own music too; it must be hard enough to play the fiddle or clarinet at the age of seven, eight or nine, even harder while trying to walk up and down the steep slope of Market Jew Street, overlooked by the portico of the Market House and the statue of Humphrey

Davy, inventor of the miner's safety lamp. Between the children's groups come the big bands—the Scottish pipers in their full highland regalia, the Falmouth Marine band in their own tartan with waistcoats in contrast to the long-sleeved jackets of the Scotsmen, the Golowan Band. There is music to last a whole midsummer's day through. And finally comes Bagas Degol—Feast Day band in Cornish. They perform in a wide variety of settings and dress, but for Mazey Day they have opted for the formal and the tartan. The basic line-up is one that will be familiar to anyone who has ever attended a Celtic folk music event in Brittany or Galicia (Spain)— the bagpipe, woodwind (in the case of Bagas Degol, usually a clarinet), the side-drum. For this event, they have chosen a light bagpipe with a lovely, playful tone that contrasts effectively with the heavier drone of the massed Scottish pipes. For other events, the clarinet may become saxophone or guitar, the drum a variety of percussion, and the pipes Scottish bagpipe or Galician *gaita*. Bagas Degol are smart and professional, highly respected far beyond Cornwall, playing lively dance and marching music, but in Penzance they are on home ground, and happy and proud to be there. Cornwall, in whatever genre, has this happy knack of being itself, or to put it more bluntly, not being England.

Chapter Eleven
WRITING CORNWALL

Goin' up Camborne 'ill, Comin' down,
Goin' up Camborne 'ill, Comin' down,
The 'osses stood still, the wheels turned aroun',
Goin' up Camborne 'ill, Comin' down.

White stockins, white stockins she wore,
White stockins, white stockins she wore,
White stockins she wore, the same as before,
Goin' up Camborne 'ill, Comin' down.

Traditional

INTRODUCTION: PROMOTING CORNWALL
The historian A. L. Rowse may be taken as the archetype of the bright, young Cornishman who makes his way in the world "up country" but maintains throughout his life a commitment to Cornwall. Born at Trego-nissey, near St. Austell, in 1903, and dying in 1997 at Trenarren, St. Austell, his life fits neatly within a twentieth century that saw the decline

of Cornish industry, the rise of tourism and the increasing sense of Cornwall's special identity within Great Britain. Rowse was often a very angry young man indeed. He won a scholarship from elementary school to St. Austell Grammar School and thence a scholarship at Christ Church, Oxford. He hated the poverty and narrowness from which he had emerged (his father was a china clay worker). He fought the Penryn and Falmouth seat for the Labour Party in 1931 and 1935, not a good time to be a Labour candidate in Cornwall or anywhere else. Later in his life, his political views moved rightwards. Despite a successful career as one of the leading academic and popular historians of his generation, as well as a respected writer, the chip remained firmly on his shoulder throughout his life. He quarrelled with colleagues, with reviewers, with anyone who had an opinion different from his own.

Cornwall remained his great enthusiasm, and it is thanks to the efforts of Rowse and women and men like him, that the view of Cornwall has persisted and thrived as a place with a distinctive history and politics, distinctive economic and social problems, always marginal—to England, to Europe, to wherever. Rowse was able to link his Cornish commitment to his interests in sixteenth-century history, publishing *Tudor Cornwall* in 1941. He explored how Cornwall, a remote corner of England with its own Celtic language, had become the front-line in the conflicts with Catholic Spain. He spent time in the USA and wrote *The Cornish in America* in 1969. But the book that most interests us here is his *A Cornish Anthology*, first published in 1968. In this he collected together many of the writers who have helped to define Cornwall down through the centuries, some of them Cornish by birth, some by adoption, still others simply passing through. Some of these we shall meet later in the chapter. There is Thomas Hardy sorrowing over youthful love and the sadness of old age and loss on the "wild weird western shore" at Beeny Cliff; there is D. H. Lawrence enthusing that "I like Cornwall very much. It is not England. It is bare and dark and elemental, Tristan's land." Of the locals there is Charles Causley, whom we met briefly in the previous chapter, another Cornish elementary schoolboy, who saw active service in the Second World War, wrote about it in verse, trained as a teacher and subsequently taught for thirty years in his native Launceston. In his short poem "The Seasons in North Cornwall" he saves the best for winter. Winter in Cornwall is an active season, the season of winds and storms, the season when the tourists have retreated beyond the Tamar, the season when incomers finally decide whether they are going to become Cornishmen and women or not:

> My room is a bright glass cabin
>> All Cornwall thunders at my door
> And the white ships of winter lie
>> In the sea-roads of the moors

Then there is R. S. Hawker, vicar of Morwenstow, an underemployed cleric to match Sabine Baring-Gould. We shall speak of him a little later. There is the rather busier John Wesley facing down a riot in Falmouth. And finally the unlikely Kenneth Grahame, who loved the Fowey River, and was almost certainly thinking of Cornwall rather than the Thames when he wrote some of the most memorable passages in *Wind in the Willows*, including that magical opening chapter "The River Bank".

DU MAURIER'S CORNWALL

There are a few women writers in Rowse's *Cornish Anthology*, but one notable name is absent—Daphne du Maurier, already a distinguished novelist when she published *Vanishing Cornwall* in 1967, the year before Rowse's anthology. If the sailors of Falmouth gave John Wesley a hard time, she observes, then the tinners did more so. She notes that their hostility more often than not turned to repentance once he began to speak. Wesley himself said that the people of St. Just were "the chief of the whole country for hurling, fighting, drinking and all manner of wickedness; but many of the lions are become lambs, are continually praising God, and calling their old companions in sin to come and magnify the Lord together." Du Maurier remarks on the ubiquity of the Methodist chapels in Cornwall, the way they brought respect and dignity to harsh labour and poor homes, the use they made of the old mine-workings at Gwennap Pit near Redruth as a natural amphitheatre for preaching, away from the prying ears of land-lord or priest. But of course the downside of Methodism was precisely the decline of some of the rowdier forms of popular culture that are once more coming back to the fore in our own godless, pleasure-seeking age. It is a pity that Rowse ignored du Maurier. Popular novelist she may have been, but she was also a woman who took Cornwall and the Cornish to her heart and produced in *Vanishing Cornwall* one of the best travel books on the subject.

Of her Cornish novels, *Frenchman's Creek* is a swashbuckling yarn that yields up unexpected depths to the attentive reader. The story is simple enough. Dona (Lady St. Columb) is a married woman fleeing from her husband, and from the dissolute life of Restoration London with its theatres, gaming clubs and elaborate fashions. She gradually becomes aware of the presence of a French ship and its handsome captain, there is a brief affair, the Frenchman leaves, life goes on. The fiction is based on an unlikely premise—that a French privateer could anchor in a creek off the Helford River unsuspected by local people for sufficient time for our heroine Dona to conduct a passionate affair with its skipper. Unlikely, that is, until you visit the Helford River. Between Gweek and its seal sanctuary and the sea there is only one point at which a road comes close to the river—at Helford Passage where there is a ferry and where a modest settlement has grown up on the wooded banks of the river. Walking through the woods is hard work, the undergrowth thick and vicious, the canopy dense and matted overhead. It is hard work rewarded perhaps by an occasional glimpse of silver water and dark grey mud-banks. From Falmouth a number of pleasure boats seek out the Helford River, nosing cautiously across Falmouth Bay and round the exotically named but jagged and savage shoreline of Rosemullion Point into the Helford River. They may even show you where "Frenchman's Creek" lies, a mysterious black arm of water disappearing almost immediately round a bend between steep wooded banks. At times, this seems more Amazon than Cornwall.

This is a river of moods, and du Maurier's novel is a moody novel. On a benign autumn day, especially in the vicinity of Helford Village and Passage, this can seem a very lived-in landscape, low hills falling to the sea, thick woods, mainly oak, overhanging the high tide mark. There is a little wooden octagonal bird-watching house built up from the river's edge on stone pillars, and there are swans and egrets; the trees are green and brown and yellow, their leaves hanging on grimly against the encroaching winter. A squall has passed, the sun is out and the river, if not blue, is a rich amethyst. It is warm, sheltered and domestic. Yet two days later, near Gweek, the lanes are awash with water, mud, sticks and stones. At low tide, the bird-calls sound mournfully across the mud-flats, the brown water ebbing between shining silver banks of mud. The red and green buoys marking the narrow high tide channel up to Gweek are stranded. There is oak and hazel, holly and beech. The woods are the haunt of foxes, badgers and hedgehogs, the river of curlews, oyster-catchers and gulls. The gulls mew plaintively in the wind, the wind moans in the trees, the trees drip constantly to the sodden earth.

Du Maurier simplifies where true nature writers such as W. H. Hudson and Richard Jefferies complicate and detail. In the novel the trinity of heron, oyster-catcher and curlew stand for the rich and varied bird-life of the estuary, with the nightjar making nocturnal appearances to keep Dona company on her romantic excursions. Later in the novel sanderlings appear and also a pair of swans, an obvious symbol for the lovers. The sanderlings are more problematic—an Arctic bird that is a very rare winter visitor indeed to Cornwall, even rarer than Dona's French sea-captain. And the action of the novel takes place at mid-summer with swimming and beach picnics.

Although du Maurier is inexplicit about sex, there is a lot of undressing in *Frenchman's Creek*. But in many ways it is the dressing up that is more interesting. Dona dresses in doublet and hose and joins in a raid on the port of Fowey. She manages that very du Maurier double-act, of being the intensely feminine heroine, yet also the tomboy, the vigorous, almost mannish comrade-in-arms of the Frenchman and the trickster who outwits the great local landowner Godolphin (a historical character, of course), riding cross-saddle rather than the feminine side-saddle of the seventeenth century. She refers to the "lovely freedom" of putting aside petticoats and ribbons, and at one point exclaims: "I too would find my ship, and go forth, a law unto myself." The other women in the novel are pretty pathetic characters by contrast—keepers of the household, or in the case of Lady Godolphin dismissed as a baby factory. There is biography in this too. Du Maurier was a great walker, a keen sailor, a fisherwoman, a rider. There is more, far more to *Frenchman's Creek* than historical romance, including the fact that it was written in wartime, with France occupied by German soldiers and the Free French in London, so England and France must appear as friends rather than the enemies they had been throughout history.

The depths of du Maurier are even more apparent in Jamaica Inn, now a tourist stop on Bodmin Moor and scene of the infamous snowstorm in November 2005 when many motorists and lorry-drivers found themselves stranded by blizzard conditions on the main road that now runs past the hotel, café, pub and du Maurier memorabilia collection of the modern-day Jamaica Inn. Du Maurier explained in an author's note that "Jamaica Inn stands today, hospitable and kindly, a temperance house on the twenty-mile road between Bodmin and Launceston." Well, temperance it no longer is, but hospitable it needed to be in that strange November storm of 2005. In the novel, rain and fog are the main hazards to be dealt with. Our heroine Mary arrives from "that lost blue heaven that had mantled Helford yesterday" to find:

> ...a lashing, pitiless rain that stung the windows of the coach, and it soaked into a hard and barren soil. No trees here, save one or two that stretched bare branches to the four winds, bent and twisted from centuries of storm, and so blackened were they by time and tempest that, even if spring did breathe on such a place, no buds would dare to come to leaf for fear the late frost should kill them. It was a scrubby land, without hedgerow or meadow; a country of stones, black heather, and stunted broom.

People's lives are seen to be determined by weather and environment:

> No human being could live in this wasted country, thought Mary, and remain like other people; the very children would be born twisted, like the blackened shrubs of broom, bent by the force of a wind that never ceased, blow as it would from east and west, from north and south. Their minds would be twisted, too, their thoughts evil, dwelling as they must amidst marshland and granite, harsh heather and crumbling stone.

Perhaps it is because this harsh moorland landscape was so different from the landscape of the Fowey River where the author lived that she delights so much in the descriptions—the tors with the stones shaped like "giant furniture, with monstrous chairs and twisted tables", the bogs and morasses, and always that wind, the unrelenting wind of North Cornwall. Above all, there is that sense of something remote and pagan, moments of peace, but "a stranger, older peace, that was not the peace of God." The strange albino vicar of Altarnun, Francis Davey, turns out to be not a man of God at all, but the leader of the wrecking gang in which Mary's uncle

Joss is implicated—not only a violent and vindictive man but one who kills the survivors of wrecks and carries off their cargoes. This is 1820 and before the time of R. S. Hawker, who, as we shall discover, sought to give a kindlier face to North Cornwall and its shipwrecks. And what of Mary, the brave young woman who rides across the moors night and day, in good weather and foul? Again, we must say there is much of du Maurier here, and indeed in Chapter Eleven of *Vanishing Cornwall* she recounts a horse-back excursion on Bodmin Moor with a woman friend, where only the sure-footed horses bring them back safely through the dark and the rain to the real Jamaica Inn, to a turf fire, a kindly landlord, and a cosy supper of eggs and bacon and tea.

There is little in *Frenchman's Creek* or *Jamaica Inn*, but rather a lot in *Vanishing Cornwall*, to prepare the reader for du Maurier's comic master-piece *Rule Britannia* (1972). Emma is trying to make her way in the world, between her father (Pa), a London-based international financier and her grandmother Mad, with whom Emma lives in Cornwall. Mad is not really mad, just extremely eccentric. Du Maurier pokes fun throughout the book, just as presumably it had given her pleasure thirty years before to have her Frenchman raid her home port of Fowey. Here is Pa on the West Country:

> The trouble is that standards become lower every mile you travel west, I've noticed it for years. Passable in Hampshire, shaky in Wiltshire, doubtful in Dorset, on the definite down-grade in Devon, and once you cross the Tamar you might as well be in Tibet—in fact, I would think conditions are superior in Tibet, especially with the Chinese in control.

The United Kingdom is in economic crisis, and in return for bailing it out, the US adopts it as a dependency. Most people accept the situation, but the Cornish do not. And the fun begins as they wage generally light-hearted guerrilla warfare on their American liberators/occupiers.

But there is serious comment within this. The new regime sees the future of Cornwall, indeed of the whole UK, as a heritage playground, and to some extent is this not what has happened since 1972? But then at Padstow and at Helston in May, and at Penzance on Mazey Day, the answer seems very different. There are local solutions, local ways of living, as Joe, one of Mad's adopted family points out:

By the way, as much milk as we want from them tomorrow and Mr Trembath [neighbouring farmer] is killing a pig which we can share in. They're going to have a load of wood from me in exchange… You see, it does work, community living. Our neighbours support us, we support them. We don't need any money, we can live without it. If everyone did this, throughout the country, there wouldn't be any need for trade outside. We shouldn't get rich but we'd be happy, we'd be free.

Perhaps things will be more like this in the future. Who knows? Tongue-in-cheek, du Maurier even manages to anticipate a mock vision of Guantánamo Bay, "a regular concentration camp", in the unlikely and paradisiacal setting of the Isles of Scilly. Needless to say, Cornwall wins its war against the US.

SOME CORNISH GARDENS

On the Helford River between Rosemullion Point and Helford Passage are two great gardens lying side by side, Trebah and Glendurgan. It is unusual to find two such magnificent gardens in such close proximity, and enquiries into the why and wherefore open up a magnificent range of gardens in this one area, all owing their existence to the Fox family of Falmouth, Quakers and traders. Slightly closer to Falmouth is Penjerrick Garden, in private hands but open to the public, and in Falmouth itself the municipal Rosehill Garden, a legacy to the people of Falmouth at the end of the Second World War. Of the first two mentioned Glendurgan is now National Trust and Trebah a charitable trust that has received large funding from the Heritage Lottery Fund and the European Social Fund.

So who were the Fox family? They were people of simple faith but wide vision, capable business people with interests in timber, fishing, mining and shipping. Falmouth, with its international connections, was a broad-minded town in which Quaker and Jewish-owned businesses could flourish. They exploited the balmy climate of South Cornwall to establish many kinds of exotic plants brought from all corners of the earth. At Rosehill in Falmouth, Robert Were Fox, Fellow of the Royal Society, established the scientific basis for the growing of exotic plants in Cornwall. It was his three sons who were responsible for developing the gardens we know and love today: Alfred the businessman at Glendurgan, Robert the scientist at Penjerrick and Charles the man of letters at Trebah.

The Foxes were not the only gardeners in nineteenth-century Cornwall. As Tim Smit found when he was uncovering the no-longer-lost gardens at Heligan, the records of the Cornwall Garden Society reveal a world of both co-operation and fierce competition in garden design and innovation. We shall work gradually northwards, lest the reader become confused by such a wealth of gardens. So not Heligan yet, but Trelissick, accessible by the regular boat-service from Falmouth to Truro, regular but not timetabled, as tide conditions are a great influence on its timing. Falmouth retreats to starboard and St. Mawes Castle to port), as the ferry ambles past Mylor and Feock and, if the season is right, past the small sailing boats and nets of the Falmouth oyster fleet, specially designed to limit both the catch and damage to the oyster beds on the river bed. This is the way to experience a garden, to arrive in a way honoured by time and practice.

From the landing-stage there is a short, sharp walk up to the garden and its exposed hilltop position, which has greatly influenced what will grow here. These gardens are older than those in the Falmouth area, with a small park and tree-planting having begun as early as 1750. In 1805 a new owner rode into town, Ralph Allen Daniell. An odd name but his father Thomas Daniell had made a fortune partly out of mining but also by marrying the niece and heiress of Bath's own Ralph Allen. (If it was not true, you could not invent it.) His ambitions for the house, including a mock-castle water-tower that is now one of the most instantly recognizable features of Trelissick, outran his fortune, and a sudden slump in mining in 1832 led him into bankruptcy. The gardens continued to change hands, and not only survived on this windswept hilltop but flourished, passing to the National Trust in 1955. Its main contribution has been to re-establish several acres of orchard, planted with traditional Cornish varieties. Good gardens need good gardeners as well as good owners and designers: Mike Roskilly and Jack Lilly are remembered at the summer-house up by the Celtic Cross, commanding a view of the wooded banks of the Fal and the romantic King Harry's ferry, the only road link between the equally romantic Roseland peninsula and the rest of Cornwall, without going the long way round via Truro.

The King Harry Ferry, with the aid of a good map, will also lead one from Trelissick to Heligan. If Heligan has been much written about and has been the subject of television programmes, it is surely due to the indefatigable energy of Tim Smit, the brains and the energy behind both the Lost Gardens of Heligan and the Eden Project. What's in a name? If the success of Smit is anything to go by, a lot. There is no doubt that the naming of both projects has helped to fire the public imagination, to quicken expectations: the "Lost Gardens" conjure up the recovery of a magical, lost world of childhood; Eden is both the garden of Eden to which we aspire (like the Quaker Coxes' heaven on earth) and the paradise from which we have been expelled by our foolish disregard of both the beauty and the fragility of the earth's eco-system. Heligan as we see it today is a place of light and colour, of birdsong and cheerful chatter. Heligan when Smit first saw it was dank and gloomy, brooding and silent. This great estate of the Tremayne family, a garden (if that is not too modest a term for Heligan) that stretched from the big house almost to the little fishing village of Mevagissey, had fallen victim to the First World War. Of the 22 gardeners who had been employed before the war, half were killed; the big house itself became an army convalescent home. It was a blow from which, like countless other great houses and gardens in England, Heligan never recovered.

The gardens became a place of myth and fantasy, part buried in the memories and annals of the Tremayne family, part in the fantastical popular imagination of Cornish people given to story-telling. This suggested, among other unlikely factoids, that half the population of Mevagissey had been conceived among the palm-trees and bamboo groves of a lost tropical garden. Children and poachers alike spoke of strange discoveries, of hidden temples amid the undergrowth. How, then, had it all begun? In essence, Heligan is a late eighteenth-century garden, a basic framework added to by successive members of the Tremayne family. It includes the Jungle garden, developed to the south of the house in mid-century to create a setting for the very Victorian, very Cornish, passion for collecting exotic plants from all over the world.

If part of Heligan is about pleasure gardens and enjoyment, there is another story to tell, of a more-or-less self-sufficient estate producing all the vegetables, herbs and fruit needed on the estate. Fruit included not only the "common-or-garden" apples, pears, plums, quinces and medlars, but fruit such as grapes, melons and pineapples to tempt the jaded palate and to impress important visitors and (just as important) rival gardeners. In order to achieve this, ranges of greenhouses were erected and curious systems devised to produce the intense heat needed to cultivate tropical fruit. To supply sufficient water for both house and garden, hydraulic rams were installed in 1880 in a valley a mile away, capable of pumping water at nine gallons per minute into a reservoir in the higher part of the estate.

Let us return for a moment to the silent, gloomy chaos that confronted Smit in the early 1990s. Fortuitously, the hurricane of 1990, which was as dramatic an event in the south-west as the 1987 great storm had been in the south-east, created the conditions in which a start could be made on the recovery of Heligan. The Countryside Commission made available funds to repair storm damage, and Heligan received a good slice of the money. Over the years Smit used all his skills as an entrepreneur to secure funding from a wide variety of sources. There were other factors in his favour too. In 1988 Tony Hibbert, fresh from the heroic retirement task of restoring Trebah gardens, had started the Cornwall Gardens Trust to record and survey the gardens of Cornwall. He had written off Heligan, but was delighted that someone else was prepared to take on the task. Smit visited Trebah, they looked at budgets together and promises were made of practical help in the future. And between them they recreated the conditions of Victorian Cornwall in which gardening, now in competition, now co-operatively, became a private and a public obsession.

Just one story will suffice here, since Smit himself has written so vividly of the gardens at Heligan. Tree ferns were needed for the Jungle garden. Trebah needed tree-ferns too. Hibbert and Smit got together, and formed a consortium to bring a container load across from Tasmania. The trees arrived and were rehydrated in a pond. They were planted, it rained, they grew.

One of the most interesting features of Heligan, and one which has certainly set a standard for other gardens to follow, is the attempt to recreate the productive garden. This allows the visitor to experience the day-to-day life of the Victorian garden—labour-intensive, plant-loving and in modern terms organic and sustainable. Where the nineteenth century took self-sufficiency for granted, our own century is working hard at sustainability, at the local sourcing of food. Again, Heligan struck a chord, not so much with its exotic pineapples and grapes, but with the very ordinariness of its Cornish apples (eighty varieties have been recorded), its broad beans and lettuces, many of them heritage varieties that over the years have dropped off the end of the average seed catalogue. The throbbing heart of

The Eden Project

all this growing is the vegetable garden, with its trim, bright green, lightly scented box hedges, its rows of alternating red and green lettuces marching across the plot, its beans scrambling up their poles, its asparagus rising from the secret earth like a visitor from another planet, its potatoes with white and pink and mauve blossom. Here then is something the average gardener can both admire and aspire to. We shall not all grow pineapples and melons, gunnera and bamboo, rhododendrons the size of a house, but with a little effort we can probably all manage a broad bean with exquisite carmine flowers and plump pods of tasty goodness.

And so on to Eden, somewhere in a worked-out clay pit above St. Austell. This is not a pretty part of Cornwall. On the contrary, it is a scarred, blighted landscape from which human beings have extracted what they thought was of value and left nothing in return. And here Smit and his associates have created something entirely different. Not a restoration, not depending on the usually benign climate of south and west Cornwall, but starting from scratch to reproduce largely under cover a unique educational and environmental resource. As Tony Kendle, the director of the

Eden Foundation, writes in his foreword to the guide, the environment is not something outside of us, but is "shorthand for issues that impact on us in a thousand ways every day, from the food we eat and the clothes we wear to the weather we enjoy or suffer." Eden does not believe in talking down to people, and patronising them, but in challenging them to face the fragile realities of this earth. It works through a series of biomes—the outdoor biome, the warm temperate biome and the humid tropical biome. Within these indoor biomes are reproduced the conditions of distinct parts of the earth, and the crops on which people depend for food, for clothing, for their livelihood. These indoor biomes are formed by the geodesic domes now so closely identified with Eden, so familiar that it is scarcely believable that Eden only opened in 2001, a child of our times.

The design is largely the work of Nicholas Grimshaw. At the Bath Spa project he produced a building which while extremely costly is understated, conscious of its need to allow the historic city to absorb and to learn to live with it. Eden marks the other extreme of his work, exciting, challenging, a landmark building if ever there was one, using all the latest building materials and technology. Essentially it is a steel frame covered in a lightweight, translucent material, like a vast heap of frog-spawn, as adapted to its clay-pit site as is the frog-spawn to its pond.

Eden is an educational charity, and much of its educational work is of the most informal variety. It is possible to drift round Eden simply enjoying the colour and spectacle, the warmth of the indoor biomes on a wet or cold day. But there are many displays which give further information about the plants, their natural habitat, the human use to which they are put. And part of the challenge is the art-work, the sculptures, a challenge to experience the world in a more creative, imaginative way. How much of this rubs off on the casual visitor is unknown.

Eden is popular, enormously so. It has contributed in a major way to the revival of the Cornish economy, as a creator of jobs. It employs some 400 full-time staff (in addition to some seasonal staff and volunteers), most of whom are recruited locally. When it first opened, three-quarters of staff came from the ranks of the local unemployed. It sources most of its needs locally, which in turn creates and sustains more jobs. It recycles. It saves rainwater and re-uses much of the grey water that has to be pumped from the site, the bottom of which is well below the water-table. It is commercial in the best possible way, drawing in money which is then not drained off to turn a profit elsewhere but which remains within the business—a social enterprise in the full sense of the term. Development continues at Eden, with the ongoing involvement of Nicholas Grimshaw and Partners. The Core is the most recently completed building. This is where the more formal education takes place with the visiting school parties and the training courses. A further building is planned—The Edge—which will reproduce conditions in the dry tropics, where so much of the world's population and so many of the world's intractable problems such as drought and poverty are located, as well as providing performance space for theatre and music groups.

ROMANTICS AND WRECKERS

> O the opal and the sapphire of that wandering western sea,
> And the woman riding high above with bright hair flapping free—
> The woman whom I loved so, and who loyally loved me.
> Thomas Hardy, "Beeny Cliff", March 1870-March 1913

It is hard to turn aside from the optimism of the Eden project and a very twenty-first-century vision of Cornwall and to turn back to earlier visions which still somehow dog the efforts of Cornwall to re-establish itself as a place for itself, more than just a playground for visitors and incomers. There is Tintagel, for example. Why is it so difficult to resist the allure of Tintagel on a sunny day, when the temperature suddenly drops and the mist begins to blow in off the sea, wreathing the cliffs in mystery? Do children still read the stories of King Arthur? Even more, do adults still believe that Arthur, or some other mythical Celtic king, once held court here, promoting chivalry and dealing in magic?

The composer Arnold Bax certainly thought so. Bax was fascinated by the world of the Celtic twilight, by Ireland and by romance. He wrote poetry, including some fiercely nationalistic lines at the time of the 1916 Dublin Rising, though most feel now more comfortable with the plaintive sounds of harp, flute and oboe in the "Elegiac Trio", written with the same event in mind. Tintagel was important to him. He composed an extensive tone poem called simply "Tintagel" and a poem "Tintagel Castle" in which he muses on love, past and present:

> Though Iseult's arms and bosom
> Were shadowy as her shame
> And dusty brains have proven
> That Arthur's but a name
> We have a certain token
> How hearts of old were broken
> And English, Celt or Norman
> Love hurt them still the same.

Sabine Baring-Gould, the wandering vicar of Lewtrenchard, was here too, spreading stories and confusion in every direction. Of the hump in the landscape around which the little village of Bossiney grew, he wrote:

> According to Cornish tradition, King Arthur's golden Round Table lies deep in the earth buried under this earthen circular mound; only on midsummer night does it rise, and then the flash of light from it for a moment illuminates the sky, after which the golden table sinks again. At the end of the world it will come to the surface again and be carried to Heaven, and the Saints will sit and eat at it and Christ will serve them.

The mound is an ancient defensive earthwork, used in time of danger until the building of bigger Tintagel Castle. As the local website informs us: "From the Mound writs for the election were read and results declared. Here too Cornishmen raised their hands to send Francis Drake to Parliament. He was returned as MP for the Borough of Bossiney in November 1584."

Hardy's North Cornwall experience was a story of romance gone sour. St. Juliot's church has become a Thomas Hardy shrine above the Valency valley and reached by a lovely flower-decked springtime walk from Boscastle past bubbling brook, bluebells and wood anemones. Hardy, sent as a young architect to draw up plans to restore the little church, met and fell in love with Emma Gifford, sister-in-law of the vicar, and director of the church music. A novel, *A Pair of Blue Eyes*, ensued in 1873, not very successfully. But forty years later, with Emma dead and Thomas married to his secretary, he wrote as sad a set of love poems as any in the language. Emma is remembered at St. Juliot's, if at all, in a severe grey stone plaque. The Thomas Hardy Society celebrated the new millennium with a window commissioned from Simon

Whistler, Laurence's son. It was an opportunity missed, perhaps, to right the wrongs that Thomas had done to his Emma. Had not Whistler (father) celebrated the lives of both Edward Thomas and his widow Helen at Eastbury in Berkshire? As it is, the window celebrates and illustrates three poems: "When I Set Out for Lyonnesse", "Under the Waterfall" and "Beeny Cliff". It is a beautiful, but sad place.

At Morwenstow, up on the cliffs just short of the Devon border, R. S. (Robert Stephen) Hawker was an archetypal Victorian vicar from 1834 for the next forty years. We have already come across him as the author of "And Shall Trelawney Die"; he also managed to "invent" the Harvest Festival service, which remains one of the staples of rural Anglicanism. (And there was the small matter of converting to Roman Catholicism on his death-bed.) One of the more bizarre National Trust properties is his driftwood hut on the cliffs, where he gazed seawards, wrote poetry and hymns and took opium. He is also rumoured to have sat on rocks his head covered with seaweed pretending to be a mermaid. What a field-day the modern gutter-press would have with R. S. Hawker.

One of the things Hawker may have been looking for as he gazed seawards was bodies. After storms he posted look-outs on the cliffs and paid men to drag dead bodies from the surf. He was determined to break the ancient taboo that said that it was bad luck to retrieve bodies from the sea; better to send them on their way to another shore or to be eaten by the fishes. Such had been the common belief. To retrieve the goods from shipwrecked ships (the normal activity of wreckers, rather than the deliberate attempt to lure ships on to the rocks and kill survivors) had always been the preferred activity, preferred that is to the retrieval of the already dead. Hawker placed great stress on the importance of Christian burial. After the wreck of the *Caledonia* in 1842, he wrote the lines:

> They came in paths of storm; they found
> This quiet home in Christian ground.

The men of the *Caledonia* lie in the churchyard at Morwenstow, beneath the proud figurehead of a Scottish warrior queen, a sword in her right hand, a shield decorated with a thistle in her left.

In his carefully researched reconstruction of the shipwreck of the *Caledonia* on Sharpnose Point, which includes some fictional elements,

Jeremy Seal is not the first to catch out the Revd. Hawker. He was not perhaps a liar in the most blatant sense of the word, but certainly one capable of dealing a little expansively with the truth. This in turn raises doubts about Hawker's true motives. Seal plays on these doubts, uncertainties and inconsistencies very cleverly. For a while we are inclined to believe that Hawker, like du Maurier's fictional vicar of Bodmin Moor, was actually in league with the wreckers. It is almost a disappointment to find Hawker's reputation as a Christian soul upheld. Life was harsh and difficult for everyone in nineteenth-century Cornwall; in sailing and fishing communities sympathy with the shipwrecked was high. Unsurprisingly, as Charles Kingsley noted, there was less sympathy in agricultural communities, and among the tinners even less. Just as those who raided the containers washed ashore at Branscombe in Devon in early 2007 were mainly townsfolk, so it now seems likely that if atrocities were committed in those days before the advent of a well organized and watchful coastguard service, they were more likely to be miners than Hawker's quiet parishioners. But "wrecking", the recovery of goods from shipwrecks, remains a good story. It is surprising to hear that of the famous seventeen BMW motorbikes taken from Branscombe Beach, two have been recovered, thirteen declared to the authorities and only two remain unaccounted for. And what are we to make of the tidy villager who recycled empty wine barrels as garden seats for himself and his friends?

LIGHT AND DARK AT ZENNOR

Beyond St. Ives the hills and cliffs of Penwith stretch out towards Lands End, a jumbled countryside of rocks and moors. On a day of alternating rain and sunshine, sea and sky are a thousand shades of grey and silver and indigo. The fields are small and hard-won from the wild, often surrounded by the stones that have been dragged from the earth to make an area for cultivation. There are foxgloves in the hedges and buzzards in the sky. There are abandoned mine workings in abundance, Cornish daffodils and potatoes in their seasons. This is a land, too, of pre-history, of enigmatic quoits—great slabs of rock suspended on uprights, probably once covered by turf mounds and used for burials. The turf has worn away in the rain, only the stone remains. There is the Men-an-Tol, the stone of the hole, like a millstone with a great hole in it; this too may have been placed at the opening of a burial chamber, but later superstitious Cornish people believed that crawling through it, especially three times, would cure any number of common ailments. Standing stones, hawthorn and furze are sculpted by the constant wind into twisted, tortured forms; it is obvious why sculptors like Barbara Hepworth found such inspiration here.

It is also easy to see at Zennor why the Cornish needed faith, whether pre-historic ceremony, medieval superstition or Wesley's Methodism. Sheltering from a thin warm Sunday midday rain in the church porch, listening to a fine rendering of that lovely hymn "Lord of all Faithfulness, Lord of all Joy", another hymn of the common round, any religion seems like a refuge from the world. And as the sundial on the tower reminds us, "The glory of the world passeth." Inside there is warmth, a slight suggestion of incense, the vicar and his congregation taking tea and coffee in decidedly up-country voices.

Zennor is in the care of St. Senara. Stories are told of her and her son Budoc that stretch credibility to the limit, but it was all a long time ago, in the sixth and seventh centuries AD, as Breton and Irish missionaries spread the new Celtic faith to Cornwall. Perhaps the seafaring saint prepares us for Zennor's mermaid. Other churches in Cornwall have depictions of mermaids, but Zennor is alone in having a wooden relief pew-end mermaid, her breasts and belly swelling provocatively above her scaly tail. In pre-Christian times Aphrodite, goddess of love and of the sea, held a quince—a love-apple. The Christians replaced it by the mirror, a symbol of vanity. Unsurprisingly the Zennor mermaid has a story too. In brief, a beautiful young woman sits at the back of the church each Sunday in a long dress.

A chorister Matthew Trewhella falls in love with her. She lures him to the cove below Zennor, and they swim away together into the sunset.

In her tender and passionate 1994 novel *Zennor in Darkness* Helen Dunmore sets an important scene in Zennor church. She weaves her story from a local girl who comes to know D. H. Lawrence and his wife Frieda during that period in 1916-17 when they lived at Zennor. The novel begins with Clare and her cousin Hannah bathing naked near Hayle, something they have been doing since childhood. It is, of course, the prelude to loss of innocence and worse. Clare's soldier boyfriend, John William, back from France, blows his head off at a training camp, but not before getting Clare pregnant. Hannah's boyfriend Sam is a deserter, holed up somewhere in London, waiting for better times. And in the middle of this fine book, Clare is in Zennor church with D. H. Lawrence. Brought up a Catholic, Clare has always loved the carving of the mermaid, to her another incarnation of Mary, "star of the sea, virgin most pure". Lawrence says people hate her because "she makes people think that there's something more—something they haven't been told about." Clare is soon to discover what happens when the mermaid sheds her tail and takes the man into her. The mermaid was there, and yet she troubled people. The medieval church found a way round it, using the mermaid, human and fish, in the Cornish mystery plays to explain the dual nature of Christ as god and man. But as Lawrence knows and Clare is discovering, there is more to it than that.

Clare will find fulfilment, one trusts, in her baby and her art. But what of the real Lawrence and his Frieda? How, if at all, did they belong in this surreal, elemental world of rocks and cliffs and sea? Cornwall could manage artists, their models (clothed or unclothed) and tourists, but the proud, arrogant Lawrence and his German wife? It was in the end the war that made the difference, the war that brought out something tribal, a gathering together, a closeness, something that alienated the men who went away (Sam the deserter, John William the soldier) but bound together those who stayed. Frieda Lawrence remembered it thus:

> In the first year of the war Cornwall was still not quite engulfed by it: but slowly, like an octopus, with slow but deadsure tentacles, the war spirit crept up and all around us. Suspicion and fear surrounded us. It was like breathing bad air and walking on a bog.

Cornwall was a back-to-the-earth experience for Lawrence, "the powerful, pre-human earth, showing its might," as he put it, but gradually, then with increasing speed, the war came between him and Cornwall.

There is a gap before Lawrence writes of all this, placing it in the unlikely setting of his Australian novel *Kangaroo* (1923). William James Trewhella is the Cornish character, an exile and wanderer like so many, distanced from the tribe and sardonically aware of its limitations. But Somers and Harriet (the Lawrence characters) have also been to Cornwall, and the landscape calls, insistently:

> And they talked for a while of the bleak, lonely northern coast of Cornwall, the huge black cliffs with the gulls flying away below, and the sea boiling, and the wind blowing in huge volleys: and the black Cornish nights, with nothing but the violent weather outside.

Padstow? Zennor? Cornwall, certainly. Lawrence devotes a whole chapter ("The Nightmare") to Somers' wartime experiences in Cornwall. It is a cruel chapter, as hard to read as anything Lawrence wrote, hard to comprehend either the experience or Lawrence's lingering bitterness about it: the local people petty and vindictive, the police both vindictive and laughable. And yet this is Coleridge and the Wordsworths in the Quantocks, a farce if ever there was one, repeated as tragedy. The Lawrences are expelled from their Eden.

Cornwall, the earth, remains, but it is no use pretending that the footsteps of men and women tread lightly on this earth. To be aware of a landscape is already to be at a remove from it: Jefferies, Hardy, Coleridge, Lawrence. Simply to be in a landscape, not knowing, not asking the why or the wherefore, that would be paradise. But who would know? At Zennor the moors are grey flat slabs of granite piled untidily one on the other; below the fields the bracken, gorse and foxgloves, then the sea, turquoise, orange, grey-blue. A buzzard, big, mottled brown and savage, floats effortlessly between the sun and the earth. Lawrence, Hardy, Hawker, du Maurier—all gone. But Cornwall remains. Beyond the sea lies America. But before America there is Scilly.

Epilogue

SCILLY

I am in a small boat. The September sun is shining. I am among the Isles of Scilly, and the dolphins have come out to greet me. There are a good number of people on the boat. The dolphins approve of that; they like people. On a day like today I think that I do too.

If Cornwall is remote, then Scilly is remoter still, a cluster of rocks and islands located some thirty miles off the Cornish coast. I met the dolphins playing excitedly out in the channel that separates St. Mary's, the largest island, from the other isles: Samson, uninhabited, with its gentle profile and two symmetrical hills, Tresco with Bryher beyond it, St. Martin's, low and spreading, the Eastern Isles protecting us from the open sea. Only St. Agnes and the wreck-strewn Western Rocks with the Bishop's Rock lighthouse are not visible.

An aerial view of Scilly reveals many surprises. Beneath the shallow waters are many prehistoric remains, field boundaries and burial mounds to match those on the present-day islands, the suggestion at least of causeways between the islands. The Bronze Age people who colonized Scilly

Stone maze, Bryher

were settling on a relatively large land-mass which included all the main islands except St. Agnes. The lost land of Lyonnesse is on our doorstep, the island of Ennor. In calm weather and at low tide it is still possible, if not sensible, to wade between Tresco and Samson. At low tide on Samson the old field walls are clearly visible, used in the nineteenth century to trap fish.

Samson seems to have had a particular attraction for the Bronze Age people. Both the North and South hills have a particular concentration of burial mounds. Perhaps these people worshipped the goddess and found the rounded breast-like form of the hills especially appropriate for ceremonial activities. There is talk, too, of Scilly as the "Islands of the Dead", a place where ashes or even bodies were brought from the mainland. Here certainly is the greatest concentration of burial chambers in Britain. And yet the artefacts found at these sites suggest ordinary, local people. Scilly was thriving, but gradually the sea was encroaching as the polar ice-caps continued to shrink. By Roman times it is likely that St. Mary's had already become detached. Over the centuries life on Scilly became more difficult.

What of Scilly today? The islands are delicately poised. They welcome both scientists and archaeologists who come to study the wealth of Scilly's wild life, while they also welcome the tourists who take a passing interest in such matters. The *Scillonian* still plies between St. Mary's and Penzance, a difficult crossing made more difficult by the shallow draft required to berth at Hugh Town harbour. There are light planes from a number of airports and a quick if rather expensive helicopter service from Penzance. The tourists are not the issue, it seems to me. The issue is how much longer real communities can exist on Scilly, communities of work and leisure, where families can grow, where the sick and the elderly can find care. These are issues for every West Country community, but Scilly has that quality of emphasis: more remote, more ancient, more separate, more beautiful even. I went to Tresco to think about these matters.

In 1834 Scilly acquired a new landlord of the "improving" sort—Augustus Smith. Smith revitalized the island economy, for example by building a new quay at St. Mary's and setting up schools. He acquired the crumbling remains of Tresco Abbey, and started to build. He also started to garden, on a grand scale, creating shelter belts of salt-tolerant trees such as the Monterey pine and terraces of tender plants from Australia, South Africa and the Americas. And so it went on, each successive generation of the (now) Dorrien-Smith family adding to and consolidating the collection of palms, agapanthus, yuccas, olives, proteas, banksias, pelargoniums, bamboos and aloes.

Tresco remains a wonderful garden and rightly one of the star attractions of Scilly. But it seems curious, in a decade when climate change and global warming are on everyone's lips, that only twenty years ago we were worrying about snowy winters. In January 1987 Scilly was hit by heavy snow followed by several weeks of icy, easterly gales. Many tress lost boughs under the weight of snow, palms and aloes literally froze to death and many other tender plants succumbed. But gardeners are resourceful people, and with the support of Kew and many other gardens throughout Britain, Tresco was restocked. Then came the hurricane of January 1990, which wiped out most of the Victorian shelter belt. Over the years since, led by head gardener and curator Mike Nelhams, clearing and replanting has gone ahead. The garden survives.

Nelhams arrived on Tresco as a student; he married a local woman and now has Scillonian children of his own. One of the features of the gardens is David Wynne's sculpture. His "Gaia" is a giant female nude in South African marble, not perhaps as I might have imagined this earth-spirit. The life-size bronze of the "Tresco Children" in which two stretching figures bear a third bird-like aloft against a (hopefully) blue sky moved me deeply. If Scilly has a future then what happens to the children is crucial. St. Agnes, St. Martin's, St. Mary's, Tresco—each has its primary school. St. Mary's has a secondary school with a boarding-house, but at tertiary level, students must move to the mainland. Only a vibrant economy and a vibrant social and community life will make them want to stay or return.

The book proper finished with a flourish and a proper sense of finality at Zennor. But there is a zed in Scilly too, the Zen of Scilly, which John Fowles summarizes as "the elemental compound of sky, sea, sand, rock, the forms and textures of simplest things, the cleansing, as the sea itself will cleanse, of over-artifice, over-knowledge and over-civilisation." It is "one huge Zen garden of the Atlantic". For once in my life, I am happy to leave the last word to another.

Further Reading & References

Prologue
  Woodbridge, Kenneth, *The Stourhead Landscape*. London: National
    Trust, 2002.

Chapter 1
  Bosley, Kate, *John Aubrey 1626-1697* (pamphlet). London: National
    Trust/Alexander Keiller Museum, Avebury, 1997.
  Gillings, Mark and Pollard, Joshua, *Avebury*. London: Duckworth,
    2004.
  Golding, William, *Moving Target*. London: Faber, 1982.
  Golding, William, *The Spire*. London: Faber, 1964.
  Hoskins, W. G., *The Making of the English Landscape*. London:
    Hodder & Stoughton, 1955.
  Whistler, Laurence, *The Initials in the Heart: A Celebration of Love*.
    London: Weidenfeld & Nicolson, 1987.
  Whistler, Laurence, *The Image on the Glass*. London: John Murray,
    1975.

  The Churches Conservation Trust http://www.visitchurches.org.uk/
  White Horses in Wiltshire http://wiltshirewhitehorses.org.uk/

Chapter 2
  Hudson, W. H., *Nature in Downland* (1900). London: J. M. Dent,
    1951.
  Richard Jefferies, *The Story of my Heart* (1883). London: Staples Press,
    1946.
  Jefferies, Richard, *Selections of his work, with details of his life and cir-
    cumstance, his death and immortality*, ed. Henry Williamson.
    London: Faber, 1937.
  Jefferies, Richard, *At Home on the Earth*. Totnes: Green Books, 2001.
  Mabey, Richard, *Flora Britannica: the Definitive New Guide to Wild
    Flowers, Plants and Trees*. London: Chatto & Windus, 1996.
  Tanner, Heather, *Wiltshire Village* (1939). London: Impact Books, 1987.
  Tanner, Robin, *Double Harness: An Autobiography*. London: Impact
    Books, 1987.

Tanner, Robin, *What I Believe: Lectures and Other Writings*. Bath: Crafts Study Centre, 1989.

Thomas, Edward, *In Pursuit of Spring* (1914). Holt (Wiltshire): Laurel Books, 2002.

Thomas, Helen, *World without End* (1931). London: Faber, 1978.

Watts, Ken. *Figures in a Wiltshire Landscape*. Salisbury: The Hobnob Press, 2002.

Williams, Alfred, *Life in a Railway Factory* (1915). Gloucester: Alan Sutton, 1984.

Williams, Alfred, *Folk Songs of the Upper Thames*. London: Duckworth, 1923.

Williams, Alfred, *In a Wiltshire Village: Scenes from Rural Victorian Life* (1912). Gloucester: Alan Sutton, 1981.

Williams, Raymond, *The Country and the City*. London: Chatto & Windus, 1973.

Chapter 3

Austen, Jane. *Persuasion* (1818). Oxford: Oxford University Press, 2004.

Beer, Patricia and Godwin, Fay, *Wessex: a National Trust Book*. London: Hamish Hamilton, 1985.

Fiennes, Celia, *The Illustrated Journeys of Celia Fiennes 1682-1712*, ed. Christopher Morris. Exeter: Webb & Bower, 1982.

Fowles, John, *The French Lieutenant's Woman*. London: Little, Brown, 1969.

Hardy, Thomas, *Under the Greenwood Tree* (1872). Oxford: Oxford University Press, 1999.

Hardy, Thomas, *Far from the Madding Crowd* (1874). London: Penguin, 2003.

Hardy, Thomas, *The Return of the Native* (1878). Oxford: Oxford University Press, 2005.

Hardy, Thomas, *Tess of the d'Urbevilles* (1891). London: Penguin, 2003.

Trewin, J. C. (ed), *The West Country Book*. Exeter: Webb & Bower, 1981.

Loughwood Meeting House http://www.kbc.org.uk/history.html

Chapter 4

Bond, Lilian, *Tyneham: a Lost Heritage* (1956). Wimborne, Dovecote Press, 1984.

Gardiner, Rolf, *England Herself: Ventures in Rural Restoration*. London: Faber, 1943.

Lawrence, T. E., *Seven Pillars of Wisdom* (1926). Ware: Wordsworth Editions, 1997.

Lawrence, T. E., *Revolt in the Desert* (1926). London: Leonaur, 2008.

Massingham, H. J., *A Mirror of England: an Anthology of the Writings of H.J. Massingham (1888-1952)*, ed. Edward Abelson. Bideford: Green Books, 1988.

Matless, David, *Landscape and Englishness*. London: Reaktion Books, 1998.

Powys, Llewelyn, *Dorset Essays*. Bristol: Redcliffe Press, 1983.

Powys, Theodore, *Mr Weston's Good Wine*. London: Chatto & Windus, 1927.

Stinton, Judith, *Chaldon Herring: Writers in a Dorset Landscape*. Crediton: Black Dog Press, 2004.

Whistler, Laurence, *Scenes and Signs on Glass*. Woodbridge: The Cupid Press, 1987.

Williamson, Henry, *Goodbye West Country*. London: Putnam, 1937.

Woolsey, Gamel, *One Way of Love*. London: Virago, 1987.

Wright, Patrick, *The Village that Died for England: the Strange Story of Tyneham*. London: Jonathan Cape, 1995.

The Dorset Coast www.explorethesouthwestcoastpath.co.uk/lulworth2chapmanspool.html

Chapter 5

Ashworth, Nancy (ed), *Voices from the Peat: An Oral History of the Avalon Marshes*. Taunton: Somerset County Council, 2004.

Copas, Liz, *A Somerset Pomona: The Cider Apples of Somerset*. Wimborne: Dovecote Press, 2001.

Diocese of Bath and Wells, *Keeping the Faith: a Celebration of the Life of Thomas Ken 1637-1711*. Wells: Diocese of Bath and Wells, 1995.

Lynch, James, *Skylines: Visionary Paintings of Wessex*. Taunton: Furlong

Fields Publishing, 2006.

Lynch, Kate, *Willow: Paintings and Drawings with Somerset Voices.* Taunton: Furlong Fields Publishing, 2003.

Powys, John Cowper, *A Glastonbury Romance* (1932). Woodstock, NY: The Overlook Press, 1996.

Thorne, Roger, "A Landscape of Chapels and Churches". Frome (Somerset): Rook Lane Chapel Tercentenary Lecture, 10 November 2007.

Glastonbury Tor http://www.glastonburytor.org.uk/

Chapter 6

Blackmore, R. D., *Lorna Doone* (1869). London: Collins, 1952.

Clifford, Sue and King, Angela, *England in Particular*. London: Hodder & Stoughton with Common Ground, 2006.

Darley, Gillian, *Villages of Vision: a Study of Strange Utopias* (1975). Nottingham: Five Leaves Press, 2007.

Davis, Lindsey, *The Silver Pigs* (1989). London: Century, 2006.

Holmes, Richard, *Coleridge: Early Visions*. London: Hodder & Stoughton, 1989.

Karpeles, Maud, *Cecil Sharp: His Life and Work*. London: Routledge & Kegan Paul, 1967.

Layley, Charles, *St. Beuno's Culbone: The Smallest Complete Parish Church in England*. Culbone: Culbone Parochial Church Council, 1985.

Staelens, Y. and Bearman, C. J., *The Somerset Folk Map*. Taunton: Somerset County Council, 2006.

Toulson, Shirley and Yarrow, Judith, *Woods and Water: West Country Landscapes in the Footsteps of Samuel Palmer*. Witney: Windrush Press, 2006.

Watters, Reggie, *Samuel Taylor Coleridge: the West Country Years*. Nether Stowey: The Friends of Coleridge, 2003.

Hannah More http://www.wringtonsomerset.org.uk/morelocke/more-locke2.html

"The Seeds of Love" www.folkinfo.org/songs/

Chapter 7

Aughton, Peter, *Bristol: A People's History*. Lancaster: Carnegie Publishing, 2000.

Austen, Jane, *Northanger Abbey* (1818). London: Random House, 2007.

Beckford, William, *Vathek* (1786). Oxford: Oxford University Press, 2008.

Bennett, Robert, *Selina Countess of Huntingdon: a Brief Celebration of a Remarkable Eighteenth Century Lady*. Bath: Building of Bath Museum, n/d.

Cunliffe, Barry, *The City of Bath*. Gloucester: Alan Sutton, 1986.

Fielding, Henry, *Tom Jones* (1749). Oxford: Oxford University Press, 2008.

Fielding, Sarah, *The Adventures of David Simple* (1744 and 1753). Oxford: Oxford University Press, 1987.

Green, Kim, *Valley of the Sacred Spring*. Bath: Second Nature Press, 2004.

Hoskin, Michael, *The Herschel Partnership, as Viewed by Caroline*. Bath: William Herschel Society, 2003.

Lane, Maggie, *A Charming Place: Bath in the Life and Novels of Jane Austen*. Bath: Millstream Books, 1986 (amended reprint 1993).

Lee-Milne, James, *William Beckford* (1976). London: Century, 1990.

Mowl, Tim, *Palladian Bridges: Prior Park and the Whig Connection*. Bath: Millstream Books, 1994.

Swift, Andrew, *The Ringing Grooves of Change: Brunel and the Coming of the Railway to Bath*. Bath: Akeman Press, 2006.

Various authors, *Obsession: John Wood and the Creation of Georgian Bath* (exhibition catalogue). Bath: Building of Bath Museum, 2004.

Winchester, Simon, *The Map that Changed the World*. London: Viking, 2001.

Bristol history www.discoveringbristol.org.uk/

Chapter 8

Acland, Anne, *A Devon Family: the Story of the Aclands*. London: Phillimore, 1981.

Acland, Anne, "History of Killerton", in National Trust guidebook to Killerton. London: National Trust, 2000 (revised 2005).

Baring-Gould, Sabine, *A Book of Dartmoor* (1900). London: Wildwood House, 1982.

Dartmoor National Park, *Military on Dartmoor: Dartmoor Factsheet*. Newton Abbot: Dartmoor National Park Authority, 2006.

Doyle, Arthur Conan, *The Hound of the Baskervilles* (1902). London: Penguin, 2001.

Eliot, T. S., *Four Quartets* (1944). London: Faber, 2001.

English Heritage, *Merrivale: an Archaeological Landscape*. Newton Abbot: Dartmoor National Park Authority, 2004.

Gribble, David (ed), *That's All Folks! Dartington Hall School Remembered*. Self-published, 1987.

Kumar, Satish, "Earth Pilgrim", first broadcast BBC2, 18 January 2008.

Small, Ken with Rogerson, Mark, *The Forgotten Dead*. London: Bloomsbury, 1989.

Sabine Baring-Gould, "Songs of the West" http://www.sbgsongs.org/
Exeter history www.exetermemories.co.uk/
Ontario Heritage Trust http://www.heritagefdn.on.ca/

Chapter 9
Bateman, Martyn, *Lydford Lives*. Lydford: Lydford Parochial Church Council, 1991.

Kingsley, Charles, *Westward Ho!* (1855). London: Macmillan, 1939.

Kipling, Rudyard, *Stalky and Co.* (1899). London: Booksurge Publishing, 2000.

Landmark Trust Guide to Lundy Island (1987), revised edition. Maidenhead: Landmark Trust, 2004.

Langham, A. F., *The Island of Lundy*. Gloucester: Alan Sutton, 1994.

Williamson, Anne, *Henry Williamson: Tarka and the Last Romantic*. Gloucester: Alan Sutton, 1995.

Williamson, Henry, *Tarka the Otter: His Joyful Water-life and Death in the Country of the Two Rivers* (1927). London: Putnam, 1945.

Chapter 10

Causley, Charles, *Collected Poems 1951-57*. London: Macmillan, 1992.

Day, Brian, *Chronicle of Celtic Folk Customs*. London: Harrap, 2000.

du Maurier, Daphne, *Vanishing Cornwall: The Spirit and History of Cornwall* (1967). London: Virago, 2007.

Dunbar, Janet, *Laura Knight*. London: William Collins, 1975.

Harrison, Charles, *Ben Nicholson* (exhibition catalogue). London: Tate Gallery, 1969.

Knight, Laura, *Oil Paint and Grease Paint*. London: Macmillan, 1936.

Knight, Laura, *The Magic of a Line: the Autobiography of Laura Knight DBE, RA*. London: William Kimber, 1965.

Newton, Laura (ed), *Painting at the Edge: British Coastal Art Colonies 1880-1930*. Bristol: Sansom & Co., 2005.

Shanes, Eric, *Turner's Picturesque Views in England and Wales 1825-1838*. London: Chatto & Windus, 1979.

Val Baker, Denys, *The Timeless Land: The Creative Spirit in Cornwall*. Bath: Adams and Dart, 1973.

Federation of Old Cornwall Societies http://www.oldcornwall.org/

Penzance and the Golowan Festival www.golowan.com/traditions.html

Tate St. Ives and Barbara Hepworth Gallery www.tate.org.uk/

Chapter 11

Bax, Arnold, *Ideala* (ed. Scott-Sutherland, Colin; contains poems Bax wrote under pseudonym Dermot O'Byrne). Petersfield: Fand Music, 2001.

du Maurier, Daphne, *Jamaica Inn* (1936). London: Virago, 2003.

du Maurier, Daphne, *Frenchman's Creek* (1941). London: Virago, 2003.

du Maurier, Daphne, *Rule Britannia* (1972). London: Virago, 2004.

Dunmore, Helen, *Zennor in Darkness* (1993). London: Penguin, 2007.

Eden Project: The Guide. London: Random House Transworld, 2001 (and yearly thereafter).

Fox, Charles, *Glendurgan: A Personal Memoir of a Garden in Cornwall*.

Penzance: Alison Hodge, 2004.

Hardy, Thomas, *A Pair of Blue Eyes* (1873). Oxford: Oxford University Press, 2005.

Lawrence, D. H., *Kangaroo* (1923). London: Penguin, 1997.

Lawrence, Frieda, "Not I But the Wind", in Jackson, Rosie, *Frieda Lawrence*. London: Harper Collins Pandora, 1994.

Ollard, Richard (ed), *The Diaries of A. L. Rowse*. London: Penguin, 2004.

Rowse, A. L., *A Cornish Anthology*. London: Macmillan, 1968.

Seal, Jeremy, *The Wreck at Sharpnose Point: a Victorian Mystery*. London: Picador, 2002.

Taylor, Helen (ed), *The Daphne du Maurier Collection*. London: Virago, 2007.

Dictionary of National Biography (on-line), A. L. Rowse

Tintagel and Bossiney www.tintagelweb.co.uk

Trebah Garden www.trebahgarden.co.uk/

Epilogue
Fowles, John and Godwin, Fay, *Islands*. London: Jonathan Cape, 1978.

Nelhams, Mike, *Tresco Abbey Gardens: a Personal and Pictorial History*. Truro: Truran, 2000.

Reid, Neil, *Isles of Scilly Guidebook*. Penzance: Cormorant Design, n/d.

Index of Literary & Historical Names

Index of Places & Landmarks

Affpuddle 46
Alfoxden Park 112-3
Alton Barnes 6
Alton Priors 6
Ashburton 162
Ashclyst Forest 149
Athelney 92, 98
Avebury 1-5
Avebury Trusloe 5
Avon, River (Bristol Avon) xix, 126
Avon, River (Hampshire) 10

Badbury Rings 46
Barbury Castle 22
Barnstaple 169-73
   Barnstaple Pannier Market 172
   Barnstaple Museum and Heritage
      Centre 172
Barry 107
Bath ix, xvii-iii, 3, 42, 98, 108, 124,
   125-38, 152
   Bath & Camerton Archaeological
      Society 123
   Bath & West Show 98, 137
   Bath City Football Club 131
   Bath Royal Literary & Scientific
      Institution 137
   Beckford's Tower 133, 135-6
   Beechen Cliff 110, 129, 134
   Holburne of Menstrie Museum 35
   Thermae Bath Spa 127-9, 225
Beeny Cliff 214, 226
Bemerton, Lower 13, 37
Bendigo (Australia) 194
Beth Car (East Chaldon) 64
Biddestone 34
Bideford 169-70, 175, 186
Bindon Heath 76
Blackdown Hills 92-3
Blackmoor Vale 42

Blagdon 109
Blaise Hamlet 116
Blandford Forum 42-4, 62, 64
Bockhampton 51, 54
Bodmin Moor xxi, 217-9
Bolt Tail 156
Boscastle 197, 209, 227
Bournemouth 45
Bovington Camp 73-6
   Bovington Camp Museum 78
Boyton 18
Branscombe 229
Brean Down 103, 106
Brent Knoll 92
Bridgwater 93-4, 100, 121
   Somerset Willow Company 95
Bridport 47
   Bridport Food Centre 64
Bristol ix, 3, 94, 108, 110, 125, 138-
   46, 174
   Commonwealth Museum 143
   St. Mary Redcliffe 138-40
   Society of Merchant Adventurers
      108
Bristol Channel 93, 104-6
Broadclyst 149, 153
Broughton Gifford 37
Brue, River xvi
Bryher 233
Burderop Down 22
Burrow Bridge 92
Burrow Mump 92

Caen Hill locks 6
Calstock xix, 184
Camborne 192-3, 213
Camel, River 206
Castle Cary 100
Cerne Abbas 46-7, 62
Cerne, River 46

THE COTSWOLDS
A Cultural History
Jane Bingham

The Cotswolds have featured on a thousand country calendars, but what is the real story behind the picture-perfect rural scene? Jane Bingham reveals a history of privilege and poverty, idyll and conflict, through the eyes of travellers, writers and artists.

Lying in the heart of Southern England, the Cotswolds occupy a significant place in the history of the nation. Ancient stone circles and ruined Roman villas provide reminders of a distant past. Fine churches and manor houses survive from the prosperous Middle Ages, and the landscape also bears the scars of Civil War. The home of kings and nobles since Saxon times, the region is famous for its grand estates, while signs of an industrial age can be seen in its mills and factories.

After the wool trade reached its peak in the fifteenth century, the fortunes of the Cotswolds suffered a slow decline as its villages sank into picturesque decay. But in the 1890s the region began to experience a remarkable transformation. It was then that William Morris and his followers discovered the area, establishing thriving centres for Arts and Crafts. In the following century, writers and artists moved to the Cotswolds and there followed a steady rise in tourism. Today, the region continues to attract visitors, as well as country-weekenders and celebrities.

Observing all these changes, and picturing the landscape, has been a lively company of writers, artists and musicians. Some, like Laurie Lee, belong to a particular place, while others have viewed the Cotswolds as outsiders. In their writings, art and music, they have all celebrated the distinctive, and sometimes surprising, character of the Cotswolds.

Jane Bingham writes on history and art. A prolific author of books for young people, she has also written on English heritage for the national and local press. She is currently a Royal Literary Fund Fellow at Oxford Brookes University.

FAMOUS FIGURES: Elizabeth I at Woodstock; Charles I at Edgehill; Marlborough and Churchill at Blenheim; The Mitford sisters at Swinbrook; Prince Charles at Highgrove; Damien Hirst at Toddington Manor.

THE ARTS AND CRAFTS MOVEMENT: William Morris at Kelmscott and Broadway; C. R. Ashbee at Chipping Campden: Ernest Gimson and the Barnsley brothers at Sapperton.

WRITERS AND MUSICIANS: William Shakespeare in the northern hills; Alexander Pope at Cirencester Park; Laurie Lee in the Slad Valley; T. S. Eliot at Burnt Norton; Ralph Vaughan Williams and A. E. Housman on Bredon Hill.

256pp
203x133mm
Pbk £12.00
978-1-904955-62-7
TRAVEL

THE FRENCH RIVIERA
A Cultural History
Julian Hale

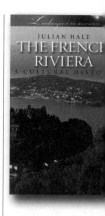

We all have our image of the French Riviera: the azure blue of the sea and the swimming pools; the dark green of the pines and the swaying palms; the yachts and the sports cars on the Corniche roads; the hovering croupiers raking in the chips in the Monte Carlo casino. And all these are true.

But there is another Riviera. Above Monaco towers a ruined reminder of Roman power, the Emperor Augustus' Trophy of the Alps. Monuments to Napoleon and Maginot Line forts testify to turbulent times, while statues and gravestones recall the years from the belle époque to the 1930s when the British, then the Russians and Americans swept in with their money, and their weak lungs, for relaxation and rest cures.

The Côte d'Azur is now French. But for centuries, until 1860, the land from Nice eastwards to Menton and the Italian border, were part of the Kingdoms of Savoy and Sardinia. Local dialects still remind us of the Ligurian past. Churches and chapels all along the coast and in the inland, hilltop villages and towns contain pictorial and architectural treasures from the Brea family during the Renaissance to Picasso and Matisse in the twentieth century. Grand hotels and villas, gardens both historic and showy (and often both), the film festival at Cannes all place the Riviera at the centre of showbusiness and artistic enterprise.

If the Riviera has had its critics—Somerset Maugham famously used the phrase "a sunny place for shady people"—it remains the epitome of glamour. Julian Hale reveals how a piece of rugged, inaccessible coastline was transformed into a byword for luxury and hedonism—but always with a special beauty of its own.

Julian Hale is a writer and broadcaster who divides his time between London and Menton.

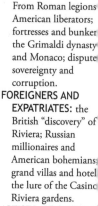

CONFLICT AND POWE
From Roman legions
American liberators;
fortresses and bunker
the Grimaldi dynasty
and Monaco; dispute
sovereignty and
corruption.

**FOREIGNERS AND
EXPATRIATES:** the
British "discovery" of
Riviera; Russian
millionaires and
American bohemians
grand villas and hotel
the lure of the Casino
Riviera gardens.

**ARTISTS, ARCHITECTS
AND WRITERS:** Ren
Chagall and Bonnard
Baroque churches and
belle époque hotels;
Somerset Maugham a
Cyril Connolly; Scott
Fitzgerald and Edith
Wharton; Chekhov a
Diaghilev.

256pp / 30 illus
215x150mm
Pbk £12.00
978-1-904955-58-0
TRAVEL

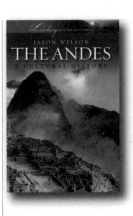

HE ANDES
Cultural History
on Wilson

Andes form the backbone of South America. Irradiating from
zco—the symbolic "navel" of the indigenous world—the mountain
ge was home to an extraordinary theocratic empire and civilization,
Incas, who built stone temples, roads, palaces and forts. The clash
ween Atahualpa, the last Inca, and the illiterate conquistador
arro, between indigenous identity and European mercantile values,
forged Andean culture and history for the last 500 years.

Jason Wilson explores the 5,000-mile chain of volcanoes, deep
leys and upland plains, revealing the Andes' mystery, inaccessibility
power through the insights of chroniclers, scientists and modern-
novelists. His account starts at sacred Cuzco and Machu Picchu,
ves along imagined Inca routes south to Lake Titicaca, La Paz,
osí and then follows the Argentine and Chilean Andes to Patagonia.
hen moves north through Chimborazo, Quito and into Colombia,
ng the Cauca valley up to Bogotá and then east to Caracas.

Looking at the literature inspired by the Andes as well as its
bulent history, this book brings to life the region's spectacular
dscapes and the many ways in which they have been imagined.

Jason Wilson is Professor of Latin American Literature at
University College London and the author of books on
Buenos Aires (Signal, new edition 2007), Borges and Pablo
Neruda.

**DRAMATIC SCENERY AND
EVENTS**: the mythic
peaks of Chimborazo
and Aconcagua; the
ruins of Machu Picchu
and the fabled mines of
Potosí; plane crashes,
earthquakes and high-
altitude cities; guerrilla
war from Tupac Amaru
to Che Guevara and
Sendero Luminoso.
**INDIGENOUS CULTURE
AND RESISTANCE**: the
Inca empire; conquest
and oppression;
Quechua, Aymará and
Mapundungu languages;
coca, quinoa and
potatoes; the political
renaissance and
migration to the cities.
**WRITERS, EXPLORERS
AND MUSICIANS**: the
Spanish chroniclers;
Humboldt and Darwin;
Pablo Neruda, Vargas
Llosa and Francisco
Vallejo; indigenous
music and urban popular
culture.

256pp / 30 illus
215x140mm
Pbk £12.00
978-1-904955-54-2
TRAVEL

THE CAMARGUE
Portrait of a Wilderness
Edwin Mullins

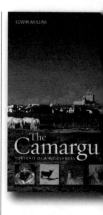

One of Europe's last remaining wildernesses, the Camargue forms a unique landscape of salt-marsh, lagoons, cultivated farmland and seashore. Where the turbulent River Rhône meets the Mediterranean in southern France lies this huge delta, home to a rich array of wildlife—flamingos, a host of other migrating birds and marshland flora—as well as a complex mix of agricultural and tourist interests. The whole region is now under increasing threat from commercial and ecological pressures.

Edwin Mullins, whose acquaintance with the Camargue dates back many years, evokes the area's natural beauty and also its appeal to artists and writers. From Dumas père to the great champion of Provençal culture, Frédéric Mistral, and Vincent van Gogh, he considers the aesthetic inspiration offered by a romantic emptiness that was once despised as a mosquito-infested swamp. Assessing the impact of the nineteenth-century renaissance of local identity, and in particular the defining role of the Marquis Folco de Baroncelli-Javon, he explores how myth and vibrant local culture—white horses, bull-fighting, the gypsy-influenced Marian cult of Les Saintes-Maries-de-la-Mer—have contributed to our fascination with the Camargue. His portrait includes the architectural beauty of St.-Gilles and Arles as well as the haunting beauty of the region's open spaces.

This accessible survey looks at the Camargue's early Roman settlement and its medieval role as an embarkation point for Crusaders and pilgrims en route to Santiago de Compostela. It then considers its more recent history as a religious battleground and neglected backwater until its modern-day renaissance as a tourist attraction. Explaining the region's turbulent religious past, Mullins describes how the Camargue has survived environmental challenges to remain a place of mystique and legend.

Edwin Mullins, who lives in London and Provence, is the author of the award-winning *In Search of Cluny: God's Lost Empire*, *Avignon of the Popes* and *The Pilgrimage to Santiago*, all published by Signal Books.

• *An accessible history of one of Europe's last remaining wildernesses, where the River Rhône meets the Mediterranean in southern France*

• *Written by an award-winning historian*

208pp / 30 illus
215x150mm
Pbk £12.99
978-1-904955-57-3
TRAVEL